Marx Through Post-Structuralism

Continuum Studies in Continental Philosophy
Series Editor: James Fieser, University of Tennessee at Martin, USA

Continuum Studies in Continental Philosophy is a major monograph series from Continuum. The series features first-class scholarly research monographs across the field of Continental philosophy. Each work makes a major contribution to the field of philosophical research.

Adorno's Concept of Life, Alastair Morgan
Badiou, Marion and St Paul, Adam Miller
Being and Number in Heidegger's Thought, Michael Roubach
Deleuze and Guattari, Fadi Abou-Rihan
Deleuze and the Genesis of Representation, Joe Hughes
Deleuze and the Unconscious, Christian Kerslake
Deleuze, Guattari and the Production of the New, edited by Simon O'Sullivan and Stephen Zepke
Derrida, Simon Morgan Wortham
Derrida: Profanations, Patrick O'Connor
Derrida and Disinterest, Sean Gaston
The Domestication of Derrida, Lorenzo Fabbri
Encountering Derrida, edited by Simon Morgan Wortham and Allison Weiner
Foucault's Heidegger, Timothy Rayner
Gadamer and the Question of the Divine, Walter Lammi
Heidegger and a Metaphysics of Feeling, Sharin N. Elkholy
Heidegger and Aristotle, Michael Bowler
Heidegger and Logic, Greg Shirley
Heidegger and Philosophical Atheology, Peter S. Dillard
Heidegger Beyond Deconstruction, Michael Lewis
Heidegger, Politics and Climate Change, Ruth Irwin
Heidegger's Early Philosophy, James Luchte
Merleau-Ponty at the Limits of Art, Religion and Perseption, edited by Kascha Semonovich and Neal DeRoo
Merleau-Ponty's Phenomenology, Kirk M. Besmer
Nietzsche, Nihilism and the Philosophy of the Future, edited by Jeffrey Metzger
Nietzsche's Thus Spoke Zarathustra, edited by James Luchte
The Philosophy of Exaggeration, Alexander Garcia Düttmann
Sartre's Phenomenology, David Reisman
Time and Becoming in Nietzsche's Thought, Robin Small
Who's Afraid of Deleuze and Guattari? Gregg Lambert
Žižek and Heidegger, Thomas Brockelman

Marx Through Post-Structuralism
Lyotard, Derrida, Foucault, Deleuze

Simon Choat

continuum

Continuum International Publishing Group
The Tower Building   80 Maiden Lane
11 York Road   Suite 704
London SE1 7NX   New York NY 10038

www.continuumbooks.com

© Simon Choat, 2010

First published 2010
Paperback edition first published 2012

All rights reserved. No part of this publication may be reproduced or transmitted in any form or by any means, electronic or mechanical, including photocopying, recording, or any information storage or retrieval system, without prior permission in writing from the publishers.

British Library Cataloguing-in-Publication Data
A catalogue record for this book is available from the British Library.

ISBN: HB: 978-0-8264-4275-8
       PB: 978-1-4411-8508-2

Library of Congress Cataloging-in-Publication Data
Choat, Simon.
  Marx through post-structuralism/Simon Choat.
    p. cm. – (Continuum studies in Continental philosophy)
  Originally published: 2010.
  Includes bibliographical references (p.   ) and index.
  ISBN 978-1-4411-8508-2 (pbk.)
  1. Marx, Karl, 1818-1883. 2. Poststructuralism. I. Title. II. Series.

B3305.M74C483 2012
193–dc23   2011031472

Typeset by Newgen Imaging Systems Pvt Ltd, Chennai, India
Printed and bound in Great Britain

Contents

Acknowledgements	vi
Introduction	1
1. Marx and Postwar French Philosophy	8
2. A Writer Full of Affects: Marx Through Lyotard	38
3. Messianic Without Messianism: Marx Through Derrida	66
4. The History of the Present: Marx Through Foucault	94
5. Becoming Revolutionary: Marx Through Deleuze	125
6. Marx Through Post-Structuralism	155
Notes	177
Bibliography	191
Index	203

Acknowledgements

Numerous people have offered invaluable advice and encouragement while this book was written. In particular I would like to thank Alex Callinicos and David Owen, and past and current staff and students in the Department of Politics at Queen Mary, University of London, especially: Diana Coole, Madeleine Davis, Paul Rekret, John Grant, Ljuba Castelli.

Introduction

Marx and post-structuralism: an incongruous partnership, perhaps. One that should not be attempted, it might be said, for the two sides have little in common. Certainly when the theories and arguments of post-structuralist thinkers first entered the Anglophone world, they met some hostility, not least from Marxist commentators. It would not be wrong to say that the relation between post-structuralism and Marxism was at first characterized by mutual suspicion. Those sympathetic towards post-structuralism tended to view it as a superior alternative to a Marxism still based on outdated metaphysical arguments: post-structuralism could at the very least act as a corrective to the shortcomings and naiveties of classical Marxism, and might even supersede it entirely. For their part, Marxists tended to see post-structuralism either as a retrograde step or an unwelcome threat. Both sides tended to assume that post-structuralism begins with a rejection of Marx, or at least with a desire to move the argument elsewhere. Over time a different relationship also developed, in which attempts were made to reconcile or combine the two philosophies. Indeed, some might argue today that the problem with any new attempt to analyse the relation between Marx and post-structuralism is not so much a fundamental incompatibility but rather that this ground is now barren, with all possible combinations exhausted or leading nowhere.

It is the wager of this book that a productive and novel engagement between Marx and post-structuralism is possible, but only if we take a different approach: what follows is not a critique of Marxism from a post-structuralist perspective, or vice versa, yet nor is it an attempt to combine the two sides into a 'post-structuralist Marxism'. Rather than offering a comparative exercise in which I assess the relative merits of two isolated systems of thought, I begin from the recognition that Marx has been an enormous influence on post-structuralism and that each thinker has written about and used Marx in various ways that merit further attention. This will be Marx *through* post-structuralism, not just Marx *and* post-structuralism. I do not treat post-structuralism as either a homogeneous system of thought or as a loose term covering a general tendency, but instead focus on four specific philosophers – Jean-François Lyotard, Jacques Derrida, Michel Foucault, and Gilles Deleuze – using the term 'post-structuralism' to cover these four thinkers, and looking specifically at what they have said about Marx alone, rather than examining their links to Marxism in general (though these more general links will inform my analysis of their work on Marx).

Analysis of the ways in which these four post-structuralists have read and used Marx can reveal something about both Marx and the post-structuralists – their respective strengths and weaknesses – and about political philosophy more generally. While I treat each post-structuralist as an individual thinker rather than simply as a representative of a wider trend, throughout I shall highlight common threads running through their uses of Marx, and in so doing build up a series of interrelated arguments. First and foremost, I argue that there is a distinct and original post-structuralist approach to Marx – an approach that reflects both the contextual situation within which post-structuralism arose and its wider interests and influences. Moreover, this approach is not marked by a dismissal of Marx: rather than rejecting him, the post-structuralists engage productively with Marx's work, drawing upon his innovations and affirming his political and philosophical significance for the contemporary world. It will be seen both that Marx anticipates certain post-structuralist themes and arguments, and that post-structuralist readings of Marx allow us retrospectively to view Marx in a new and different light. This does not mean that Marx was a post-structuralist *avant la lettre*, nor that the post-structuralists were really Marxists, but in a strong sense they are all engaged in the same endeavour: all are driven by a desire to provide a genuinely materialist philosophy. A central task of this book will be to illuminate the contours of this new materialism. The claim that Marx is a materialist is, I would think, relatively uncontroversial. Yet the status and nature of Marx's materialism is more open to debate. From at least 1845 onwards, Marx is clear that existing forms of materialism are inadequate: a new materialism is needed. This new materialism must be distinct from idealist thought, yet cannot simply be the opposite of idealism, for then it will only be a mirror image and will not escape the framework of idealism; it must also be distinct from crude or mechanical materialisms, from 'all previous materialism' as Marx puts it in his 'Theses on Feuerbach' (Marx, 1976*b*: 3). The brevity of Marx's notes on Feuerbach from 1845 lends them a certain clarity – Marx is clear that a new materialism is needed, and begins to outline its parameters – yet it also makes them somewhat enigmatic: these notes are only the beginning of a task that will occupy Marx for the rest of his life.

It is my contention that Lyotard, Derrida, Foucault, and Deleuze are also materialists, and that their readings of Marx can enable us to distinguish between that in Marx which he uncritically inherits and that which is new and unique. One way in which they do this is through a critique of a residual idealism that can be found in the writings of Marx, who does not always live up to the task that he has set himself. The concept of idealism that I shall use is drawn from another thinker: Louis Althusser. For Althusser, idealism is a philosophy of Origins and Ends, relying at once on an ontology – defined here as a conception of the essential nature of the world – and a teleology – referring all events to a pre-established destiny. In seeking to subvert Marx's ontology and teleology, the post-structuralists push the critique of his idealism further than before, thus both revealing a different Marx and helping us to think about what a materialist philosophy looks like. Yet the post-structuralist engagement with Marx is not merely a critical exercise in which he is disrobed of particular outdated encumbrances. In their discussions of power, subjectivity, desire, history, and capitalism, the post-structuralists develop concepts and arguments that can supplement Marx and contribute to a materialist political philosophy. The encounter between Marx and post-structuralism is not a one-sided encounter in which the latter comes to the rescue of the former, however: for although I think that Marx can benefit from being submitted to post-structuralist readings, he has the potential to offer something that post-structuralism does not. The pursuit of materialism brings with it various difficulties: there is a risk not only of failing fully to escape idealism, but also a danger specific to materialism, that of losing the ability to orient critical reflection at all. In the end, it may be that some kind of solution to these problems is found in Marx rather than the post-structuralists – yet it will be a Marx filtered through post-structuralism. Thus Marx emerges an invigorated figure after his encounter with post-structuralism: on the one hand, he is shorn of certain objectionable elements and supplemented with new concepts and perspectives; on the other hand, his strengths emerge in contrast to post-structuralist weaknesses. At the same time, analysis of the ways in which they read Marx sheds light on the relations between the four post-structuralists, and their aims and arguments.

The bulk of the book is dedicated to detailed analysis of each engagement with Marx. Chapter 1 acts as a kind of extended introduction, and as such is more narrative than the other chapters: it provides contextual background, offers provisional definitions of certain terms, and helps frame the arguments developed later. We shall look at the intellectual environment within which post-structuralism developed, in order to get a better understanding of what links these four thinkers and of what had previously been done with Marx in France. In order later to establish the distinctness of the post-structuralist approach to Marx, I examine the contribution to the study of Marx made by Althusser, who acts as something of a forerunner of post-structuralism, yet whose work differs from post-structuralism in significant ways. It is from Althusser that I take the definition of idealism as a philosophy of Origins and Ends. Finally, I want to highlight the limitations of another way of approaching the relation between Marx and post-structuralism – that offered by British Marxist critics of post-structuralism.

With this groundwork completed, chapters 2 to 5 offer a more analytical investigation, assessing the reading of Marx given by each post-structuralist – where 'reading' refers not only to direct comments, but also to unspoken uses and implicit criticisms. Each thinker's engagement with Marx is placed in relation to their wider philosophical interests, as I sketch their particular paths to

Marx and assess their specific arguments. Given that consistency is not always highly prized by the post-structuralists, we shall also trace their changing positions on Marx, making sense of their sometimes inconsistent and even contradictory remarks. I extract common features and themes both from within each individual engagement and between the four different engagements. The chapters have been arranged so as to build up a set of arguments cumulatively. In Chapter 2, I deal with Lyotard's changing relation to Marx, beginning with his early Marxist writings and following his different positions thereafter. Lyotard engages with Marx over a forty-year period, and the breadth of his engagement allows me to set out certain themes which are key to all four readings of Marx. Lyotard well expresses the central post-structuralist charge against Marx: he relies on a concept of lost naturality that will one day be restored – in other words, he relies on an idealist philosophy of Origins and Ends. It is possible to identify three different positions taken by Lyotard in response to the problems he finds in Marx, but each position has its own problems, reflecting the difficulty of pursuing critical philosophy beyond idealism. Lyotard also tends to overlook alternative possibilities in Marx, and increasingly sidelines him. Derrida, whom I discuss in Chapter 3, came to Marx by a very different path but he makes very similar accusations. I use Derrida to show that one can – like Lyotard – attack Marx's teleology without – like Lyotard – marginalizing Marx. However, I claim that the alternative to teleology that Derrida finds in Marx – messianicity without messianism – resembles the philosophy of the event that Lyotard opposes to Marx, and brings with it similar difficulties. I critically examine Derrida's discussion of Marx's ontology in order to think about what a concrete study of reality can mean.

Using Foucault, in Chapter 4 we look at how Marx offers concrete analysis of power relations and the production of subjectivity without reference to a metaphysical ontology. In addition, I use Foucault to show that the alternative to teleology in Marx is not messianicity but something like what Foucault calls a history of the present. However, Foucault suffers similar problems to Derrida and – especially – Lyotard. Sometimes Foucault seems to imply that there is no alternative to the present, while at other times he lapses into a kind of vitalism. This vitalism is shared by Deleuze, whom I discuss in Chapter 5, and whose work also demonstrates the risks of pursuing a materialist philosophy. Yet I finish with Deleuze because he read Marx with the most imagination and interest, and ties together many of the features of the three other engagements. In Chapter 6, I offer a more detailed analysis of post-structuralism, using their readings of Marx and comparison with Althusser to provide a sharper assessment of the similarities between the four post-structuralist thinkers. I then look at the Marx that emerges from these readings: this will not be a straightforward return to Marx, however – for it is a 'return' to a Marx newly understood in the light of post-structuralism. We shall end by revisiting the question of materialism.

Having outlined the arguments, aims, and structure of the book, further clarification can be gained through some brief comments about its omissions. First, this book is not primarily about the relation between post-structuralism and Marx*ism*. That relation has been explored elsewhere – usually, as I suggested earlier, using one side to criticize the other: offering post-structuralism as a corrective to Marxism, or defending Marxism against the unwelcome encroachments of post-structuralism.[1] My focus is more specific: it is on the relation that the post-structuralists have to Marx. It does not frame that encounter in terms of a conflict in which one has to declare oneself in favour of one contender over the other, nor as the search for some third-way compromise in which we recognize good and bad points on both sides. My account of the strengths and weaknesses of Marx and post-structuralism comes not from weighing up the benefits of two as yet unrelated philosophies, but from looking at what the post-structuralists have done with Marx.

But even if post-structuralism and Marxism are not measured against each other, it might be argued that it is important to place the former in relation to the latter: to compare and contrast post-structuralist readings of Marx with those already offered within the Marxist tradition. It would certainly be possible – and potentially fruitful – to draw parallels between post-structuralism and certain Marxist thinkers. (The work of Gramsci and Adorno might be interesting places to start.) It is in part restrictions of space that prevent me from doing so: there is only so much that we can examine. But more importantly, it is because I am interested in the relation that the post-structuralists have to Marx rather than to Marxism. A key argument presented here is that the post-structuralists throw new light on Marx by offering original readings of his work. But in order to defend this claim, rather than contrasting post-structuralism with every writer who has ever commented on Marx, I shall contrast them with the Marxist thinker to whom they are closest: Althusser. In this way, I aim to show that although the post-structuralists come near to existing readings of Marx within the Marxist canon, they nevertheless offer something new.

Just as there are other Marxist thinkers whom I could have discussed, so I could have included a number of other writers under the term 'post-structuralism': this is, after all, a relatively flexible term, and has been used to describe a variety of positions. I shall offer a fuller definition of the term in the next chapter, but for now I want to explain why I am including only Lyotard, Derrida, Foucault, and Deleuze under this label. Once again, it is not only constraints of space that have limited my focus; there are significant theoretical reasons for restricting myself to analysis of these four thinkers. Although unique, the readings of Marx that the post-structuralists produce are similar to those offered elsewhere. Some commentators have linked them to so-called 'post-Marxism'.[2] The work of the post-structuralists certainly resembles some of the work produced by Ernesto Laclau and Chantal Mouffe and their attempt to move to a 'post-Marxist terrain' (Laclau and Mouffe,

2001: 4). Without anticipating the following analyses too much, it can be said that like the post-structuralists, Laclau and Mouffe do not simply repudiate Marx. Their post-Marxism takes the form of a 'process of reappropriation of an intellectual tradition, as well as the process of going beyond it' (Laclau and Mouffe, 2001: *ix*), and as such borrows from parts of the Marxist tradition while rejecting others: 'the deconstruction of Marxist tradition, not its mere abandonment, is what proves important' (Laclau, 1990: 179). The critical content of this post-Marxism also resembles post-structuralist critiques of Marx: wary of Marx's 'manifold dependence on crucial aspects of the categories of traditional metaphysics' (Laclau and Mouffe, 1987: 106), Laclau and Mouffe reject all forms of essentialism and reductionism, and emphasize a logic of contingency against claims of historical necessity.

But this congruence of interests and arguments is not unexpected or merely fortuitous, for the authors of *Hegemony and Socialist Strategy* explicitly cite post-structuralism as the key influence on their work, claiming in the preface to the book's second edition that 'post-structuralism is the terrain where we have found the main source of our theoretical reflection' (Laclau and Mouffe, 2001: *xi*).[3] Consequently, it is better to see Laclau and Mouffe as descendents rather than contemporaries of Derrida et al.: where they contribute to a post-structuralist approach to Marx, it is largely derivatively; where they bring new insights, they tend to distance themselves from post-structuralism by drawing on influences unused by the post-structuralists (most obviously Gramsci). In fact, Laclau and Mouffe draw far more often from Marxism than from Marx: *Hegemony and Socialist Strategy* offers a critical history of Marxism rather than a reading of Marx; they do not provide detailed analyses of Marx's work or even take directly from his work.[4] Above all, they operate in a different context to that of the post-structuralists; like Hardt and Negri (2000, 2004), they have produced work that is informed by but distinct from post-structuralism.

One thinker who shares a contextual background with the post-structuralists is Jean Baudrillard. Born in France in 1929, Baudrillard was an intellectual contemporary of the post-structuralists, and his approach to Marx has much in common with their work. It would not be inappropriate to name him a post-structuralist. But as Douglas Kellner argues, after criticizing Marx in the early 1970s, Baudrillard began to move 'toward a totally different theoretical and political universe, one that will become increasingly hermetic and idiosyncratic' (Kellner, 1989: 58). Kellner is referring to Baudrillard's distance from Marxism, but his idiosyncrasies also distanced him from the other post-structuralists, as he began to follow his own unique path. Kellner's criticisms of Baudrillard have been challenged, but it can be said that Baudrillard's work – his interests, concepts, and frame of reference – became increasingly remote from both Marx and post-structuralism; as such I have not included him among the post-structuralists I am examining (though where appropriate I have indicated points of convergence).[5]

Introduction

I should finally say something about a figure whose presence runs throughout this work, but in somewhat ghostly form: Hegel holds a key role in all four post-structuralist readings of Marx. All the post-structuralists are suspicious of Hegel, and this suspicion inevitably impacts on their approach to Marx: while the idealism in Marx they wish to challenge is not simply a residual Hegelianism, they do seek to produce a Marx distinct from Hegel. It would not be wrong to claim that hostility towards Hegel is the starting point for each post-structuralist engagement with Marx. But while I examine how that hostility affects each reading of Marx, I shall not analyse the respective critiques of Hegel in any depth, and I make no judgement on the veracity of those critiques. I take their criticisms of Hegel as given: my interest is in where those criticisms lead with respect to Marx.[6] With this in mind, I want now to examine the background to the post-structuralist readings of Marx.

Chapter 1

Marx and Postwar French Philosophy

What can it mean to say that we should simply *be Marxists (in philosophy)?*
(Althusser, 1976: 132)

This first chapter traces the background to the post-structuralists' engagements with Marx. It will help define some terms and frame the arguments: by looking at what else has been done with Marx in France, it will set the post-structuralists' work in context and lay the foundations for an understanding about what is distinctive in the post-structuralist approach. The first section follows the changing intellectual currents of postwar France and the place of Marx in these changes. The post-structuralism of Lyotard, Derrida, Foucault, and Deleuze followed on from an earlier structuralism, itself developed in opposition to a still earlier humanist tendency. In outlining some of its main features, I shall offer a preliminary definition of post-structuralism – preliminary because it is by looking at what they say about Marx that a better picture of the contours of post-structuralism will be reached. Having established the context, the second section looks in more detail at the work of Althusser, a philosopher who occupies a unique position in tying together various strands of thought. I look at Althusser because his work in particular sets the scene well: both because he is a kind of forerunner of post-structuralism, clearing the ground of humanist and Hegelian Marxisms, and because he usefully frames the terms of the debate, explicitly criticizing idealism as a philosophy of Origins and Ends. It is not, however, my contention that Althusser is somehow a post-structuralist: Althusser is examined not only as a precursor, but also so he can be contrasted with the post-structuralists, who have their own approaches to Marx. Indeed, I shall argue in Chapter 6 that Althusser's later work offers evidence that he was in turn influenced by post-structuralism. Finally, the third section of this chapter looks not at what the post-structuralists have said about Marx, but at what Marxists have said about post-structuralism. In particular, I examine the criticisms made of post-structuralism by British Marxists, arguing that these critiques leave much left undone.

Marxism, Structuralism, Post-Structuralism

French philosophy was enormously productive in the twentieth century, especially in its latter half. Alain Badiou has compared this 'moment', stretching from Sartre and Bachelard to Deleuze and Badiou himself, to two other great periods in philosophy: that of classical Greece, from Parmenides to Aristotle, and that of German idealism, from Kant to Hegel (Badiou, 2005: 67–8). The difficulty lies not in recognizing the inventive productivity of French philosophy in this period, but in attempting, as Badiou does, to define it further: to identify its specific characteristics and coordinates without resorting to caricature; to pull some order from what might otherwise be a formless imbroglio, while avoiding the reduction of complex networks of differences and connections to a neatly arranged table of alliances and enemies.

One way to proceed would be to offer a kind of who's who of French philosophy, following Richard Rorty's suggestion that Continental philosophy can be distinguished from analytic philosophy by virtue of the fact that the former trades in proper names rather than in propositions (Rorty, 1989: 81n3). Certainly much of what follows in this chapter will deal with proper names, for the story of postwar French philosophy is in large part one of changing influences. Vincent Descombes, for example, divides between that generation after 1945 that worked under the influence of 'the three Hs' (Hegel, Husserl, Heidegger) and that generation after 1960 influenced by 'the three masters of suspicion' (Marx, Nietzsche, Freud): broadly, a distinction between phenomenology and structuralism (Descombes, 1980: 3). Yet as Derrida points out in his 1968 essay 'The Ends of Man', what dominated before 1960 was not simply the influence of the three Hs, but a particular way of reading them – an anthropological reading that Derrida emphatically rejects, while nevertheless continuing to draw on the three Hs (Heidegger and Husserl in particular) (Derrida, 1982: 117). So if the story of twentieth-century French philosophy can be told in proper names, this tale must also take into account that what changes over time are not simply the names that are referenced, but the way these authors are read: there are changes of problematic which alter the kinds of questions that are being asked and the kinds of answers that are sought, and which mean that Heidegger (for example) is not the same from one generation to the next.

Marx, of course, was not immune to the vicissitudes of theoretical currents. He did not suddenly appear only after 1960, along with the other masters of suspicion; but he appeared in a very different way after 1960, assimilated to new trends and joined to new themes. In this section, we shall look briefly at what was done with Marx in the period 1945–60 – a period when the post-structuralists, born 1924–30, were learning their philosophical craft – before tracing the general change of atmosphere after 1960 and outlining the key features of post-structuralism as distinct from structuralism.

Humanist Marxisms

'For thirty years', wrote Raymond Aron shortly before his death in 1983, 'Parisian ideological fashions have always been accompanied by a reinterpretation of Marxism' (Aron, 1990: 380). This sentence might be read as the weary bemusement of a staunch anti-communist, disdainful of his contemporaries' persistent obstinacy in defending and praising a totalitarian ideology. But it gives something else away, perhaps despite itself, and that is the relative brevity of the period in which Marx was a vital name in French philosophy, in which Marx and Marxism were favoured by Parisian ideological fashions (to use Aron's disparaging phrase). No more than three decades; in fact, essentially from 1945 to 1968.[1] After the student-worker May revolts, Marx was overtaken by other thinkers, and through the 1970s he was turned upon with a vengeance. The self-styled *nouveaux philosophes* now competed with each other to heap opprobrium on Marx's head. Philosophically without merit, the *nouveaux philosophes* nonetheless stand as a useful sign of a time when the theoretical vogue in Paris, disseminated by an eager and uncritical mass media, was accompanied by a condemnation of Marxism and Marx: a time when it became, in Althusser's words, 'the fashion to sport Gulag buttons in one's lapel' (Althusser, 2006: 10).[2] Before the war, Marx had been a similarly marginalized thinker, though he was largely simply ignored rather than abused. His work had begun to find an audience but he was not yet a dominant figure. Marxism had been something of a latecomer to France. Other names – Blanqui, Proudhon, Sorel – dominated her labour movement and her intelligentsia tended to treat Marxist philosophy with hostility or disdain. When Marxism did begin to make a first tentative impression in the 1920s and 1930s, it took on a distinctive hue, influenced by both the recent publication of the *Economic and Philosophic Manuscripts* and the eruption of Hegelianism triggered principally by the translations, commentaries, and lectures of Alexandre Kojève and Jean Hyppolite. In the following years and in their own distinctive and differing ways, Henri Lefebvre, Lucien Goldmann, Jean-Paul Sartre and Maurice Merleau-Ponty all forged a subjective, humanist, Hegelian Marxism.

It was this type of Marxism that came to dominate after the war, when Marx gained a stronger foothold. Sartre announced his intention to 'reconquer man with Marxism' (Sartre, 1963: 83), while Merleau-Ponty, writing in 1947, agreed with the notion that '*Capital* is like a concrete *Phenomenology of Mind*' (Merleau-Ponty, 1969: 101). The French Communist Party (PCF), meanwhile, had played a major role in the wartime Resistance and was in a strong position come the Liberation. Yet with the Party's leadership guided largely by a doctrinaire adherence to Stalinism, and offering qualified support for French colonial adventures in South-East Asia and North Africa, most French communist intellectuals had a fitful, ambivalent relationship with the PCF, a relationship in which professions of loyalty competed with statements of defiance, expulsions, and resignations. As Merleau-Ponty remarked at the time: 'It is impossible to be an anti-Communist, and it is not possible to be a Communist' (Merleau-Ponty, 1969: *xxi*). Nonetheless, after the death of Stalin, patterns in French Marxism inside and outside the PCF came to mirror each other. After Khrushchev's Secret Speech at the Twentieth Congress, the French Party was initially somewhat reluctant to 'de-Stalinize', but soon proceeded with enthusiasm. The marginalization of Stalin and his legacy left a theoretical hole, which would be filled by a philosophy of humanist Marxism formulated by Roger Garaudy, the Party's newly established intellectual guru. This inflation of a Hegelian, humanist Marxism inside the Party was aided by external theoretical movements: not only the indigenous efforts to reconquer man within Marxism but also translations into French of Lukács, Korsch, and Marcuse. So by 1960, both inside and outside the PCF, French Marxism found its roots in Hegel and its nourishment in the young Marx: Man was at the centre of this Marxism.

This all forms part of the background to the post-structuralist engagements with Marx. Politically and organizationally, postwar French Marxism was close to the Soviet Union, while philosophically and academically it was close to Hegel: post-structuralism will want to distance itself from both these poles, while holding on to Marx. Uses of Marx in the immediate postwar period were marked by idealism, albeit sometimes of a surreptitious kind: behind everything is Man, in whose name critique is pursued, and whose freedom is the desired end. While it is true that the work of a thinker like Merleau-Ponty cannot necessarily be reduced to these kinds of formulae, this was the atmosphere in which Marx was disseminated in the universities, where the post-structuralists – young students after the Liberation – would have faced Marx.

Dissolving Man

The subject-centred philosophies of the 1940s and 1950s gave way to new trends, however; the post-structuralists were not the first to challenge humanism of the type that dominated after the Second World War. It was in explicit opposition to Sartre that Claude Lévi-Strauss announced in 1962: 'I believe the ultimate goal of the human sciences to be not to constitute, but to dissolve man' (Lévi-Strauss, 1966: 247). Here, in the final chapter of *The Savage Mind*, one can see the philosophical plates shifting. This is the move that Descombes describes: from phenomenology to structuralism. It is this latter term that I wish now to examine. 'Structuralism' should be seen as a convenient label for a certain tendency or attitude rather than the name for a coherent school or doctrine. There is no manifesto or set of principles that define 'structuralism', but Lévi-Strauss, Althusser, Roland Barthes, Jacques Lacan, and others shared some common assumptions that distinguish them from the generation of Sartre and Merleau-Ponty.³ In moving the terrain of study to the systems of difference that both constrain and enable the subject's acts, this tendency was characterized by its anti-humanism.

Although it moved the focus of study to the symbolic order, away from phenomenology's interest in the body, structuralism was not a new form of idealism, obsessed with language to the neglect of material elements and factors. The work of Saussure was certainly a dominant influence on structuralism, but rather than simply leading a turn to language, Saussure's methodological innovations provided a new template for studying the humanities and social sciences. It is possible to identify three key aspects of Saussure's influence on structuralism. First, he shifted attention from conscious acts and intentions to the unconscious systems that limit, shape, or determine these acts and can only be revealed by careful study. Second, within those systems elements were analysed not as self-sufficient units but as a set of related elements which find their place only through differentiation from other elements: as Saussure put it, in a well-known phrase, 'in language there are only differences *without positive terms*' (Saussure, 1960: 120). Finally, he undertook a synchronic rather than a diachronic analysis which focused on the 'essential' rather than the 'accessory' or 'accidental' (cf. Saussure, 1960: 14). Each of these aspects is replicated somehow in the work of the structuralists. There was an attack on the sovereignty of Man, now taken neither as the origin of all meaning and action nor as an ethical or political end, but rather as a product of relations and forces which he did not control and of which he might only be dimly aware. Structuralism proceeded not by breaking things down into isolated constituent elements but by analysing a proliferating series of constitutive relations. Finally, if structuralism sought 'laws' of any kind – underlying explanations of phenomena – these were not laws of history through which events could be determined by reference to an anticipated *telos*.

That these aspects – which are general characteristics rather than strict rules – were recognized and acknowledged by at least some of the structuralists themselves is evident if we look at some lines from Lévi-Strauss, who was important in introducing Saussure into France and ensuring that his influence spread beyond linguistics. Lévi-Strauss did not come to Saussure directly, but instead approached him through other linguists like Roman Jakobson and Nikolai Troubetskoy. Setting out self-consciously to establish a structural anthropology, he conveniently outlined the four operators of the 'structural method' as developed by Troubetskoy, 'the illustrious founder of structural linguistics' (Saussure himself never spoke of structures or structuralism, rather of systems):

> First, structural linguistics shifts from the study of *conscious* linguistic phenomena to study of their *unconscious* infrastructure; second, it does not treat

terms as independent entities, taking instead as its basis of analysis the *relations* between terms; third, it introduces the concept of *system* . . .; finally, structural linguistics aims at discovering *general laws*. (Lévi-Strauss, 1963: 33)

In applying the methods of structural linguistics to anthropology, Lévi-Strauss paved the way for structuralism's entry into French thought, to be taken up in psychoanalysis, literary criticism, history, and other areas. Of this generation, the thinker who engages most with Marx is Althusser, whom we shall look at in some detail in the next section. A fuller understanding of what connects Lyotard, Derrida, Foucault, and Deleuze will be gained by analysing their respective treatments of Marx, but it will be useful first to offer a preliminary survey of the affiliations which justify grouping these four thinkers together in the first place. In addition, we can begin to outline the relation of both structuralism and post-structuralism to materialism.

Defining post-structuralism

Post-structuralism, as the word suggests, can be used to name that which followed in the wake of structuralism: specifically, and for the purposes of this book, the work of Foucault, Derrida, Deleuze, and Lyotard. All the caveats about avoiding tidy narratives also apply here: an examination of the publication dates of the relevant works tends to disrupt any convenient chronology in which post-structuralism follows structuralism as smoothly and naturally as day follows night, for certain key texts from the post-structuralists were published before certain key texts from the structuralists. Nonetheless, it can be said with justification that those I am calling post-structuralists came to prominence only once the fire of structuralism had died down. In Derrida and Foucault, one can almost see the shift taking place in the successive works of each author, with their early writings demonstrating affinities to other structuralist works, before a change takes place as the 1960s gave way to the 1970s. The places of Deleuze and Lyotard are a little less obvious but they too have their own relations to structuralism. Deleuze appeared on the scene via his own unique path, but his first joint work with Félix Guattari, 1972's *Anti-Oedipus*, critically engaged with Lévi-Strauss, Lacan, and Althusser, and like Derrida, Deleuze had carefully reflected on the question of structuralism.[4] Lyotard arrived as something of a latecomer, having focused his early attention on Marxist analyses of events in North Africa, but he can be seen grappling with structuralism in a book like *Discours, figure* (1971) (itself praised in *Anti-Oedipus*). Overall, post-structuralism is characterized by an ambivalent attitude towards the structuralism that preceded it, an attitude expressive of neither acceptance nor rejection: post-structuralism *takes on* structuralism in both senses of this phrase – it inherits and combats structuralism. The post-structuralists set themselves against the humanist idealism they had absorbed as young men, yet their work can also be distinguished from the first wave of anti-humanism.

This ambivalence towards structuralism is perhaps most explicitly articulated by Derrida, who has said that deconstruction is at once a structuralist and an anti-structuralist gesture (Derrida, 1991: 272). To get some idea of what Derrida means by this, we can turn to his celebrated 1966 essay 'Structure, Sign, and Play in the Discourse of the Human Sciences'. Here Derrida notes approvingly that Lévi-Strauss abandons 'all reference to a *centre*, to a *subject*, to a privileged *reference*, to an origin, or to an absolute *archia*' (Derrida, 1978: 286). So Derrida does not think that structuralism offers a too-static notion of structure, fixed about a central term: structuralism, following Saussure, inaugurates a decentring, and of this Derrida approves. But at the same time he is suspicious: he sees in Lévi-Strauss's work an ambivalence, revealed as 'a sort of ethic of presence, an ethic of nostalgia for origins, an ethic of archaic and natural innocence, of a purity of presence and self-presence in speech'. Here Derrida contrasts two attitudes: 'the structuralist thematic of broken immediacy is therefore the saddened, *negative*, nostalgic, guilty, Rousseauistic side of the thinking of play whose other side would be the Nietzschean *affirmation* . . . *This affirmation then determines the noncentre otherwise than as loss of the centre*' (292). Though post-structuralism has often been presented as a kind of Nietzschean play affirmed against Rousseauistic nostalgia, Derrida himself emphasizes that there is no question of choosing between the two: post-structuralism is a refusal of both pure origins and pure play, negotiating its path between these two options.

There is nonetheless a sense for post-structuralism that what preceded it remained ensnared somehow in idealist metaphysics, unable to keep away from fixed origins and ends, or at least unable to do so without nostalgia. Post-structuralism pursues the critique of idealism with even greater rigour. If there is a proper name that dominates as an influence on post-structuralism, then it is that mentioned by Derrida – Nietzsche – and this influence marks a key distinction between post-structuralism and structuralism. A caveat must be issued here, for one should be wary of *over*stating Nietzsche's influence. Early study of Husserl and Heidegger are more significant for Derrida's work. Although Lyotard's *Libidinal Economy* has very Nietzschean moments, Lyotard himself has claimed that Freud was a greater influence on that book (Lyotard, 1994: 80). Foucault only really came to Nietzsche having already amassed a large body of work in which Nietzsche appears as no more than a striking but secondary figure. Deleuze, who in 1962 provided the most systematic treatment of Nietzsche among the post-structuralists with his book *Nietzsche and Philosophy*, has a huge range of influences, and it could be argued that among them Bergson and Spinoza are at least as important as Nietzsche. Nonetheless, it can be said that the influence of Nietzsche forms a common thread in post-structuralism, and one that is largely missing in earlier, structuralist works.[5]

Nietzsche brings a kind of flexibility into post-structuralism, and a certain perspectivism that is in contrast to structuralism's scientific search for invariant structures expressed in coherent theoretical systems, leading the post-structuralists away from depth/surface models. The post-structuralists proceed in the spirit of Nietzsche's claim that '[t]he "apparent" world is the only one: the "real" world has been lyingly added'; like him, they 'mistrust all systematizers' (Nietzsche, 1968: 36, 25). Where Lévi-Strauss sought general laws, post-structuralism rejects structuralism's conceptual formalism in favour of a sensitivity to the event. This is related to a renewed attention to history: there is an attempt to avoid the synchronic analyses offered by structuralism, but without lapsing into teleology or a crude historicism. Foucault provides a useful example of the shift from structuralism to post-structuralism on the question of historicity. All Foucault's work has sought to avoid working from a metahistorical perspective that would assign events their place in a continuous development. But with his turn to Nietzsche, Foucault moved away from his earlier, structural analyses which had suspended questions of causality and emphasized sudden breaks and ruptures. Instead Foucault began to offer careful genealogical recreations of the descent and emergence of ideas, concepts, and events. Derrida, in an essay on Foucault's *The History of Madness*, had earlier warned of the danger of renouncing 'etiological demands' (Derrida, 1978: 44) – and Derrida's 1966 essay neatly expresses the attitude of post-structuralism, praising Lévi-Strauss for rejecting a teleological, metaphysical concept of history, but also warning against simultaneously effacing history altogether and falling into an ahistoricism that is equally metaphysical (291).

The turn to Nietzsche, the mistrust of systems, and the rejection of teleology are all reflected in a common post-structuralist attitude towards Hegel. If Nietzsche is a mutual ally of the post-structuralists, then Hegel is a common enemy. Their attitudes to Hegel vary somewhat, from the violent hatred of Deleuze to the considered suspicions of Derrida (who insists on the need to continue to read Hegel), yet all four in some way define their work against Hegel. They want to think difference as difference, not as contradiction. This critical attitude towards Hegel finds its most vociferous expression in Deleuze, who has claimed that '[w]hat I most detested was Hegelianism and dialectics' (Deleuze, 1995b: 6). Yet it is there in the others too. Lyotard has said that his explosive *Libidinal Economy* 'was a matter of ridding political reflection of Hegelianism' (Lyotard and Thébaud, 1985: 89). Derrida has spoken of the 'closure of metaphysics' as the 'coming out of a certain Hegelianism' (Derrida, 1995c: 80), and has suggested that *différance* might be defined as 'the limit, the interruption, the destruction' of the Hegelian *Aufhebung* (Derrida, 1981: 62). As Foucault has said, in a suggestive remark, 'our entire epoch, whether in logic or epistemology, whether in Marx or Nietzsche, is trying to escape from Hegel' (Foucault, 1981: 74).[6] This suspicion of Hegel, and the Nietzschean suspicion of systems and teleology, will have a strong influence on the way the post-structuralists approach Marx.

So there is in post-structuralism both an affinity with and a distance from structuralism: accepting the latter's critique of humanism and teleology, post-structuralism analysed differential relations not as systems of general laws but in terms of more fluid connections, borrowing heavily from Nietzsche and formulating a more explicit anti-Hegelianism. Just as structuralism has been charged as 'idealist', so has post-structuralism – but in the case of post-structuralism the charge has even less justification. There is in post-structuralism a shift away from an interest in language and symbolic structures, with the accompanying idiom of signifier and signified, and towards a concern with extra-discursive factors and forces. Language remains a theme, but it is discussed in very different terms. Foucault again provides a useful example of this shift, his work moving from enigmatic allusions to the 'prediscursive' to explicit analysis of social and economic institutions in terms borrowed from Nietzsche rather than Saussure. Lyotard's *Discours, figure* is primarily concerned to challenge structuralist theories of language, and although there is something like a return to language in *The Differend*, it is this time inspired by Wittgenstein rather than Saussure. Like Deleuze, Lyotard also presents a form of desire that cannot be accounted for using a logic of linguistic structures. Where Deleuze deals with linguistics, he draws on Hjelmslev in place of Saussure, rejecting the signifier-signified dyad. The charge of linguistic idealism is most often aimed at Derrida, but he too has always shown an interest in what he calls the 'other of language' (Derrida, 1984: 123).

This, then, is the basic topography of the landscape that will be surveyed in the following chapters. The post-structuralist engagement with Marx does not take place in a vacuum, but builds upon and reacts against work already done. The changing intellectual scene in postwar France was not characterized by a smooth evolution in which one distinct school gives way peacefully to its natural successor – yet nor quite by sharp, sudden breaks and ruptures: rather, there are ebbs, flows, and eddies, an intricate dance of complex and shifting engagements, alliances, and confrontations from which it is nonetheless possible to identify common tendencies. The Hegelianism and humanism that had embraced (and smothered) Marx after the Second World War had been challenged by the anti-humanist tide of structuralist thought of the 1960s. In turn, this structuralist thought was itself criticized by a post-structuralism in which structuralism's decentred subject was not recentred but rethought via a series of new concepts (power, desire, machinic assemblages, discourse, textuality). Parallel to this development of post-structuralist thought – yet also quite distinct from it – was something of a loss of interest in Marx, and even a violent reaction against Marx: from the *nouveaux philosophes* who came to prominence in the 1970s but also from more credible thinkers. Merleau-Ponty distanced himself from Marxism through criticism of Sartre, and towards the end of his life Sartre himself repudiated Marxism. The post-structuralists did not succumb to the widespread anti-Marxism of the post-1968 years; yet nor did they simply assimilate themselves to an existing form of Marxism. They offered their own, distinctive readings of Marx, critical yet sympathetic. Their work is not a form of idealism preoccupied by language: they built upon the critique of idealism initiated by structuralism, but took it further and sought a Marx not caught up in idealist metaphysics. In order better to understand what 'idealism' here signifies, I want now to turn to Althusser. For Marx had not been swept away by the anti-humanism of the 1960s – rather, he was carried along the tide, guided by Althusser.

Philosophy as a Revolutionary Weapon: Marx Through Althusser

Acting as a link between French and international Marxism, structuralism, and post-structuralism, Althusser merits extended attention before I turn to the post-structuralists. His work on Marx has much in common with that of the post-structuralists. Yet, I examine him here partly in order to show that there are significant differences with the post-structuralist approach: although they build on his work, they do not simply adopt an Althusserian position on Marx. Thus, looking at Althusser will be an important step in establishing the distinctiveness of post-structuralist readings of Marx. That unique post-structuralist position in turn influences Althusser's own late-period writings. Before we examine Althusser's work, however, a couple of potential difficulties need to be addressed.

Placing Althusser

In a sense, it can seem relatively easy to find a place for Althusser in the history of twentieth-century French philosophy, for he seems to unite two dominant strands of thought: Marxism and structuralism. Thus, first there would be Althusser's structuralist Marxism, then a subtly different post-structuralist Marxism. This is not the approach I want to take, and a more nuanced appreciation of Althusser's work raises difficulties that challenge this convenient classification. Althusser's writings certainly have affinities with other works of the period that can be designated 'structuralist'. He shares the anti-humanism characteristic of the era: 'It is impossible to *know* anything about men', Althusser claimed in 1964, 'except on the absolute precondition that the philosophical (theoretical) myth of man is reduced to ashes' (Althusser, 1969: 229). He heaped praise on Lacan, and parallels can be drawn between the former's return to Marx and the latter's return to Freud. Yet Althusser could also be curtly dismissive of the work of the structuralists. Despite according Lévi-Strauss modest praise, he also mocked his ignorance of Marx (Althusser, 2003: 31, 21). In a 1966 letter to Lacan, Althusser states that 'one can . . . see clearly enough in what ways the Marxist concept of structure can be distinguished without any possible confusion from the Lévi-Straussian concept of structure (and all the more from all the idealist aberrations of the "structuralists")' (Althusser, 1996: 171). Elsewhere, Althusser expresses irritation with the term, stating bluntly that 'we were never structuralists', suggesting that 'our "flirt" with structuralist terminology [in *Reading Capital*] obviously went beyond acceptable limits, because our critics, with a few exceptions, did not see the irony or parody intended' (Althusser, 1976: 131, 127). But while one should certainly avoid labelling Althusser a structuralist and leaving it at that, his flirt with structuralism cannot simply be reduced to irony: whatever profound differences exist between Althusser and someone like Lévi-Strauss, the former clearly saw something interesting in what was called structuralism – and, moreover, saw something a little like structuralism in Marx himself. As Althusser says in a letter from 1984: 'if we "flirted" with structuralism, it was not only because it was in vogue; it was also because one finds formulas in *Capital*, well-developed formulas, that come close to authorizing the use of structuralism or, at least, "flirting" with it' (Althusser, 2006: 210–11).

Althusser's relationship with Marxism may seem more straightforward, but even here it is more complicated than it first appears. He is often aligned with Western Marxists, with whom he certainly shares some traits (a focus on philosophy, receptivity to non-Marxist influences, rejection of an uncomplicated economic determinism, critique of Stalinism). Yet most characterizations of the Western Marxist tradition posit features utterly alien to Althusser (leading, in fact, some commentators to exclude him from the Western Marxist canon [cf. Jacoby, 1981]). Western Marxists are presented as enemies of Soviet Marxism, suspicious of scientism, sympathetic to Hegel, and attracted to the young Marx, eager to re-establish his subjective, humanist side. Althusser, on the other hand, scorns humanism, rejects the young Marx, tries to eradicate all Hegelianism within Marx, seeks to establish what it is that makes Marxism a science, and rarely has anything but praise for Lenin. Althusser's work is *unique*, and cannot easily be categorized. Yet if he is unique this is not because he was isolated from his contemporaries, cut off from all existing interests and problems – but, on the contrary, because he alone was situated at a busy confluence of a number of significant streams of thought. Most importantly for present purposes, in Althusser's work one can find a foretaste of subsequent post-structuralist engagements with Marx. Althusser had his own 'three Hs' to battle, and in defending a Marx who is anti-humanist, anti-historicist, and anti-Hegelian, he anticipates many of the issues later raised by Lyotard and Derrida, Foucault and Deleuze.

This does not mean that it is possible to construct a tidy narrative in which Marx is first filtered by structuralism and then further refined by post-structuralism. Although, born in 1918, Althusser was a little older than the post-structuralists, his philosophical development was interrupted by internment in a prisoner of war camp under the Nazis and so his most influential and important essays were produced from the early 1960s to the mid-1970s, making him as much a contemporary as a precursor of the post-structuralists. Deleuze's *Nietzsche and Philosophy* and Foucault's *History of Madness* both predate *Reading Capital*; Althusser's *Elements of Self-Criticism* comes after Derrida's *Of Grammatology* and Lyotard's *Discours, figure*. Moreover, there is not one Althusser: behind the caricature of a structuralist Marxist, his texts are extremely diverse. He was engaged in an almost permanent process of autocritique, with numerous revisions and reworkings. Gregory Elliott, for example, suggests that Althusser's work can be divided into (at least) five different phases, from the early writings on Hegel to the 'aleatory materialism' of the 1980s (Elliott, 2006: 365–6). These phases do not conform to a tidy evolutionary schema: there are as many tensions and gaps in Althusser's writings as he finds in Marx's. Much of the renewed interest in Althusser's work that has blossomed over the past decade has been inspired in large part by the posthumous publication of material written in the 1980s, after the end of his formal academic career. These writings both continue Althusser's earlier work and mark something of a change of direction: I shall argue in Chapter 6 that in this later work it is possible to see evidence of the influence of post-structuralism upon Althusser. By the 1980s he looks more like a successor than a predecessor.

Yet before he can draw on their work, Althusser first acts as a forerunner of post-structuralism, at least when it comes to reading Marx. There are at least two ways in which it is legitimate to view Althusser in this manner (i.e., as a forerunner). First, there is a strong sense in which he belongs to a different, earlier intellectual generation (precisely that which it is possible to group under the name structuralism): specifically, beyond a few (albeit praiseworthy) mentions, his pre-1980 work does not engage with Nietzsche. Second, among these thinkers Althusser is Marx's primary theorist, in a double sense: he was both the first to engage seriously with Marx's work, and the one who devotes most time and care to Marx. The most interesting and significant post-structuralist work on Marx comes after Althusser. I want to examine various features of Althusser's work, including his textual strategies, his attitude towards Hegel, and his critique of idealism. We shall begin with Althusser's aims in reading Marx.

Political Marx

It is important to set Althusser's work in context. As a member of the PCF, he wanted to work within the Party in order to steer it in a different direction, seeking to combat both the Stalinism to which it had once adhered and the humanist critiques of Stalinism which, following the Twentieth Congress, it now propounded. Althusser read Marx not as a dry academic exercise, but for political reasons, searching for a 'Marxist theory brought back to life: one that is not hardened and deformed by consecrated formulae, but lucid, critical and rigorous' (Althusser, 1978: 45). This attempt to revive a radicalized political Marx, free from dogma, accords with Althusser's definition of philosophy as class struggle in theory.[7] The point for Althusser is not to establish the consistency and coherence of Marx's logical propositions and thence assign him his place in the history of philosophy; the point is to recover a political Marx who can serve practical purposes. Philosophy for Althusser 'is not a Whole, made up of homogeneous propositions submitted to the verdict: truth or error. It is a system of *positions* (theses), and, through these positions, itself occupies positions in the theoretical class struggle' (Althusser, 1976: 143). Philosophy is never 'pure contemplation, pure *disinterested* speculation. . . . Even speculative ideologies, even philosophies which content themselves with "*interpreting the world*", are in fact active and practical' (57). It is not until the mid-1960s that Althusser explicitly insists on the *political* nature and role of philosophy, criticizing his earlier work in *For Marx* and *Reading Capital* for its 'theoreticism': for '*theoretically* overestimating philosophy' and *politically* underestimating it (150). These claims for a politicized philosophy are nonetheless implicit, present in a latent form, in Althusser's earlier work: to borrow a formulation from Althusser himself, in his early work the politicization of philosophy is a problem that Althusser practises without actually posing it.

It is thus for political reasons that Althusser first undertakes his return to Marx. This return, however, is not straightforward: it is not simply a question of collecting quotations, silencing Marx's successors in Marxism so that we may better hear what he really said. To begin with, there is no one, single Marx for Althusser. At the very least, Marx's thought is divided into two key periods, one before and one after 1845. Althusser always insists on the importance of the 1845 break, the moment Marx supposedly broke with Hegel and the idealist-empiricist philosophical tradition and founded a new science – the science of history, or what Althusser refers to as historical materialism. Yet at the same time Althusser repeatedly complicates this neat periodization. Even in Althusser's early work the schema is not simple. In his 1965 Introduction to the essays collected in *For Marx*, Althusser further divides Marx's work into four phases: the early works of 1840–44 (themselves divided into a 'liberal-rationalist moment' and a 'communalist-rationalist moment'); the works of the break in 1845, principally *The German Ideology*; the transitional works of 1845–57; and the mature works after 1857 (Althusser, 1969: 34–7). In Althusser's later writings this schema becomes even more complicated. While defending the significance of the break from Hegel, Althusser thus postulates a heterogeneous diversity to Marx's texts.

This does not lead him to advocate a theoretical eclecticism that would break Marx down into distinct elements from which one could pick and choose as one pleases. Rather, he searches for Marx's problematic: its particular problems, objects, concepts. In doing this Althusser is looking for what is *new* in Marx, his special contribution: 'the irreducible specificity of Marxist theory' (Althusser, 1969: 38). At times Althusser implies that this simply means reading Marx very closely – yet he also claims that this specificity 'cannot be *read* directly in Marx's writings' (Althusser, 1969: 38). Of course Marx must be read – but 'there is no such thing as an innocent reading' (Althusser and Balibar, 1970: 14). Hence Althusser's call for a 'symptomatic reading' of *Capital*, one which pays as much attention to what Marx does not say as to what he says, to his lapses and silences as to his concepts and formulations. Only a symptomatic reading can identify the problematic within which Marx writes and allow a distinction between Marx's own conceptual innovations and the dead modes of expression that haunt his later work. To appreciate Marx fully, he needs to be worked upon, in order to hear 'the unsaid of his silence' (Althusser and Balibar, 1970: 143), and grasp the significance of his lacunae.

More than this, however, Marx needs to be built upon and added to. Marx's foundation of a new science offers the opportunity for a new philosophy, and it is this opportunity – to elaborate the philosophy that is not fully developed in Marx, that lags behind its science – that Althusser takes. 'Most of Marx's successors have done nothing but repeat (i.e. gloss or interpret) Marx himself, and blindly plunged into the darkness of night' (Althusser, 1990: 276). In order to illuminate this night, it is necessary to go beyond mere interpretation. In part, Althusser does this by playing different Marxes against each other. Indeed, it is not an exaggeration to say, as Elliott does, that Althusser simply suppressed those parts of Marx which did not fit into the Althusserian schema: Althusser's earlier writings ignore most of the *Grundrisse*, for example (Elliott, 2006: 115). In his posthumously published autobiography Althusser himself willingly concedes that

> I suppressed everything [in Marx] which seemed incompatible with his materialist principles as well as the remaining traces of ideology. . . . [T]hat is why my own version of Marxist theory, which offered a corrective of Marx's own literal thought on a number of issues, brought forth countless attacks from those who clung to the letter of what Marx had written. (Althusser, 1993: 221)[8]

But in addition to this use of Marx against Marx, and in common with many Western Marxists, Althusser also feeds Marx from various non-Marxist sources – so that the version of Marx's philosophy presented in *Reading Capital* resembles, in Elliott's words, 'a transformed, *marxisant* Bachelardian epistemology combined with certain Spinozist and structuralist theses, and with elements of Marx's own reflections' (Elliott, 2006: 49). Althusser himself would later call it 'a philosophy of Bachelardian and structuralist inspiration', and in his last writings this effort to supplement Marx becomes even more explicit: his 'philosophy of the encounter', or aleatory materialism, 'will not be a Marxist philosophy: it will be a philosophy *for Marxism*' (Althusser, 2006: 257–8). So while Althusser wants to revive Marx by returning to him, he also recognizes a diversity in Marx's texts – and, moreover, posits that this diversity entails a certain reconstruction, an inventive labour that does not simply try to recover the original, true Marx but necessarily adds to him, often using non-Marxist sources. We are never *simply* Marxists in philosophy.

Anti-Hegel

Althusser believed that the attempt to revive Marx and redirect the PCF must simultaneously be an attack on Hegel and his influence: both Stalinist determinism and its humanist critique were effectively forms of Hegelianism for Althusser. The economistic-evolutionism propounded by Stalinism was little more than an inverted Hegelianism, with Matter 'substituted . . . for the Hegelian "Mind" or "Absolute Idea"' (Althusser, 2006: 254). Its humanist adversary, on the other hand, did little more than put a Marxist gloss on Kojève's anthropological reading of Hegel, now retold as a story of the journey of Man towards Communism. Thus the anti-Stalinist humanist-historicism offered by Garaudy et al. was merely the obverse of Stalinism's ossified version of Second International economic determinism. Though Stalin may have tried to purge Hegel from Marxism, his theoretical dogmas effectively retained a Hegelian schema, while the critique offered from within the PCF, although it may have been politically opposed to Stalinism, did little to advance things: 'from the standpoint of its *theoretical problematic*, and not of its political style and aims, this humanist and historicist materialism has rediscovered the basic theoretical principles of the Second International's economistic and mechanistic interpretation' (Althusser and Balibar, 1970: 138).

Both Stalinism and humanism forced Marxism into a crude Hegelian framework, whereby history is seen as a progression of stages towards a predetermined *telos*. For Althusser, this is to misunderstand Marx's contribution: Marx does not simply adopt Hegel's concept of history and apply it to political economy. He introduces history into political economy in a unique way, constructing non-Hegelian concepts of history and society. For Hegel (according to Althusser), historical time is continuous, homogeneous, and contemporaneous with itself: each historical period expresses every other and the social totality that contains them. For Althusser's Marx, on the other hand, society cannot be reduced to a totality of which there exists a single common essence or centre: it is rather a complex unity of different levels (economic, political, legal, scientific, philosophical, etc.), and each level has its own rhythm, its own time and history which cannot be known immediately but must be constructed – produced in relation not to some continuous, homogeneous time but to the structure of the determination of the whole. Marx's reconceptualization of society means that 'it is no longer possible to think the process of the development of the different levels of the whole *in the same historical time*' (Althusser and Balibar, 1970: 99).

Althusser's attack on Hegel, then, is simultaneously an attack on humanism and historicism. In Marx there is neither an anthropolgized Hegel nor an inverted Hegel, neither Man nor *Telos*: for Marx history is a process without a Subject or Goal(s). This formulation, however, brings with it some problems – for Althusser claims that Marx takes the idea of history as process from Hegel: this is the 'kernel' he appropriates. In his 1968 essay 'Marx's Relation to Hegel' Althusser argues that 'Man' is not at all the subject of history for Hegel. In fact, if we look for a subject in Hegel we are reduced to the paradox that the only subject is the process without a subject, the process itself in its teleology. 'Take away the teleology, there remains the philosophical category that Marx inherited: the category of a *process without a subject*' (Althusser, 1972: 184–5). Minus the teleology, then, a process without Subject or Goal(s). This is the 'crucial gift' that Hegel gives to Marx: it is '*the idea of the dialectic*' (Althusser, 1972: 174). Thus there is a certain ambiguity in Althusser's attitude towards Hegel. Althusser had been something of a Hegelian in his youth, and despite the marked anti-Hegelianism of his mature writings, he never completely relinquishes all sympathy for Hegel.[9] Moreover, because Althusser wants a *dialectical* Marx, he is always haunted by the ghost of Hegel, no matter how hard he tries to exorcize it at times. Althusser wants both to rid Marx of Hegel and to retain Hegel: constantly to emphasize the non- or anti-Hegelian aspects of Marx while at the same time acknowledging that Marx took something from Hegel. In *For Marx* Althusser had claimed that 'the Young Marx *was never strictly speaking a Hegelian*'. The *1844 Manuscripts* were 'Marx's one and only resort to Hegel in his youth': a last-moment immersion into the Hegelian underworld before the inauguration of historical materialism, a moment on the threshold which reflects 'the paradox that the text of the last hours of the night is, theoretically speaking, the text the furthest removed from the day that is about to dawn' (Althusser, 1969: 35–6). Yet it seems that the shadows of the night stretch long into the next day, even as far as dusk, for elsewhere Althusser claims that of Marx's mature works only the 'Critique of the Gotha Programme' and the '"Notes" on Adolph Wagner' (two works written in the final decade of Marx's life) 'are *totally and definitively exempt* from *any* trace of Hegelian influence' (Althusser, 1971: 90). Althusser seems uncertain which Marx he wants: the Marx in debt to Hegel, or the Marx who owes Hegel nothing.

Defining idealism

This sense of uncertainty persists in Althusser's attitude to idealism, of which his attitude to Hegel might be seen as derivative. The critique of idealism is much more forceful than the critique of Hegel, however: whereas Althusser sometimes shows an active willingness to retain Hegel, the traces of idealism that remain in Althusser's own work seem to persist against his will. So keen is Althusser for a materialist Marx that he refashions Marx's conceptual apparatus where he thinks Marx fails to live up to his materialist promise. For instance, he insists that the concept of ideology must refer to the material actions of a subject engaged in certain material practices and rituals, claiming that although Marx himself approached this position, he failed to think his new concept properly: 'Marx never crossed "the absolute limit" of the material existence of ideologies, of their material existence in the materiality of the class struggle' (Althusser, 2006: 138).

The clearest articulation of the concept of idealism that Althusser wishes to undermine comes in his later work. Here he contends that idealism – which has formed 'the dominant tendency in all of Western philosophy' – is not characterized by a belief in 'the primacy of thought over Being, or Mind over matter, and so on' (Althusser, 2006: 272, 224). Rather, idealist philosophies are those that posit some Reason for the world, some ultimate, unifying principle that can bring order to the disorder of the world:

> [T]he principle according to which everything that exists, whether ideal or material, is subject to the question of the *reason for its existence* . . . and the existence of this question opens up a hinterworld (Nietzsche), a 'behind' the thing, a reason hidden beneath the appearance of the immediate, the empirical, the thing given here and now. (Althusser, 2006: 216–17)

Some essence is sought, some core to which everything must relate. So Hegel's conceptualization of the social whole, as Althusser presents it in *Reading Capital*, is fundamentally idealist: Hegel presupposes 'that the whole in question be reducible to an *inner essence*, of which the elements of the whole are then no more than the phenomenal forms of expression' (Althusser and Balibar, 1970: 186).

Idealism searches for order, giving everything an Origin and an End: everything has a place, a *telos* inscribed at birth.

> [I]n idealism, the question of the Origin is a question that arises on the basis of the question of the End. Anticipating itself, the End (the meaning of the world, the meaning of its history, the ultimate purpose of the world and history) projects itself back on to and into the question of the origin. The question of the origin of anything whatsoever is always posed as a function of the idea one has of its end. (Althusser, 2006: 217–18)

Idealism, then, requires a joint ontology and teleology: an account of the Being of things that is also an account of their End. Materialism, on the other hand, is not merely the inverse of idealism: as Althusser says in a much earlier essay, a philosophy inverted does not change its structure, problems, or meaning; it retains the same problematic (Althusser, 1969: 73). Such a philosophy would be 'a materialism of necessity and teleology, that is to say, a transformed, disguised form of idealism' (Althusser, 2006: 168). A true materialism must escape the problematic of idealism; it must be the 'rejection of all philosophies of essence (*Ousia, Essentia, Wesen*), that is, of Reason (*Logos, Ratio, Vernunft*), and therefore of Origin and End – the Origin being nothing more, here, than the anticipation of the End in Reason or primordial order' (Althusser, 2006: 188).[10]

These characterizations of idealism and materialism, although coming at the end of Althusser's career (or, more accurately, in that hinterland between the official end of his career and his death), reconfirm his earlier critiques of Hegel and readings of Marx: the original aim to dethrone 'the Gods of Origins and Goals' (Althusser, 1969: 71), an aim which stretches back to Althusser's work on Montesquieu of the 1950s. There is no Goal to history for Althusser's Marx, no necessary End that is the flower of its Origin. History has no Subject for this Marx: the end of history is not the restoration of Man. The concept of overdetermination is developed by Althusser in the early 1960s in order to combat idealism. Where Hegel (according to Althusser) reduces the complex totality of a society to a simple, central contradiction, overdetermination signifies the complex and differentially articulated structure of society as recognized by Marx. Here there is no longer an idealist conception of the whole in which all elements are expressions of an inner essence. If Althusser can be called a structuralist, it is not because he refers all phenomena to underlying laws or a single subterranean Cause, but because he overthrows the sovereignty of the subject and analyses the social structure in terms of its relations. The requirement is not for the identification of general laws (*pace* Lévi-Strauss) but the careful articulation of a complex set of relations, relations that are not determined by a pre-existing structure: the social structure is itself nothing more than the set of relations. In materialism there is a refusal of pre-established order out of respect for 'the thing given here and now'. This is what Marxism is for Althusser, who is fond of quoting Lenin on this point: '*the soul of Marxism is the concrete analysis of a concrete situation*' (Althusser, 1969: 206; cf. Lenin, 1966: 166).

For Althusser, then, Marx is in a struggle not just against Hegel but against idealism more generally. Nevertheless, in Althusser's later work, just as he is more prepared to concede that Marx did not break definitively with Hegel, so he is more prepared to admit that Marx does not necessarily rid himself of idealism: there are tensions, even irreconcilable alternatives, in Marx's work, and to an extent he remains a 'prisoner of idealism'. We have seen Althusser argue that Marx's notion of ideology was haunted by idealism; in connection with this, he also points to those passages in the section on fetishism in volume one of *Capital*, where 'we find . . . a latent idea of the perfect transparency of social relations under communism'. Marx, says Althusser, never freed himself from 'this whole idealist myth, which came to him straight from the utopian socialists' (Althusser, 2006: 36–7). While Althusser is correct to find a certain idealism in this section of *Capital*, he overlooks the fact that Marx's comments on fetishism are in fact very close to his own – strictly materialist – remarks on ideology. What is expressed in Marx's theory of fetishism is not the idea of a mystical illusion that needs to be corrected, but an analysis of the ways in which individuals *must act*, regardless of any distorted beliefs or ideas.[11]

Althusser finds materialist elements in Marx's work alongside, in tension with, these idealist elements. He claims, for example, that there are two 'absolutely unrelated conceptions of the mode of production in Marx' (Althusser, 2006: 197). On the one hand, there is a teleological-essentialist conception that conceives the mode of production in terms of an essential structure that precedes its elements: these elements – in the case of capitalism, owners of money and workers separated from the means of production – are posited in terms of necessity, as if they were *destined* to come together. Yet there is also another conception of the mode of production: a historico-aleatory one. In particular, this conception is found at the end of *Capital*, in the chapters on primitive accumulation that Althusser names 'the true heart of the book' (199). Here there are the same elements – owners of money, 'free workers' with only labour-power to sell – but they exist as independent, floating elements with their own separate histories, which come together in an aleatory encounter that might never have happened. The impoverished, expropriated masses may then be *reproduced* by capitalism, once the encounter has occurred, but they were not *produced* by capitalism in the first place: they were not created with capitalism in mind, but came to form an element of capitalism only through their aleatory encounter with the owners of money.

This second concept of the mode of production is an example of what Althusser calls a materialist philosophy of the encounter, or aleatory materialism. These terms are developed in Althusser's work from the 1980s, as part of a renewed attempt to posit a materialism that is not simply an inverted idealism: a materialism that will escape all questions of Cause, Origin, and End. They offer a way of thinking singularity without teleology, a thinking of history that recognizes that '[e]very conjuncture is a singular case, as are all historical individualities, as is everything that exists' (Althusser, 2006: 264). This emphasis on singular cases, as Warren Montag (1998: 69) has pointed out, continues the work done twenty years earlier. The earlier concept of overdetermination targeted the same enemies that aleatory materialism deals with: essentialist, teleological conceptions of the whole in which the elements of that whole are only the expression of a pre-established inner essence, a deeper unity. Antonio Negri suggests that Althusser's turn towards aleatory materialism proposes 'the destruction of every teleological horizon – therefore, the positive assertion of the logic of the event' (Negri, 1996: 61). Althusser's own claims confirm this suggestion: against idealist teleologies, aleatory materialism is 'required to think the openness of the world towards the event, the as-yet-unimaginable, and also all living practice, politics included' (Althusser, 2006: 264).

This is the nature of Althusser's materialism, then: attentive to the concrete singularity of the immediate situation, it rejects dependence on the concept of a deeper reality, a hinterworld beneath phenomena, some true Being which, though it may presently be repressed or alienated or lost, will one day be restored. The materialist philosopher 'always catches a moving train, the way they do in American Westerns. Without knowing where he comes from (origin) or where he's going (goal)' (Althusser, 2006: 290). Materialism does away with Origins and Ends: it does not bind all to a predetermined end but is sensitive to contingent events. It does not stand back to uncover the Truth of the world, but recognizes its own conditions and actively intervenes in a political struggle. This is the materialism Althusser wishes to extract from Marx.

Althusser and post-structuralism

Althusser sets the scene for what follows, in particular through his definition of idealism. He also clears the ground for a new kind of Marx, smashing open the dominant, humanist models that the post-structuralists would have been exposed to as students, and thus opening up new directions. Althusser rethinks what a materialist Marx would mean, what Marx's unique contribution is. Yet there exists a series of tensions in Althusser's work. He posits two Marxes, insisting on the importance of the 1845 break; yet he also recognizes a more fluid and complex diversity in Marx, and divides Marx into a proliferating number of periods. He wants to return to a Marx unscarred by Party formulae; yet to do so he reads Marx against himself, and supplements him with other thinkers. He wants to purge Marx of Hegelianism; yet he acknowledges Marx's debt to Hegel in the figure of the dialectic. He complicates that dialectic by bringing in the notion of overdetermination; yet he ties this notion to a determination in the last instance by the economy. He insists on Marx's recognition of a plurality of different historical rhythms; yet he does not analyse Marx's specific historical studies or produce his own histories. He emphasizes the materiality of ideology, its immanence to practices and institutions; yet he does not seem to recognize the materiality of Marx's own theory of fetishism. More broadly, there is a tension in Althusser's position on idealism. On the one hand, in notions like 'determination in the last instance' there is something like that nostalgia for centre and origin that Derrida identified in Lévi-Strauss; indeed, it is this nostalgia, through which Althusser remains tethered to the idealism that he wishes to overcome, that most clearly justifies grouping

Althusser with the structuralists. On the other hand, Althusser's later work may go too far in the other direction, succumbing to the seduction of a theory that prioritizes the aleatory but which thence can discern no patterns in the chaos and offer no explanations for what become apparently random events. In this case, rather than resembling structuralism, Althusser anticipates some of the difficulties encountered by post-structuralism. Thus, in a sense, Althusser sits between structuralism and post-structuralism, caught between nostalgia for what has been lost and an inability to orient any critical position. This point is touched on by Montag, one of Althusser's most astute commentators in recent years: he argues that in trying to present a concept of structure present only in its effects, making the diverse intelligible without reduction or unification, Althusser equivocates between two alternatives: between a rigid structural unity and coherence, and an aleatory and indeterminate disorder (Montag, 1998: 72–3). It is then possible to posit two Althussers: 'the thinker of the formal orders of history' and the 'celebrant of difference and disorder' (Montag, 2003: 14). This equivocation, I would argue, is a result of Althusser's attempt to offer a philosophy without idealism: without some notion of an Origin or End, something to ground and order a philosophy, there is always the risk that everything will collapse into indeterminacy, and critique will become impossible. The materialist philosopher must present history without iron laws or guaranteed *telos* – but what then can history be but a collection of random events? There is a risk of falling into an indeterminacy that is merely the mirror of a rigid determination.

These are the problems Althusser faces – but they are also the problems the post-structuralists will face. Althusser sets the scene well, in particular by his characterization of idealism: to target idealism is to target those philosophies which posit some essence behind the world's appearance, some End that is also its Cause, some given Being which will be recovered with the culmination of historical destiny. These, broadly, are the terms in which post-structuralism will criticize Marx. Yet although I use Althusser first to set the terms of reference, to make vivid the problems involved, this does not mean that Althusser's explicit critique of idealism is chronologically prior to post-structuralism. Although much of Althusser's work does clear a path for post-structuralist work on Marx, much of his later work reflects the influence of that post-structuralist work. Having looked in more detail at the post-structuralist readings of Marx, it will be possible to see that in characterizing idealism as a philosophy of Origins and Ends, Althusser was following the critiques of Marx made by the post-structuralists.

Nonetheless, Althusser remains in many ways an important precursor of post-structuralism, and the tensions in his work anticipate difficulties in post-structuralism. The Marx that emerges from post-structuralism in many ways resembles Althusser's Marx: a Marx separated from humanism, historicism, and Hegel – from the traditions and movements with which he had become entwined in postwar France. But post-structuralist Marxes are not just variants on Althusserian Marxes. On the one hand, the post-structuralists go further than Althusser, pushing for an even more rigorously materialist Marx. On the other hand, they bring in new elements – introducing Marx to Nietzsche, for example. But before I look in detail at what each post-structuralist does with Marx, I want to address criticisms of post-structuralism that have been made by Marxists. This will complete our survey of the contextual background.

Marxists Against Post-Structuralism

One might assume that all that needs to be said about Marxism and post-structuralism has been said, twenty years ago or more. Once post-structuralist thinkers became popularized and their ideas widely circulated, it did not take long for Marxists to offer comment. These responses were frequently highly critical of post-structuralism. I want to offer an overview of these critiques to show that they do not exhaust the potential encounters between Marx and post-structuralism – and that, ultimately, they do not much help to further understanding of the relation between the two. On the one hand, they do not tend to look at what post-structuralism actually says about Marx; on the other hand, in criticizing post-structuralism they do not tend to use Marx.

Many of the most aggressive attacks on post-structuralism came from Britain, and this is the context in which I write, so I am going to focus on the works of British Marxists. (As we shall see, each is influenced by non-British sources.) The writers examined do not speak with one voice; they do, however, have much in common with each other, and from their works it is possible to extract a number of common views. For these Marxist critics, post-structuralism is: reflective of changes in late twentieth-century capitalism; a form of anti-Enlightenment Nietzscheanism; a product of failure and defeat; conservative, regressive, and ultimately pro-capitalist; and, at its worst, typical of fashionable French pretension. Not every one of these claims is made by every one of the critics analysed, but they occur frequently enough to be identified as common themes. While the quality and tone of the different commentaries vary, they are in general hostile to post-structuralism, and each contributes something to the catalogue of objections just given. I do not intend to refute each objection, or each writer, individually, but to demonstrate their shortcomings overall.

Post-structuralism as postmodernism

These Marxist responses to post-structuralism need to be put into context in order to understand them. Writing in the 1980s and early 1990s, Marxist critics assimilated post-structuralist philosophy into a much wider category of 'postmodernism'.[12] Alex Callinicos articulates a fairly typical viewpoint when in his book *Against Postmodernism* he sets out to examine 'three distinct cultural trends' that operate under the banner of postmodernism: postmodern art (including literature, architecture, cinema), post-structuralist philosophy, and theories of postmodernity/postindustrial society (Callinicos, 1989: 2–3). In assimilating post-structuralism into postmodernism, Marxist critics were responding to existing categorizations rather than simply inventing labels better to attack an enemy: popularizing admirers of Foucault et al., especially in the United States, had already attached the label of postmodernism. But it is not a label that would be accepted by the four post-structuralist thinkers – not even by Lyotard, who has talked of the postmodern rather than postmodernism, and who later anyway suggested that even this former term is not a very useful word (cf. Lyotard, 1991*a*: 5).

Incorporating post-structuralism into postmodernism, however, serves a useful purpose for critics: blurring or collapsing the distinction between the two allows the post-structuralists to be associated with various trends that have little to do with post-structuralism. The term 'postmodern' first became popularized in relation to architecture, where it was used to refer to a populist, commercial architecture that revelled in a consumerist aesthetic.[13] Identifying Foucault and the other post-structuralists as postmodernists assimilates them into this genial espousal of consumerism – whereas in fact, as we shall see, each post-structuralist calls on Marx as a critic of capitalism. As 'postmodernists', the post-structuralists also find themselves conflated with certain trends inside philosophy – most notably Richard Rorty and his endorsement of what he (only half-jokingly) calls 'postmodernist bourgeois liberalism'. Rorty cheerfully admits that he could never be bothered to read *Capital* (Rorty, 1999: 210), and he is largely dismissive of Marx as yet another Platonic metaphysician (cf. Rorty, 1989: 120).[14] There are certainly some philosophical similarities between Rorty and the post-structuralists (e.g. like the post-structuralists, Rorty would reject idealism as I have defined it). It is these similarities, alongside the extension of the term 'postmodern', that allow critics to tar both camps with the same brush, dismissing all as bourgeois liberals while ignoring political and philosophical differences. Even where there is acknowledgement of differences, this is often lost in the heat of polemic, and post-structuralists are condemned by association. 'Postmodern bourgeois liberalism', more than a witty slogan for Rorty's own project, becomes a judgement on post-structuralism in general.

One may object that I have committed an equal sin in labelling four separate thinkers 'post-structuralist', a label they would also reject. But there is a difference between using a term of convenience in a detailed discussion of the merits and weaknesses of each individual thinker and employing a homogenizing label that covers over differences and assimilates thinkers to trends of which they are not part. The Marxist critiques do consist of more than simply the application of a label, of course. Having employed this label, they then criticized post-structuralism from a number of different angles. In doing so they were influenced largely by three different sources. Fredric Jameson, Perry Anderson, and Jürgen Habermas set the coordinates for much of what followed: post-structuralism/postmodernism as symptom of late capitalism, product of defeat, and Nietzschean conservatism.

Jameson, Anderson, Habermas

In a seminal essay from 1984 – later reproduced as the first chapter of an expanded book of the same name – Jameson identified postmodernism as 'the cultural dominant of the logic of late capitalism' (Jameson, 1993: 46). Elsewhere Jameson has offered careful, often sympathetic readings of post-structuralist thinkers, yet it is his 1984 essay and subsequent book that have had the biggest impact.[15] Here Jameson suggests that post-structuralism be viewed as 'a very significant symptom' of postmodern culture (Jameson, 1993: 12), thus relating post-structuralism to the development of late twentieth-century multinational capitalism. So, for example, the 'so-called death of the subject' is related to 'our insertion as individual subjects into a multidimensional set of radically discontinuous realities, whose frames range from the still surviving spaces of bourgeois private life all the way to the unimaginable decentering of global capital itself' (Jameson, 1993: 413). While not without its critics, Jameson's analysis has been highly influential, and has encouraged the idea that post-structuralism be seen together with postmodernism as an expression of changes in the capitalist economy. David Harvey's *The Condition of Postmodernity* picks up this thread, presenting postmodernism as a response to changes in the experience of space and time as the Fordist-Keynesian system gave way after 1973 to a new, flexible regime of accumulation: postmodernism's 'emphasis upon ephemerality, collage, fragmentation, and dispersal in philosophical and social thought mimics the conditions of flexible accumulation' (Harvey, 1989: 302).

Interesting work has come from this sort of approach, but it has severe limitations. It is unhelpfully reductive, and fails to make significant distinctions (between different thinkers, for example). Furthermore – and more importantly for the present analysis – it does not throw any light on post-structuralism's attitudes towards Marx. Jameson has sometimes suggested that post-structuralist insights might help illuminate analysis of 'late capitalism', but in his major and most influential work on postmodernism he does not deal with individual thinkers. Post-structuralism is presented as a symptom, not a diagnostic tool; Marxism offers an interpretation of post-structuralism, but there is nothing on how post-structuralism might use Marx.

A second angle of the Marxist response presents post-structuralism as an expression of political rather than economic changes: it is a reaction to revolutionary failure. This approach is adapted from Anderson's (1976) influential thesis that Western Marxism should be seen as a product of defeat: a retreat into theory for intellectuals trapped between an invigorated capitalism and a sclerotic Stalinism. This thesis is extended by Anderson himself in a later essay to cover the work coming out of France from 1960 onwards: to a generation disappointed by the failures of first Maoism and then Eurocommunism as alternatives to Western capitalism and Soviet communism, structuralism proved 'an immensely alluring form of idealism' (Anderson, 1984: 81) – with post-structuralism as its logical successor in disappointment. This image of post-structuralism and postmodernism as solace for a defeated generation of radicals has been picked up with enthusiasm by other critics. For Callinicos, postmodernism 'must be understood largely as a response to failure of the great upturn of 1968–76 to fulfil the revolutionary hopes it raised' (Callinicos, 1989: 171). Terry Eagleton thinks that the 'profound pessimism' of post-structuralism 'articulates a massive, pervasive failure of political nerve consequent upon the disillusionments of post-1968' (Eagleton, 1988: 93). Completing a circle of mutual admiration, Anderson repays this homage to his original thesis: 'Callinicos and Eagleton are right to stress immediate sources of postmodernism in the experience of defeat' (Anderson, 1998: 91). Christopher Norris claims that much postmodernism would 'tend to bear out Anderson's thesis about the retreat into theory among left intellectuals at times of widespread political disenchantment' (Norris, 1990: 25). (Norris here is referring specifically to Lyotard but he makes it clear that Lyotard is not alone on this retreat.)[16] But according to these critics, it is not just that, like the Western Marxists, the post-structuralists have retreated into theory: they have gone a step further and surrendered any opposition to capitalism – worse, they have actively embraced capitalism, so that a once potentially radical stance 'has now passed over into a species of disguised apologetics for the socio-political status quo' (Norris, 1990: 3). 'Paris today', wrote Anderson in 1983, 'is the capital of European intellectual reaction' (Anderson, 1984: 32). Post-structuralism, as part of postmodernism, is a reactionary creed. The idea of the postmodern, Anderson later claims, developed 'in one way or another [as] an appanage of the Right . . . There could be nothing but capitalism. The postmodern was a sentence on alternative illusions' (Anderson, 1998: 45–6). Postmodernism tells the disillusioned ex-radicals that Callinicos describes exactly what they want to hear: 'that there is nothing that they can do to change the world' (Callinicos, 1989: 170).

As with the first approach, this political explanation is rather reductive – and, if anything, it pushes Marx even further into the background. The Jameson approach does not tend to look at what the post-structuralists say about Marx, but it does at least use Marx in its analysis of new economic forms (though Jameson's analysis itself is rather thin, and as indebted to Ernest Mandel as it is to Marx). But with the Anderson approach Marx is almost not needed at all. The superiority of Marxist analysis and the hostility of post-structuralism towards Marxism are both assumed: there is little explicit discussion of what exactly Marx might have that the post-structuralists do not, nor of how the post-structuralists view Marx.

Another line of attack, inspired by Habermas, does offer detailed analysis of what the post-structuralists have actually written. While Habermas himself rarely talks of post-structuralism or postmodernism – and while his status as a *Marxist* thinker is open to question – he provides extended critiques of Foucault and Derrida, and his attacks on his French contemporaries have, like the work of Jameson and Anderson, been extremely influential on Marxist responses to post-structuralism. This time post-structuralism is a symptom of intellectual confusion or dishonesty rather than of economic change or political failure. A 1980 speech in which Habermas criticizes the 'anti-modern' 'young conservatism' of Foucault and Derrida (Habermas, 1981: 13) was given the title 'Modernity versus Postmodernity' when first translated into English, thus setting the tone for the British reception of Habermas's work on this subject. *The Philosophical Discourse of Modernity* takes up several of the themes hinted at in the 1980 speech: Foucault and Derrida, it is said, pursue a radical, Nietzschean self-critique of reason which '*bids farewell* to the dialectic of enlightenment' (Habermas, 1987: 86) – but like Nietzsche they get caught up in the performative contradiction of an attack on reason that uses reason's own weapons. (Elsewhere Habermas claims that both Derrida and Foucault advance 'critiques that liquidate reason' [Habermas, 2001: 12].) Derrida, argues Habermas, tries to surmount these contradictions by illegitimately dissolving the distinction between philosophy and literature, whereas Foucault gets caught up in a '*presentistic, relativistic, cryptonormative*' methodology which can only offer critical insight by surreptitiously drawing on the very standards it putatively rejects (Habermas, 1987: 276). Unable to account for the epistemological status of their own philosophy and reliant on a celebration of aesthetic values, Foucault and Derrida offer undifferentiated, levelling critiques that 'can no longer discern contrasts, shadings, and ambivalent tones' within modernity, and are unable to distinguish the emancipatory from the repressive (Habermas, 1987: 338).[17]

This Habermasian image of Foucault and Derrida as Nietzschean assailants on Enlightenment values has been extremely influential on Marxist critics, who have expanded it to cover other post-structuralists.[18] Norris, for example, protests against those postmodernists and post-structuralists who give us 'distorted aestheticist readings of Kant' 'in pursuit of [their] own irrationalist or counter-enlightenment aims' (Norris, 1993: 14–15). Deleuze and Guattari's *A Thousand Plateaus* is for Norris an 'out-and-out polemical crusade against "enlightenment" reason in every shape or form' ('by far the most sustained postmodernist assault on all the concepts and categories of Western intellectual tradition') (Norris, 1993: 231). Eagleton writes of Foucault that in his 'drastically undialectical attitude to Enlightenment, he eradicates at a stroke almost all of its vital civilizing achievements, in which he can see nothing but insidious techniques of subjection' (Eagleton, 1992: 389). Habermas's argument is taken up most explicitly by Peter Dews, who replicates many of the themes of *The Philosophical Discourse of Modernity*: a puncturing of some of post-structuralism's supposed claims to novelty by viewing it against the background of existing philosophical traditions; admiration for the sophistication of post-structuralist insights tempered by criticism of a one-sided approach to modernity which 'remains negatively bound to the philosophy of consciousness' (Dews, 1987: 236); a claim that post-structuralists oscillate between ubiquitous ontological totalizations (*différance*, power, desire) and a Nietzschean perspectivism, between an objective neutrality and a subjective critique, ultimately unable to account either for oppression or liberation; and an appeal to rational standards of normativity against the relativism of theories which necessarily call into question their own status and validity.

These criticisms are not entirely illegitimate or wholly misguided, but the problem with this Habermasian approach is that Marx gets increasingly sidelined. Habermas claims that he 'value[s] being considered a Marxist' (Habermas, 1992: 82), and he does use Marx as an alternative to post-structuralism – but it is a diluted, anaemic Marx, a Marx filtered through Habermas's own theory of communicative action. What Habermas and his acolytes are really defending is not Marx or Marxism but 'the Enlightenment', embodied by Kant. As with Jameson and Anderson, there is little on what post-structuralism actually says about Marx. Yet Marx falls even further out of sight this time, as Kant is called on to battle post-structuralism, and Marx is recalled only as an afterthought, with the reminder that he too was an Enlightenment figure. It is not only potential post-structuralist insights into Marx that get lost, but also the irreducible specificity of Marx (to borrow from Althusser), as he is absorbed into an Enlightenment tradition to which post-structuralism is supposedly opposed. This is not to say that Marx can*not* be aligned to the Enlightenment tradition, or that he was some sort of anti-Enlightenment figure: only that there are more profitable ways to explore his relation to post-structuralism, and he should not be hidden behind Kant.

Common sense

The danger of this last, Habermasian approach – in addition to effacing Marx and risking what Foucault calls 'the blackmail of the Enlightenment' (Foucault, 1997: 312)[19] – is that it can easily degenerate into a much broader and less subtle attack where what appears to require defence is neither Marx nor the Enlightenment but an outraged common sense. Here Habermas's influence is joined by that of a peculiarly Anglicized Marxism, at once rational and empirical, suspicious of too much abstract theorizing, and prizing precision, rigour, and clarity.[20] Seen from this angle, post-structuralism is part of 'the common nonsense of the age' (Anderson, 1998: 115), 'lamentably fashion-prone' (Norris, 1992: 69) and full of 'windy banalities' (Callinicos, 1989: 78). But worse than nonsense, it is French nonsense: 'the latest intellectual fad imported from Paris' (Harvey, 1989: 7), with their 'cult of flashy theoretical fashion and instant intellectual consumption'; 'new-fangled' forms of idealism, the errors of which are repeated 'in rather more modish a guise' (Eagleton, 1997: 23, 14, 43). More than simple fantasy, or illusion, these 'modish *idées reçues*' are not only 'intellectually and morally bankrupt', but also 'perverse', 'retrograde' and 'ultimately cynical, reductive or nihilist' (Norris, 1996: 109, 64–5; Norris, 1993: 288; Norris, 1992: 120). One suspects that it is not only Callinicos and Anderson who agree that Marxism is 'a kind of common sense' (cf. Callinicos, 1989: 126).

While these quotations do not on their own do justice to the range and quality of the arguments of their authors, they accurately evoke the tone of a body of criticism that at times swings between supercilious disdain and virulent fury. The echo of Edward Thompson's (1978) diatribe against Althusser resounds in British Marxism's discussion of post-structuralism. Judged as part of postmodernism, post-structuralism is seen as not simply conservative, defeatist, and regressive, but also irrationalist, relativist, and sophistical; not merely reactionary, but reactionary nonsense. Even where concessions are made to what Callinicos calls postmodernism's 'partial insights' (Callinicos, 1989: 5), the tone is one of condescension: so, for example, while postmodernism 'could be deployed to radical ends', any positive points are offset by 'its accommodations with individualism, commercialism, and entrepreneurialism' (Harvey, 1989: 353, 113).[21]

Marxists have seen post-structuralism not as something to be engaged with, but something to be exposed and resisted. What is this thing that is not Marxism but which has taken such a hold, this thing whose 'grosser political and philosophical absurdities . . . have managed to turn the heads of a whole younger generation of potentially valuable militants' (Eagleton, 1988: 93)? This is the question Marxists ask of post-structuralism. Post-structuralism, it is thought, requires explanation: economically, as a reflection of late capitalism; politically, as a response to failure; philosophically, as an irrational relativism. Post-structuralism must be seen as part of a wider postmodernism, and as such is pro-capitalist, defeatist, and anti-Enlightenment. The question that is *not* asked of the post-structuralists is: what do they have to say about Marx? To an extent, the failure to pursue this question is understandable. The apostate Lyotard can conceivably, if unfairly, be dismissed as an anti-Marxist celebrant of capitalism: no need to listen to his thoughts on Marx. Derrida maintained a noted silence on Marx until *Specters of Marx*, published long after attitudes towards Derrida's work had already hardened. Foucault said very little on Marx, and when he did it was frequently unflattering. Deleuze has been far more vocal on Marx, but until recently Deleuze was the least discussed of the post-structuralists. It is easy to see why Marxists have seen post-structuralism as a threat rather than an opportunity.

I do not want to claim that the Marxist critics I have named produce no valid criticisms of post-structuralism. Each of them at times offers astute and penetrating comments; indeed, I shall draw on some of their insights in later chapters as I formulate my own criticisms. Moreover, they have not been unremittingly hostile; they have acknowledged valuable elements in post-structuralism, especially in more recent years, as the flames of the original polemic have died down. But it is precisely because that polemic has died down that it is now a good time to revisit the scene of the debate – but this time with a different approach, one that is more productive than that taken in the 1980s and 1990s. While I do not ignore the context within which the post-structuralists wrote, it is not my aim to explain their work by reference to economic development or political defeat. Instead I want to look at how they have read, used, and criticized Marx – and how he is enriched by these readings.

Conclusion

This chapter has tried to illuminate the background to the post-structuralist readings of Marx in order better to understand them. Without assimilating the work of Lyotard, Derrida, Foucault, and Deleuze into a uniform whole, it has highlighted some common themes in post-structuralism: the influence of Nietzsche; a distrust of Hegelian dialectics; a desire to avoid both teleology and ahistoricism; an aversion to systematization; a rejection of depth/surface models. Many of these themes can usefully be elucidated in relation to an earlier structuralism: while post-structuralism also dethrones the sovereign subject and looks at relations rather than essential elements, it does not search for general laws, and moves away from the study of signs towards an interest in extra-linguistic factors. In addition to this preliminary and general characterization, this chapter also placed the post-structuralist approaches to Marx within their context, looking briefly at the humanist interpretations of Marx predominant in postwar France, and in more detail at the anti-humanist Marxism of Althusser. I highlighted several features of the latter – not just its critique of Hegelianism, humanism, and historicism, but also Althusser's call for an explicitly political and practical Marx, and his recognition of the diversity of Marx's texts and the need for an inventive reading. Yet I also noted some ambiguities and tensions in Althusser's work. In addition, looking at Althusser enabled us to examine his critical definition of idealism, a definition that will be used later as we delineate the post-structuralist critique of Marx. Idealism here is conceptualized as a philosophy of Origins and Ends: rather than recognizing the contingency of history and analysing specific and singular situations, it forces events into a pre-established order, explaining them ontologically and teleologically, reducing them to an essential origin and a predetermined end. I suggested that there is a risk in subverting idealism in this sense: a risk that critical thinking loses the ability to orient itself, and can only record a random chaos that is the mirror of a predetermined order. Finally, I examined an alternative way of approaching the relation between Marx and post-structuralism, looking at the critical evaluations of post-structuralism provided by British Marxists, and concluding that this approach tended to marginalize Marx and to treat post-structuralism as a threat to Marxism. In contrast, I want to analyse what the post-structuralists have written about Marx – beginning with Lyotard.

Chapter 2

A Writer Full of Affects: Marx Through Lyotard

Marxism has not come to an end, but how does it continue?
(Lyotard, 1988a: 171)

I start with Lyotard's engagement with Marx not because it is the simplest, most direct, or most impressive of the post-structuralist engagements with Marx – but precisely because it is the most varied, wide-ranging, and (ultimately) disappointing. Lyotard started out as a committed Marxist militant, later renounced Marxism as a revolutionary outlook, and eventually marginalized Marx as a thinker. Despite this marginalization, Marx remains a persistent figure in Lyotard's work: he is influenced by a huge range of philosophers, but his dealings with Marx span his entire career. There is no single take on Marx by Lyotard, but this should not come as a surprise: Lyotard does not aim at consistency in his philosophy in general. He has said that 'inconsistency... bears witness to the life of thought' (Lyotard, cited in Bennington, 1988: 2), and that we should 'take up' thoughts even 'at the price of self-contradiction' (Lyotard, 1984a: 16). Yet Lyotard himself has sometimes pointed to continuities in his writings (cf. Lyotard, 1984a: 17; 1988b: 300–1), and there is a certain coherence to his work. If there is a dominant thread in that work, then it is found in Lyotard's openness to new occurrences: a refusal to place things in some neatly ordered system. This idea is a persistent theme, albeit one that takes varying forms: an attack on theory, an incredulity towards metanarratives, a critique of philosophies of history. Throughout these changes of position, there remains a common respect for what Lyotard calls the *event*: a sensitivity to that which happens but eludes re-presentation, that which 'defies knowledge' (Lyotard, 2006: 46). It is a concern that runs through his engagement with Marx, which despite its furious variations and subtle transformations has its own consistency: the critique Lyotard develops after renouncing revolutionary Marxism colours his attitude towards Marx for the rest of his life. This chapter analyses Lyotard's changing relation to Marx.[1] It argues that while Lyotard highlights important issues in Marx's work, he is too ready to dismiss Marx and hence misses much that is valuable in that work. Lyotard attacks Marx's idealism as I have defined it. But on the one hand, Lyotard does not recognize as fully as Derrida, Foucault, and Deleuze that alternatives exist in Marx; and on the other hand, Lyotard's own alternatives highlight the dangers of trying to posit a materialist philosophy. The breadth and variation of Lyotard's engagement with Marx will enable us here to examine a variety of significant issues; that this engagement is ultimately rather disappointing allows these issues to be sketched in outline form so that we can later see how Derrida, Foucault, and Deleuze have better dealt with them. The chapter will undertake a broadly chronological examination of Lyotard's relation to Marx, starting with his early Marxist writings, then dealing with libidinal economics and the break with Marxism, through his attack on grand narratives to the philosophy of the differend and the postmodern fables of his final years.

Early Marxism

Geoff Bennington claims that 'there is no sense in deciding that at one point Lyotard was "a Marxist" and at another point stopped being one' (Bennington, 1988: 32). While it is true that it is important to avoid easy categorization and respect the complexity of Lyotard's relation to Marx, it is also clear that at one point Lyotard was a Marxist and that at another point he stopped being one: up to a certain period his work is replete with Marxist concepts and terminology and he is explicitly committed to revolutionary Marxist critique. It will be useful to embark on a brief survey of Lyotard's heterodox Marxism, before examining his loss of revolutionary faith and the arguments he began to develop against Marx.

Class, contradictions, exploitation

Like many others of the postwar period, Lyotard's earliest interest in Marx was joined to an interest in phenomenology. His first book – *Phenomenology*, first published in 1954 – is an introductory guide to its title subject, and raises the possibility of combining this philosophy with Marxism. Although emphasizing the positive value of phenomenology, Lyotard ultimately concludes that no 'serious reconciliation between these two philosophies can be attempted', and even states that 'phenomenology is retrograde with respect to Hegelian and Marxist philosophies' (Lyotard, 1991*b*: 127, 135). As this statement suggests, the young Lyotard did not reject phenomenology in the name of an anti-Hegelian Marxism. The Marxism he turned to from this point cannot easily be categorized among either of the dominant strands of postwar French Marxism: it was neither Hegelian nor anti-Hegelian, neither humanist nor anti-humanist. The nature of Lyotard's Marxism is better revealed by the political writings that he produced over the next decade. In the year *Phenomenology* was published, he joined *Socialisme ou barbarie*, a Marxist journal which he later described as 'the theoretical mouthpiece of a few militants, workers, employees, and intellectuals who had banded together with the aim of carrying on the Marxist critique of reality, both theoretical and practical, even to its extreme consequences' (Lyotard, 1993c: 165). A teacher in Algeria at the time, Lyotard was assigned the task of commenting on the struggle by France's North African colonies to gain independence. In 1963 Lyotard was part of an 'anti-tendency' that had formed in opposition to the ideas of Cornelius Castoriadis (who had co-founded *Socialisme ou barbarie* in 1948) and split from the main group to write for the monthly workers' paper *Pouvoir Ouvrier*. In 1966 Lyotard resigned from this second group. Marking the death of a former *Socialisme ou barbarie* colleague in 1982, Lyotard wrote in his essay 'A Memorial of Marxism':

> we had during those twelve years devoted our time and all our capacities for thinking and acting to the sole enterprise of 'revolutionary critique and orientation' which was that of the group and its journal. . . . Nothing else, with the exception of love, seemed to us worth a moment's attention during those years. (Lyotard, 1988c: 47)

It could be tempting to read Lyotard backwards, to interpret his early Marxist writings in terms of his later work and find some sort of nascent postmodernism in the early work on Algeria. Lyotard himself has come close to such an interpretation.[2] But although some of the later, postmodern themes are evident in the early work, Lyotard's writings on North Africa remain firmly within a Marxist framework. There is a constant emphasis on class analysis and the contradictions of capitalism. For example, Lyotard claimed that if nationalist ideology had buried social antagonisms and united all the classes of Algeria, then this was only a temporary situation and 'does not mean that it is advisable . . . to abandon the concept of class' (Lyotard, 1993c: 198). Nationalist ideology was a response to colonization, which rested on the economic exploitation of the Algerians. While in Morocco and Tunisia the nationalist movements against French imperialism had been led by a native bourgeoisie who sought 'to impose an indigenous ruling class as new exploiters', in Algeria a different situation prevailed: the native bourgeoisie was economically, socially, and politically weak (178, 235). 'In Algeria, direct colonization had blocked the economic development and political expression of this class' (298). Hence, after Algerian independence was proclaimed in 1962 there was something of a power vacuum: no class was strong enough to give direction to the new nation. The offer of post-independence financial 'aid' from France to Algeria amounted to 'a late contribution by imperialism to the smooth formation of an Algerian bourgeoisie': that is, an attempt to maintain the exploitation of the vast majority of Algerian society (317).

Even these excerpts from Lyotard's analyses of the situation in North Africa provide some insight into his political position at this time: clearly Marxist, but not the sclerotic Marxism of the French Communist Party. *Socialisme ou barbarie* drew on a variety of revolutionary traditions, Marxist and non-Marxist, and Lyotard's essays were frequently highly critical of interpretations given to events by those on the left, especially Stalinists and Trotskyists. Hence while Lyotard's commitment to Marxism was hardly untypical of postwar French intellectuals, the *form* of this Marxism was unusual: neither the Stalinism propounded by the postwar French Communist Party (PCF), nor the humanist Marxism it later adopted and already expounded by Sartre et al. – yet nor was it the ahumanist, anti-Hegelian Marxism that Althusser would offer. In place of these, Lyotard followed Castoriadis in applying an unorthodox, critical Marxism that was attendant to the concrete situation and resistant to crude systematization, yet worked with Marxist categories and concepts. Lyotard was always sensitive to the specificity of local circumstances, warning against 'imposing outdated political categories on this world [or] applying a political practice to it that does not correspond to reality' (Lyotard, 1993c: 256). But this suspicion of ready-made theoretical explanations is not yet the attack on theory ('the white terror of truth' [Lyotard, 1993b: 241]) of *Libidinal Economy*, nor is it the 'incredulity toward metanarratives' (Lyotard, 1984b: xxiv) of *The Postmodern Condition*. In his *Socialisme ou barbarie* writings Lyotard remains within Marxist theory and its language of class, contradictions, and exploitation. He reaffirms that 'the only solutions . . . are *class* solutions', and expresses the faith that once colonization is overthrown, class relations will re-emerge and 'all the workers will be united, Algerians and Europeans, to carry forward the class struggle' (Lyotard, 1993c: 178, 212). He never seems to doubt that socialist revolution is the ultimate answer to North Africa's problems (even if it is not yet ready for this revolution): the class solution, the resolution of contradiction, the end to exploitation. His position during these years is firmly Marxist – which only makes his subsequent, unequivocal rejection of revolutionary Marxism even more striking: he would later state that, although 'the "work" [*Socialisme ou barbarie*] did can and must be continued', 'Marxism is finished with as a revolutionary perspective' (Lyotard, 1993c: 168).

Reorientation

The reasons for Lyotard leaving *Socialisme ou barbarie* in 1963 remain rather mysterious. The 'anti-tendency' of which Lyotard was a member had formed in opposition to ideas Castoriadis expressed in an essay published in *Socialisme ou barbarie* in 1960 (reprinted as 'Modern Capitalism and Revolution' in Castoriadis, 1988). Yet it is not at all clear what Lyotard, at least, objected to.

The ideas expressed by Castoriadis seem very close to what Lyotard was proposing at the time: the search for contradictions at all levels of capitalist society, not simply the economic; the difficulty capitalism has in trying to govern both with and against the people – that central, intractable contradiction of maintaining both the participation and the exclusion of the general population; the depoliticization of the working class and the concomitant bureaucraticization of trades unions and workers' parties; and the continuing hope in the possibility of a socialist revolution that does not trust itself to the leadership of a party or the 'laws' of history.[3] In a letter published in *Socialisme ou barbarie* in 1963, Castoriadis announced his bemusement in the face of intra-group opposition to his ideas:

> [I]t is impossible to grasp hold of any positive or even negative content in this resistance and opposition. Indeed, not only is it not known till this day what the comrades who reject this analysis propose to put in its place, but it is impossible to understand to what precisely they are opposed. (Castoriadis, 1993: 84)

Lyotard himself later found it difficult to offer explanations for his opposition to Castoriadis, claiming that in the early 1960s 'I felt myself to be close to these theses, open to their argumentation', and hence still struggling, years later, 'to understand why, in spite of . . . the sympathy I had for the majority of the theses presented by Castoriadis, I found myself . . . in the group which opposed Castoriadis' (Lyotard, 1988c: 55, 59). Lyotard suggests that he was uncomfortable with the new theories because he already felt himself drifting away from Marxism, losing faith: the new theories had only displaced the classical contradictions of Marxism from the economic to the social sphere – they were 'cleaning up Marxism, giving it new clothes' (60) – while Lyotard was questioning Marxism at a more fundamental level, wondering if it was appropriate to see the world in terms of contradictions resolvable through socialist revolution. But this is not entirely convincing as an explanation, as the doubts Lyotard (claims he) was having at the time put him closer to Castoriadis than to the more orthodox Marxism of the anti-tendency. It may be that had Lyotard given more thought to all this at the time, he would not have been so quick to marginalize Marx later on.

Whatever his reasons for leaving *Socialisme ou barbarie*, by 1966 he had left *Pouvoir Ouvrier* as well. In 'A Memorial of Marxism' Lyotard tries to retrace this part of his life, explaining his creeping doubts concerning Marxism, his growing suspicions that the 'failures' of the revolutionary movement in the mid-twentieth century stemmed from Marxism itself: what had failed, in fact, was not the revolutionary movement or the proletariat but Marxist theory. Lyotard is aware that within the Marxist discourse it would be easy enough to explain away his suspicions and doubts, his disaffection with Marxism; the Marxist doctors could diagnose his condition, assign it causes, even offer remedies. But the point here, Lyotard's difficulty, is that it was this very discourse that Lyotard doubted: how could he explain his suspicions with the very thing he was suspicious of? He could not explain himself in Marxist language: he was unable to outline his disagreement with his former comrades because they 'no longer shared a common language' (Lyotard, 1988c: 49). This disagreement was thus what Lyotard will later term a *differend*: a dispute irresolvable for want of a common standard of judgement. One side of the dispute – in this case Lyotard – is silenced, unable even to articulate his wrong because his idiom is not the idiom of the dispute.

Yet these doubts did not lead Lyotard to a straightforward rejection of Marx or Marxism: 'It was not a question . . . of refuting theses, of rejecting a doctrine, of promoting another more plausible one, but rather of leaving free and floating the relation of thought to that Marxism' (Lyotard, 1988c: 54). Instead of a simple refutation, there was a reorientation: no longer completely devoted towards Marxism and the Marxist cause, Lyotard now saw Marxism as one figure among many rather than as the whole picture. This new orientation frees up Lyotard's relation to Marx, and he begins to produce new insights into Marx's work. In a series of essays written from the late 1960s onwards, Lyotard repositions himself. What he targets in Marx is the postulation of an external ground of critique: some force that is supposed to ground the whole critique of capitalism, as a reserve of energy that capitalism draws upon and on which it will ultimately founder. Lyotard's move here cannot be reduced to an attack on the concept of alienation (an attack which, after all, could conceivably be dismissed as irrelevant to Marx's later writings): it is a more fundamental point about the architecture of Marx's analysis, in which the role of the Outside might just as well be taken by labour-power as by species-being. In contrast, Lyotard begins to rethink capitalism in terms of a fluid, dynamic system that feeds on its own internal force or power. This conceptualization persists throughout Lyotard's work, and is even echoed in late writings in which the tendency is to talk of 'systems of development' rather than simply of capitalism. It is tempting to see this new position as one inspired by Nietzsche: in place of the *ressentiment* which speaks in the name of some victim seeking redress, there is an active driving force, a kind of will-to-power. Yet while Nietzsche is undoubtedly an inspiration, Lyotard himself, as mentioned in the previous chapter, has suggested that Freud was a more significant influence on this period of his intellectual life.

From Freud Lyotard takes not just an interest in desire – and hence how capitalism is invested with desire – but also something more opaque, and that is this rethinking of energy in terms of a kind of thermodynamic system, drawing on its own forces rather than some exteriority (an idea which Lyotard thinks against Freud as well as with him). If Freud is a strong influence, then Hegel is a key target – yet so is Marx himself. Two essays from 1972 – one on Adorno

(Lyotard, 1974) and one on Deleuze and Guattari's *Anti-Oedipus* (Lyotard, 1977) – typify Lyotard's approach at this time. Marx is acknowledged for recognizing the subversive, fluid energy of capitalism, but he is then attacked for 'maintaining the positive perversion of capitalism inside a network of negativity, contradiction and neurosis': alongside the affirmative recognition in Marx, almost a celebration of capitalism's energy, there is a negative, Hegelian movement which constrains this affirmation and mourns the loss of a natural subject (Lyotard, 1977: 17). Marx posits some 'exteriority beyond the reach of capital', some force outside the system which resists it; Lyotard rejects this 'nihilism', this 'nostalgia', and instead exalts the force and energy 'in the very interior of the system' (Lyotard, 1977: 13, 15). In these essays, Lyotard offers a conceptualization of capital which does not refute or renounce Marx but significantly reworks Lyotard's own position on Marx. These arguments are expanded in his 1974 book *Libidinal Economy*, which should thus not be seen as a straightforward rejection of Marx or Marxism but as the explosive culmination of this process of reorientation.

Libidinal Economics

No refutation, but a clear alteration of position: even Bennington acknowledges that *Libidinal Economy* 'marks something of a break' (Bennington, 1988: 32). This does not entail a new silence on Marx: in fact the book offers Lyotard's most extended and imaginative treatment of Marx. I shall argue that in attacking Marx's idealist ontology, Lyotard misses much else in Marx, at times caricaturing his work and overlooking Marx's own alternatives to idealism. Nonetheless, *Libidinal Economy* is certainly not without merit. On the one hand, it identifies problematic aspects of Marx's work, and opens up new possibilities (by looking at the relation between capitalism and desire, for example). On the other hand, the book's flaws usefully highlight the dangers of repudiating idealism, as Lyotard oscillates between a renunciation of critique and dependence on a libidinal vitalism.

Stroking Marx's beard

Lyotard himself called *Libidinal Economy* 'a book of desperation' (Lyotard, 1988*b*: 300). It can be seen simultaneously as a cathartic release of energy, a celebratory liberation from the constraining bonds of Marxism, and a tumultuous search for a way out of Lyotard's 'crisis' as his devotional relationship to Marxism fell apart. He later wrote that it 'was a matter of ridding political reflection of Hegelianism' – but also of 'a Marxism of the Althusserian type', and even 'of Marx's Marxism as well' (Lyotard and Thébaud, 1985: 89).

At times Lyotard seems to be settling scores with his old self. He directs 'a parenthesis of hatred' against the *Socialisme ou barbarie* group, in particular Castoriadis and his 'great cesspool of consolations called *spontaneity* and *creativity*'; but also against all 'bourgeois, privileged smooth-skinned types' who in commiserating with the proletariat 'are like priests with sinners. . . . [Y]ou have to tell yourselves: how they must suffer to endure that!' (Lyotard, 1993*b*: 116.) The object of mockery here is not simply Castoriadis et al., but also his former self, Lyotard the Marxist – and Marxism in general.

While Lyotard's break with revolutionary Marxism is – like his original commitment to the cause – not untypical of the development of ideological fashions in postwar France, it would be hasty and superficial simply to assimilate him to the Solzhenitsyn fans of the *nouveaux philosophes*. Lyotard can sometimes seem to place himself in this camp – for example, asking in one essay:

> What was the happy ending told by the Marxist left? The abolition of injustice. And what news do we hear from the countries where this scenario was obstinately put into practice by the government and officially acted out by thousands of men and women? Thousands of uncomfortable little stories have recently been brought back by Solzhenitsyn's books, by eye-witness accounts from dissidents and by travellers. (Lyotard, 1989: 127)

Yet in this same essay he calls most of the arguments of the *nouveaux philosophes* 'insultingly naïve' (Lyotard, 1989: 123–4). Lyotard does not set out to blame Marx for later atrocities in order to warrant his excommunication or interment. The position Lyotard takes up ultimately precludes grouping him with the *nouveaux philosophes*, yet leaves him difficult to place: no longer Marxist, but still dealing with Marx, launching an attack on Hegelianism that is simultaneously an attack on that most anti-Hegelian of Marxisms, Althusser's. The stance adopted in *Libidinal Economy* deserves attention for its novelty alone: it also happens that it is an intelligent and entertaining, albeit flawed, engagement with Marx.

The book is not concerned solely with Marx or Marxism but it contains long sections on Marx and on capitalism – indeed, it is often in these sections that the Nietzschean playfulness found elsewhere is suspended in favour of dense but innovative analysis. Lyotard does not want to reveal where Marx went wrong, or to correct Marx; to give the 'true' reading of his work, or to disclose what he 'really meant': 'we have neither the hope nor the intention of setting up a portrait of the work, of giving an "interpretation" of it' (Lyotard, 1993*b*: 95). He directs sarcastic jibes towards 'the little Althusserians' who, according to Lyotard, read *Capital* in order 'to interpret it according to "its truth"' (96). As discussed in the previous chapter, Althusser himself admonishes those who would simply interpret Marx – yet Lyotard clearly thinks that the Althusserians remain too serious, too pious, and restricted in their return to Marx. Lyotard offers no critique of Marx: 'There is no need to criticize Marx, and even if we do criticize him, it must be understood that it is in no way a critique' (95). This refusal of critique is not limited to Marx. In common with other post-structuralists, Lyotard seeks to question and undermine the theoretical mechanisms and procedures of representation – but there should be no critique of representation, because for Lyotard, all critique is simply another form of representation: thus it would merely sustain and perpetuate that which it criticized.[4] Instead, he wishes to expose that which representation both depends upon and conceals: to show that the identity of the concept, the unity of the subject, notions of negation, opposition, value, truth, and falsity are all effects – effects of the 'disintensification' or stabilization of a primary flux or tumult whereby 'ebbing intensities stabilize themselves into configurations' (26). These libidinal intensities – obscured by the theoretical apparatus of representation that is parasitic upon them – are something like the notion of the 'figure' introduced by Lyotard in his earlier work *Discours, figure*, as well as what he will later call events: they are what cannot be accounted for in any representational thinking. Lyotard's difficulty in *Libidinal Economy* is therefore that he is trying to present to us – to re-present – that which cannot be represented, and to do so without resorting to nostalgia for some alleged lost object or absent meaning (a motif he refers to as the 'Great Zero'). This (at least in part) accounts for the book's occasionally frenzied prose style: as the author later noted, in *Libidinal Economy* 'my prose tried to destroy or deconstruct the presentation of any theatrical representation whatsoever, with the goal of inscribing the passage of intensities directly in the prose itself without any mediation at all' (Lyotard, 1988c: 13). Against the religiosity of critique Lyotard affirms a 'paganism' that respects each act as a singular intensity.

Though this aim effectively remains constant throughout Lyotard's work after about 1970, what makes *Libidinal Economy* so important is the book's attention to Marx – for although Marx remains a constant presence in Lyotard's later work, that presence does fade after *Libidinal Economy*. The book marks a vital point in Lyotard's work with respect to Marx: a point at which Lyotard has abandoned militant Marxism to pursue new themes, yet still discusses Marx at length. It demonstrates the extent to which Lyotard's philosophy of the event is developed not simply in conflict with Freud and structuralism, but in conflict with Marx. That is not to say that Lyotard simply opposes Marx (or, indeed, Freud or structuralism): far from dissolving his relationship with Marx, Lyotard's apostasy opens up that relationship in new and imaginative ways. Rather than treating Marx as a theory to be understood and applied, he now wishes 'to take Marx as if he were a writer, an author full of affects, take his text as a madness and not as a theory' (Lyotard, 1993b: 95). He does not want to treat Marx's work as a system whose coherence needs establishing, nor in Althusserian fashion as a science whose philosophy needs reconstructing; Lyotard takes this work as a piece of art whose 'force erupts here and there, independently of the consistency of the discourse, sometimes in a forgotten detail, sometimes in the very midst of a solid conceptual mechanism, well articulated and rooted' (103). If he does not criticize Marx this is not because he agrees with everything Marx says – far from it – but because he wishes to abandon critique in general. In common with the general line of the book, Lyotard wants to bring out the libidinal drives and forces behind the theoretical discourse: not to read Marx as a critic, nor even to approach Marx via an inventive labour of reading, but to 'stroke his beard as a complex libidinal volume, reawakening his hidden desire and ours along with it' (95).

Nostalgia for (in)organic unity

Lyotard offers two Marxes, or rather a Marx who is 'a strange bisexual assemblage':

> the little girl Marx, offended by the perversity of the polymorphous body of capital, requires a great love; the great prosecutor Karl Marx, assigned the task of the prosecution of the perverts and the 'invention' of a suitable lover (the proletariat), sets himself to study the file of the accused capitalist. (Lyotard, 1993*b*: 96–7)

But the great prosecutor Marx is as fascinated as he is scandalized by capitalism. So fascinated that he constantly postpones the completion of his work, submerging himself in his study of the accused. Marx cannot mould his studies into an artistic whole; he cannot form a unified body from them – a 'cancerization' of theory (Lyotard's phrase) that is readily recognizable in Marx's work, in which the unfinished volumes of *Capital* were supposed to be followed by further volumes, and together were only one part of a projected six-part work to be called *Economics*. Even a 'finished' work like the first volume of *Capital* is later added to with prefaces, postscripts, appendices. Marx's work is never finished. Lyotard plays on this theme, this inability to complete his work; but rather than locating it in some psychological defect, he draws parallels with capitalism itself.

The unified whole into which Marx strives to fashion his oeuvre is modelled on the unified whole that Marx (according to Lyotard) thinks he sees in both pre-capitalist societies and in his anticipated communism. Marx wants to form his work into an (in)organic unity, just as he opposes to capitalism the (in)organic unity of communism. Lyotard is here drawing on Marx's own references, in various places, to the 'inorganic'. In the *Grundrisse*, for example, he says that the Earth is the individual's inorganic body: 'not his product but something he finds to hand – presupposed to him as a natural being apart from him' (Marx, 1973: 488). Lyotard comments that

> the body of the earth is called *inorganic* [by Marx] only so as to be distinguished from the organic body of the worker himself; in fact it is a body organically bound up with the organic body and identical to it in every way in that, like it, it is *given* and not produced. (Lyotard, 1993*b*: 131–2)

Hence Lyotard writes of the (in)organic – rather than simply the organic or inorganic – as a way of highlighting this ambiguity, in order at once to use Marx's term *inorganic* and to elicit Marx's desire for an *organic* body: a body that is unified and complete – both his own theoretical body of work and the social body that would be communism. This is the crux of Lyotard's non-critique of Marx, already anticipated in the post-*Socialisme ou barbarie* essays and never really abandoned. Lyotard undertakes a joint attack on Marx's ontology and teleology, on Marx's reliance on a natural given that will one day be restored. Yet while correctly identifying a certain impulse in Marx's work, Lyotard goes too far in wanting to reduce Marx to this impulse.

Lyotard claims that Marx believes that in pre-capitalist societies the body of the individual, the social body, and the body of the Earth form a natural unity; under capitalism, in contrast, this unity is ruptured, a rupture reflected in the division between use-value and exchange-value. Marx wants 'to *do away with the scission* and to establish the great full common body of natural reproduction, communism' (Lyotard, 1993*b*: 134). In place of the alienation of capitalism, in which all relations are mediated by money, Marx pines for the immediacy, transparency, and naturality of pre-capitalist societies: he is nostalgic for a paradise which also acts 'as secure ground for a critical perspective and a revolutionary project. This is the paradise of the "inorganic body"': 'a quasi-exteriority on which all critique relies in order to criticize its object' (130–1). Searching for an Outside, 'for an *elsewhere*, for an organic body hidden beneath the abstract body of capital, for a force lodged underneath or *outside* power relations' (146), Marx posits the use-value of labour-power as an exterior force, capable of grounding his critique. (Hence this theme is not merely, or even primarily, reflected in the humanism of the young Marx: labour-power is there at the centre of *Capital*.)

But for Lyotard all this is a fantasy: there is no exterior region from which the critique can take place; Marx's longed for reconciliation will not take place. Marx's metaphysical oppositions – between use-value and exchange-value, natural union and capitalist estrangement, fixed and artificial needs – must be collapsed. 'Use and need are not exteriorities, naturalities, or references from which one would be able to criticize exchange, they are a part of it' (Lyotard, 1993*b*: 161). Rather than looking for some 'natural', original force outside the system, by which the former can be used to judge and criticize the latter, Lyotard instead urges the reader to recognize the force of desire within capitalism. Yet he warns (probably with *Anti-Oedipus* in mind) that desire should not itself become a 'quasi-exterior' region, a firm ground from which the critique can take place: Lyotard does not want to show how a 'good', original desire has been repressed or alienated, and is now waiting to be freed or rescued; he does not want desire to become another ontological given to replace labour-power or need.[5] There is no alienation for Lyotard (and hence no 'non-alienated' region); there are only different investments of desire. Lyotard wants to show that desire is not tainted or thwarted by capitalism but directly invests in capitalism. Marx refuses this recognition: he will not allow it, instead insisting on 'the idea that capitalism deprives us of intensities as affects. . . . [Marx's] whole critique draws its impetus from the following denial: *no, you cannot make me come*' (139). Likewise, the Marxists of the *Socialisme ou barbarie* group saw in the force of capitalism only something negative: only domination, alienation, apathy, passivity, lack (of creativity, invention, communication). Lyotard in contrast claims that in capitalism '*all the modalities* of *jouissance* are possible and . . . none is ostracized' (140). This leads Lyotard to make the provocative claim that there is *jouissance* in exploitation: the English proletariat that Marx and Engels studied and commiserated with '*enjoyed* the hysterical, masochistic, whatever exhaustion it was of *hanging on* in the mines, in the foundries, in the factories, in hell, they enjoyed it' (111).

This is not a question of a misplaced desire channelled in the wrong direction, but a direct investment of desire. Lyotard wants us to stop mourning, commiserating with the 'exploited' ('like priests with sinners'). Far from denying pleasure, suppressing desire, reducing everything to a grey uniformity, capitalism activates desire, generates countless new pleasures – or, rather, it does both these things at once, both this reduction and this generation. It is true that all intensities under capitalism must be submitted to the law of the market: evaluated, assigned a price, exchanged – but at the same time this necessarily implies the circulation of new intensities, with new connections made, new desires provoked and satisfied, as everything, *anything* is brought into circulation; nothing is sacred. All must be reduced to exchange, repetition, reproduction – yet at the same time, and for the same reason, '[c]apital is also positive delirium, putting authorities and traditional institutions to death, active decrepitude of beliefs and securities' (Lyotard, 1993*b*: 254). Thus Lyotard identifies a kind of rhythm to capitalism composed of two impulses: a destructive drive, maximizing intensities, towards enrichment, speculation, and innovation; and a reproductive drive, reserving intensities, annulling them in a structural law of equivalences so that they can be reproduced, repeated, exchanged, and reinvested.

Rather than acting in nostalgia for a lost unity, positioning oneself in a fantasy Outside in order to rescue some frustrated given (need, use-value, labour-power, nature, the (in)organic body), Lyotard wants to work within capitalism. He is not about to tell anyone what to do, to lay down some model of the good life, for to do so would be theatrical, religious, metaphysical. Lyotard's anti-teleological stance is thus reflected not only in his opposition to theories that posit the recovery of a lost paradise, but also in a refusal to offer programmes of action. 'No need for declarations, manifestos, organizations, provocations, no need for *exemplary actions*.' Instead, '[w]hat would be interesting would be to stay put, but quietly seize every chance to function as good intensity-conducting bodies' (Lyotard, 1993*b*: 262). To become a libidinal economist is not to criticize capitalism but to work within it: to activate its destructive drive against its reproductive drive, to maximize intensities and disrupt the law of equivalences; not to mourn for what has been denied, but to push the whole system even further. As Lyotard says in his essay on *Anti-Oedipus*, 'capitalism will never croak from bad conscience, it will not die of a lack or of a failure to render unto the exploited what is owed them. If it disappears, it is by excess' (Lyotard, 1977: 17). Lyotard's renunciation of critique, then, covers not only Marx but also capitalism itself:

> [W]e must completely abandon critique, in the sense that we must put a stop to the critique of capital, stop accusing it of libidinal coldness or pulsional monovalence, stop accusing it of not being an organic body, of not being a natural immediate relation of the terms that it brings into play, we must take note of, examine, exalt the incredible, unspeakable pulsional possibilities that it sets rolling, and so understand that *there has never been* an organic body, an immediate relation, nor a nature in the sense of an *established site of affects*, and that the (in)organic body is a representation on the stage of the theatre of capital itself. Let's replace the term critique by an attitude closer to what we effectively experience in our current relations with capital, in the office, in the street, in the cinema, on the roads, on holiday, in the museums, hospitals and libraries, that is to say a horrified fascination for the entire range of the *dispositifs* of *jouissance*. (Lyotard, 1993*b*: 140)

Criticizing Lyotard

The analyses of both capitalism and Marx that are found in *Libidinal Economy* are exciting and innovative, but also have their flaws. The depiction of capitalism adds something to Marx's analysis – illuminating the dynamic of capitalism and bringing in the notion of desire – but it also loses something, having none of the concrete historical and contemporary detail of Marx's account. Lyotard is a little too quick to do away with Marx – or, better still, it can be said that he does not in fact do away with him, and in seeking to subvert him only reaffirms Marx's importance. As Lyotard presents Marx fascinated with what he is called upon to prosecute, so Lyotard reveals a fascination with what he seeks to subvert; just as critique remains caught within the field of its object, so Lyotard's non-critique of Marx remains to a large extent dependent on the insights of Marx's original analysis. It is to Lyotard's attack on Marx's idealist ontology that I want to turn first.

The figure of the (in)organic body is vital to the discussion of Marx's idealism, for Lyotard claims that the '"disappearance" of the organic body is the accusation, in sum, made by Marx . . . by which the *dispositif* of capital stands condemned' (Lyotard, 1993*b*: 139).⁶ Partly in order to show that this nostalgia is not just a theme found in the young Marx, Lyotard cites various passages from the famous pages of the *Grundrisse* in which Marx discusses pre-capitalist forms of production. Here Marx clearly states:

> It is not the *unity* of living and active humanity with the natural, inorganic conditions of their metabolic exchange with nature, and hence their appropriation of nature, which requires explanation or is the result of a historic process, but rather the *separation* between these inorganic conditions of human existence and this active existence, a separation which is completely posited only in the relation of wage labour and capital. (Marx, 1973: 489; cited in Lyotard, 1993*b*: 133)

In large part Marx's aim here is to contrast capitalist production with pre-capitalist communal production, where the individual has property but only because he is first a member of the commune (this membership is the presupposition of individual property). What Marx is seeking to do is to emphasize the specificity of capitalist production, its key preconditions – namely the separation of the worker from the means of production, and the exchange of labour for money in order to reproduce and realize money rather than to produce goods for direct consumption. Lyotard at once recognizes this and dismisses it: we cannot rid ourselves 'of this theme of lost naturality by saying that Marx merely *made use* of precapitalist forms in order to facilitate the concretion of their opposition to the capitalist form and to make this latter manifest in its full particularity' (Lyotard, 1993*b*: 133). It cannot be that contrast with pre-capitalist societies merely highlights the separation (of worker from the means of production) at the heart of capitalism, for there would be nothing to explain in the first place, no impetus for enquiry, without this separation: the scission lies at the root of both the possibility and necessity of explanation; it is not merely a feature revealed by analysis, but the motivation for analysis.

Yet *pace* Lyotard, this does not mean that Marx is nostalgic for that which preceded the separation, as if those pre-capitalist societies can be used as a standard by which to judge and condemn capitalism. Marx names various types of pre-capitalist society, among them communal forms (including ancient, Asiatic, and Germanic), slavery, and feudalism. In these last two as much as in communal forms there still does not exist the separation between the worker and the objective conditions of his labour – though the 'unity' between worker and conditions takes on a different form in slavery and feudalism, for the slave or serf is *himself* considered an inorganic condition of production (Marx, 1973: 489, 493). Clearly Marx is not nostalgic for slavery or feudalism: he is not positing the slave or the serf as an example of a (now lost) harmonious unity with nature. These are class societies, brutal in their forms of domination, and not models for any future society. The separation Marx needs to explain is not the dissolution of a natural harmony but the separation of the worker from that which he needs to work. This separation has not yet taken place in the communal forms Marx describes, but even in these communal forms there is not the 'immediacy' that Lyotard thinks he sees: the worker here is not in an immediate relation with the earth, his inorganic body, for this relation is mediated by the commune itself. The point is not that the individual, nature, and the commune all form one great (in)organic body, but that the commune is a precondition for the individual's relation to nature. Marx is providing an analysis of material social relations rather than an ontology of the unity of man and nature. The individual worker in pre-capitalist societies is chained to his community, while under capitalism the worker is unchained, 'freed' – what Deleuze calls 'deterritorialized'. So there is mediation in both pre-capitalist and capitalist societies, but in the latter it is mediation through money 'in which all political etc. relations are obliterated': 'for exploitation, veiled by religious and political illusions, it has substituted naked, shameless, direct, brutal exploitation' (Marx, 1973: 503; Marx and Engels, 1998: 5). Far from contrasting capitalist relations unfavourably with pre-capitalist ones, Marx clearly states that the 'connections' formed under capitalism are 'preferable to the lack of any connection, or to a merely local connection resting on blood ties, or on primeval, natural or master-servant relations' (Marx, 1973: 161). Rather than indulging in nostalgia for an original unity, he objects that '[i]t is . . . ridiculous to yearn for a return to that original fullness' – an 'original fullness', Marx makes clear, that is only apparent, an invention of bourgeois romanticism (Marx, 1973: 162).

And yet: although Lyotard's charges fall short, he does shed light on an important issue. While Marx's critique of capitalism cannot be reduced to nostalgia for the paradise of a unified (in)organic body, this theme is not completely absent in his work. He does indeed write (in the *Grundrisse*) of 'the natural unity of labour with its material presuppositions': the unity of humanity and its inorganic conditions (Marx, 1973: 471, 489). To make his case further, Lyotard points to *Capital*'s section on commodity fetishism as evidence of Marx's desire for 'transparency, naturality, or immediacy' (Lyotard, 1993b: 134). These are the very same pages that Althusser pointed to in accusing Marx of succumbing to the 'idealist myth' of transparent social relations. Marx here contrasts 'the magic and necromancy' of commodity production with both pre-capitalist forms and communism as 'an association of free men': the 'social relations of the individual producers . . . are here transparent in their simplicity'. 'The religious reflections of the real world', he continues, 'can, in any case, vanish only when the practical relations of everyday life between man and man, and man and nature, generally present themselves to him in a transparent and rational form' (Marx, 1976a: 171–3). These passages are reminiscent of the demands in *The German Ideology* for man's 'control and conscious mastery', in place of a society where 'man's own deed becomes an alien power opposed to him, which enslaves him instead of being controlled by him' (Marx and Engels, 1976: 51, 47). Even where he mocks the absurdity of yearning for an original fullness, he emphasizes the need to gain mastery, to establish communal control of our social interconnections. This is not so much a question of the persistence (or not) of the concept of alienation in Marx's work, but rather the very issue that Lyotard raises: positing a notion of natural immediacy as both the ontological ground for critical reflection and the *telos* of social development. One might object that Marx is not seduced by nostalgia, because rather than anticipating the simple return of a lost origin, he views communism in terms of the progressive socialization of labour. To frame things in these terms, however, is in effect still to be caught within idealism: the End is still anticipated in the Origin – it is just that the End is the natural development of the Origin rather than its mere reproduction. Communism is still posited as the *telos* of a predictable development.

Lyotard is right to identify in Marx a wish to do away with the 'mystery' of capitalism and commodity production in order to establish simpler, more transparent social relations, and he is right that this desire cannot be dismissed as a residue from Marx's youthful preoccupations – yet by focusing on this aspect of Marx's work, he overlooks much else that is valuable. There is much more to Marx: while he retains an idealist viewpoint in places, Marx also makes a significant break with idealism, introducing an analysis of society that does not root itself in nostalgia for a lost Whole, but instead sets out to distinguish the specificity of different social formations by analysing their particular forms of social relations and struggles. There is tacit recognition by Lyotard that Marx offers something more – for his own portrayal of capitalism, though apparently formed in opposition to Marx, is strongly reminiscent of Marx's own analysis: a simultaneous enrichment and annulment, both creative and repetitive, sweeping away all traditional, established practices and institutions yet reducing everything to the commodity form. It calls to mind the extraordinary pages of *The Communist Manifesto* in which Marx relates the revolutionary power of capitalism ('All that is solid melts into air . . .'). Yet, whereas Marx seeks to explain the concrete historical processes by which the commodity-form emerges, Lyotard offers an account that is richly descriptive but drained of historical reference, tending to hypostasize the rhythm of capitalism identified by Marx by translating it into the terms of libidinal economics. If in *Libidinal Economy* Lyotard begins to resemble Nietzsche rather than Marx, then it is the Nietzsche of *The Birth of Tragedy* rather than *On the Genealogy of Morality*: repudiating myths of the noble savage but still reliant on the idea of an inaccessible metaphysical substratum beneath all phenomena (will for the still Schopenhauerian Nietzsche, desire for Lyotard). Lyotard himself would reject this characterization of his work, but accusations of this kind are easy to make because he does not – as Deleuze and Guattari do in *Anti-Oedipus* – offer any historical genealogy of the representation that he seeks to subvert. Why and how do mechanisms of representation develop historically? These are the questions, I would argue, that should be addressed by any materialist account of representation. Without this historical orientation, it begins to seem as if desire acts as an ontological reference point for Lyotard, just as the harmony of man and nature is supposed to act as an ontological reference point for Marx. Although he explicitly refuses all critical judgement, rejecting it as so much metaphysical piety, Lyotard does in effect adopt a critical position with respect to capitalism, urging us to exalt its subversive drive against its reproductive drive: 'let everything go', he implores, 'become conductors of hot and cold, of sweet and sour, the dull and the shrill, theorems and screams, let it make its way over you, without ever *knowing* whether it will work or not' (Lyotard, 1993*b*: 259). Yet he only maintains this position by relying on an affirmation of desire. He thus equivocates between refusal to offer alternatives to the current system and dependence on a libidinal vitalism that undercuts claims to have abandoned essentialist ontology.[7] This is a significant potential difficulty with materialist philosophy, one we shall come across again and again: how to maintain a critical perspective – and hope for the future – without relapsing into reliance on ontological foundations which have supposedly been repudiated. In *Libidinal Economy* Lyotard does not quite manage to negotiate this difficult path.

Lyotard later acknowledges that there is a problem. 'It is not true the search for intensities or things of that type can ground politics', he commented in 1979, 'because there is the problem of injustice' (Lyotard and Thébaud, 1985: 90). Lyotard is not talking simply about the need to criticize capitalism here, but identifying a general problem: 'following nothing but the intensities of affects does not allow us to separate the wheat from the chaff' (Lyotard, 1988*c*: 15). Having gone through the catharsis of *Libidinal Economy*, Lyotard then reintroduces the neglected theme of *judgment*. This new focus on judgement is reflected in a renewed willingness to criticize capitalism – and it is Marx who is called upon to help in this critique. Yet this renewed critique of capital and somewhat more sympathetic attitude towards Marx are not accompanied by a more rigorous analysis of capitalism or a deeper engagement with Marx – on the contrary, the analysis is thinner, the engagement weaker. At the very moment Marx is called upon once more in resistance to capital, he fades into the background of Lyotard's work. Kant and Wittgenstein are the figures dominating this later work, not Marx or Freud. Marx certainly has a place in Lyotard's work after *Libidinal Economy*, but it is a place of reduced importance. At times *Libidinal Economy* reads like an attack on Marx, and yet (almost against itself) it succeeded in reaffirming Marx's significance: the challenge to Marx's alleged 'nostalgia' does not sweep Marx away but brings into focus certain issues in his work, while the presentation of capitalism mirrors Marx's own analysis. Many of the book's themes – an attack on Marx's ontology, a refusal of teleology, an investigation of the dynamics of capitalism in non-dialectical terms – are taken up by other post-structuralists, as we shall see in subsequent chapters. For now, however, I want to look at the next stage of Lyotard's work on Marx.

The Grand Narrative of Marxism and the Differend of Capital

Where in *Libidinal Economy* Lyotard had called for a 'pagan theatrics', in 1979's *Just Gaming* he calls for a pagan politics. Paganism, he says, 'is a name . . . for the denomination of a situation in which one judges without criteria.' (Lyotard and Thébaud, 1985: 16). A pagan politics would be what is called for at the end of *The Postmodern Condition*: 'a politics that would respect both the desire for justice and the desire for the unknown' (Lyotard, 1984b: 67). A politics, he says elsewhere, 'which is both godless and just' (Lyotard, 1989: 135). James Williams suggests there is 'a shocking reversal' between the two uses of the term pagan, that is, between its use in *Libidinal Economy* and its new use in *Just Gaming* and after (Williams, 2000: 100). But while the insistence on the necessity of judgement is certainly new, the qualification 'without criteria' maintains a connection with the earlier work. Lyotard is no longer happy simply to 'let everything go', but evaluation and discrimination cannot take place on the basis of pre-set norms: he continues to oppose that 'piety' which 'implies the representation of something that of course is absent, a lost origin, something that must be restored to a society in which it is lacking' (Lyotard and Thébaud, 1985: 20). There remains the anti-metaphysical, anti-humanist trend of *Libidinal Economy*, which rejected grand, systematizing theories – but it is reworked to account for justice. So there is both change and continuity here, and the same can be said of Lyotard's attitude towards Marx and capitalism. Marx remains under fire: he is identified as one of those pious thinkers who holds 'the deep conviction that there is a true being of society, and that society will be just if it is brought into conformity with this true being' (Lyotard and Thébaud, 1985: 23). Similarly, in *The Postmodern Condition* Marxism is identified as one of the 'metanarratives' that, the book announces, have had their time (Lyotard, 1984b: 36–7). What Lyotard is concerned with here is a need for openness and respect for the plurality of the social bond; he thinks Marx does not show this respect, instead trying to enclose and explain everything within a single metanarrative. While the nature of the social bond in *Just Gaming* and *The Postmodern Condition* is discussed in terms of a multiplicity of language games, by *The Differend* Lyotard has changed his terminology: the concept of language games is dismissed as too anthropomorphic and instead there are 'phrase regimens' and 'genres of discourse'. What also comes across with greater strength in *The Differend* is the violation that capitalism does to this plurality. This is a big change from *Libidinal Economy*: what is now emphasized is that drive towards equivalence, exchange, homogenization. Whereas in *Libidinal Economy* Lyotard had found creative and subversive potential *within* capitalism, now this potential is more likely to be found in opposition to capitalism – but still not in some lost naturality. And though Marx and Marxism are criticized, they are also called upon in resistance to capitalism: 'This is the way in which Marxism has not come to an end, as the feeling of the differend' (Lyotard, 1988*a*: 171). In order to unpack what is meant here, it will be necessary to look briefly at Lyotard's philosophy of the differend in general, before examining his new claims about Marx and Marxism.

The relevance of Marxism

I have (in relation to Lyotard's break with *Socialisme ou barbarie*) already touched upon what a differend is: 'a case of conflict, between (at least) two parties, that cannot be equitably resolved for lack of a rule of judgement applicable to both arguments' (Lyotard, 1988*a*: *xi*). Differends arise because there is no single correct way to respond to events, only a number of different, disputed, and incommensurable ways. What Lyotard calls a 'phrase' is something like an event – an occurrence, a happening – and hence he refuses to define it: but a phrase is not necessarily linguistic; it might be a gesture, a signal, even a silence. Phrases belong to heterogeneous regimens (the descriptive regimen, the prescriptive, evaluative, cognitive, etc.) and are linked together according to the stakes of a particular genre of discourse, each of which offers some end aimed at (to persuade, to teach, to make laugh, to make cry, etc.). It is not possible that there is no phrase (for even silence is a phrase), and one phrase must be followed by another, but there is no universally applicable standard of judgement that can say which new phrase should follow. 'To link is necessary, but a particular linkage is not' (80). Genres of discourse provide rules for linking, but no genre is supreme, and there is no ultimate measure to decide between genres, no single, universal end. Hence, there are differends: conflicts between genres without an independent judge. A tribunal can be set up to regulate a conflict but 'applying a single rule of judgement to both [sides of the conflict] in order to settle their differend as though it were merely a litigation would wrong (at least) one of them (and both if neither side admits this rule)' (*xi*). In any conflict there will be a loser; yet not only has the loser suffered an injustice, he is also unable to articulate this injustice because the genre of discourse used by the tribunal is not his own: he must remain silent – as Lyotard had to when faced with his own differend with Marxism.

For Lyotard politics is precisely this competition between genres of discourse. Politics is not a genre in itself, but rather 'the multiplicity of genres, the diversity of ends': it is the arena in which competing genres battle and as such is always 'the threat of the differend' (Lyotard, 1988*a*: 138). If politics is this threat of the differend then philosophy is a particular response to this threat: it involves keeping open the political space in which genres of discourse compete, allowing differends to appear so that the philosopher can bear witness to them. 'One's responsibility before thought consists . . . in detecting differends and in finding the (impossible) idiom for phrasing them. This is what a philosopher does' (142). 'Impossible' because no single idiom can express both sides of a differend at the same time. Unlike other genres, the philosophical genre does not really have any rules: its only rule is that the rule of the discourse is what is at stake.

This philosophical role is necessary because within political conflict different genres try to present themselves as supreme and determine the only correct form of concatenation. This is Lyotard's objection to capitalism: it gives hegemony to what Lyotard calls the economic genre, and this genre attempts to impose its rules at the expense of other genres. This genre of economic discourse is one of the main targets of *The Differend*. Capital subordinates everything to its stakes of profitability. It does not admit 'the heterogeneity of genres of discourse. To the contrary, it requires the suppression of that heterogeneity' (Lyotard, 1988*a*: 178). Traces remain of *Libidinal Economy*'s insistence on capitalism's creative, subversive side: within capitalism's economic genre, Lyotard says, 'under the conditions of [its] end, the most unheard of occurrences are greeted and even "encouraged"'. Yet here Lyotard is taking a shot at Hegel, declaring 'capitalism's superiority over the speculative genre' (138–9); overall the emphasis in *The Differend* is on that side of capitalism which annuls the event, forecloses possibility. 'The economic genre with its mode of necessary linkage from one phrase to the next dismisses the occurrence, the event, the marvel' (178). Lyotard gives a specific example of a differend that occurs and is suppressed under capitalism. The worker becomes a victim of a differend:

> contracts and agreements between economic partners do not prevent – on the contrary, they presuppose – that the labourer or his or her representative has had to and will have to speak of his or her work as though it were the temporary cession of a commodity, the 'service', which he or she putatively owns. This 'abstraction', as Marx calls it . . . is required by the idiom in which the litigation is regulated ('bourgeois' social and economic law). (Lyotard, 1988*a*: 9–10)

Under the dominant capitalist idiom, labour-power is simply a commodity like any other, and the exchange between worker and capitalist is free and just. As Marx says:

> They [the worker and the capitalist] contract as free persons, who are equal before the law. Their contract is the final result in which their joint will finds

a common legal expression. . . . [E]ach enters into relation with the other, as with a simple owner of commodities, and they exchange equivalent for equivalent. (Marx, 1976a: 280)

The worker is unable to protest that he is coerced into selling his labour-power, that the exchange is unequal, that he has been exploited in any way. The economic genre of capital is dominant, and according to this genre the worker has been involved in a fair exchange and has no cause for complaint. There has been no injustice according to the rules of capitalism:

> The justice of the transaction between agents of production consists in the fact that these transactions arise from the relations of production as their natural consequence. . . . The content [of the transaction] is just so long as it corresponds to the mode of production and is adequate to it. It is unjust as soon as it contradicts it. (Marx, 1981: 460–1.)

These excerpts from Marx invoke debates about his attitude to the concept of justice as well as broaching his account of the relations between exchange and production. Rather than dealing with these issues here, I use these quotations in order to demonstrate how Lyotard can draw on Marx for his claim that capitalism suppresses differends, establishing a hegemony that denies particular responses. The worker suffers a double blow: he is compelled to sell his labour-power to the capitalist and he is also denied the means to argue that this is unjust. He is a victim of a wrong in Lyotard's specific sense of this word: 'a damage accompanied by the loss of the means to prove the damage' (Lyotard, 1988a: 5) This is how Marxism remains relevant for Lyotard:

> The wrong is expressed through the silence of feeling, through suffering. The wrong results from the fact that all phrase universes and all their linkages are or can be subordinated to the sole finality of capital . . . and judged accordingly. Because this finality seizes upon all phrases, it makes a claim to universality. The wrong done to phrases by capital would then be a universal one. Even if the wrong is not universal (but how can you prove it? it's an Idea), the silent feeling that signals a differend remains to be listened to. Responsibility to thought requires it. This is the way in which Marxism has not come to an end, as the feeling of the differend. (Lyotard, 1988a: 171)

Philosophies of history

So Lyotard calls on Marx in resistance to capitalism, as a voice for the victims of capitalism and as testament to their differend. However, although praised for highlighting the alleged differend of capitalism, Marx cannot be fully accepted by Lyotard as a philosopher of the differend: not content to testify to a radical conflict, Marx proposes a new metanarrative as a solution, and in doing so suppresses more differends. Rather than keeping open the space of politics, respecting the incommensurability of genres of discourse, Marxism 'claimed to be able to transcribe all genres' (Lyotard, 1988*c*: 53). Lyotard criticizes Marx for remaining 'a prisoner of the logic of result', trapped in the 'speculative genre' (Lyotard, 1988*a*: 172). The allusion here is to Hegel, who is criticized at length earlier in the book. Rather than acting in accordance with the philosophical genre, in which the rule of the discourse is what is at stake ('the discourse makes links any way it can, it tries itself out'), Hegel's speculative genre presupposes its rules in order to ensure that they are engendered at the end (Lyotard, 1988*a*: 97). Against Hegel, whose discourse consumes everything, submitting all to its presupposed ends, Lyotard pits (his own reading of) Kant. Kant looks for events that are signs of history (the example is the enthusiasm of spectators to the French revolution); these signs indicate the validity of certain Ideas of progress, freedom, and the like. These Ideas are what Kant calls *ideas of reason*, that is ideas which cannot be confirmed through experience by the presentation of an intuition: 'a concept formed from notions and transcending the possibility of experience' (Kant, 1964: 314). What Lyotard admires in Kant is his respect for (in Lyotardian terms) the heterogeneity of phrases: an Idea cannot be validated in the way that a cognitive phrase can. In contrast, Marx, too much the Hegelian and too little the Kantian, confuses things: he interprets the sign that is the enthusiasm aroused by workers' struggles as a demand from a presupposed, Ideal self, and then confuses this Ideal of a revolutionary subject with the real political organization of the real working class (Lyotard 1988*a*: 172). This confuses two senses of the proletariat: as cognitive reality and as an Ideal object.

Against this attempt to interpret events according to a discourse which would act like a final judgement, Lyotard again advocates paganism, praising the 'pagan sense of humour' – a humour which leaves the question of judgement open, which recognizes that '[t]he history of the world cannot pass a last judgement. It is made out of judged judgements' (Lyotard, 1988*a*: 8). Far from validating some philosophy of history, for Lyotard the signs of history disrupt such philosophies: 'The "philosophies of history" that inspired the nineteenth and twentieth centuries claim to assure passages over the abyss of heterogeneity or of the event. The names which are those of "our history" oppose counter-examples to their claim.' And among these claims: 'Everything proletarian is communist, everything communist is proletarian: "Berlin 1953, Budapest 1956, Czechoslovakia 1968, Poland 1980" (I could mention others) refute the doctrine of historical materialism: the workers rose up against the Party' (Lyotard, 1988*a*: 179). Lyotard is not here offering the same arguments as the *nouveaux philosophes* who discarded Marx because he was supposed to have led to Stalinism. He does not dismiss their claims entirely, and he certainly does not think that Marxism can continue unaffected by that which happened in the twentieth century in states calling themselves communist. For Lyotard, however, it is not that Marx has ineluctably led to the gulag, but rather that both the crimes perpetrated under Stalin and others and the resistance to those crimes signal the impossibility of any reconciliation in a universal history – 'the impossibility of inscribing them in any *destiny*' (Lyotard, 1974: 135).

That this last remark is made in Lyotard's essay on Adorno from 1972 is revealing, for it highlights the persistence of certain motifs and ideas in Lyotard's work.[8] The claims made in *The Differend* concerning the bankruptcy of modern philosophies of history have their roots in the work Lyotard produced after his break with Marxism, in the Adorno essay and other pieces. By the time of *The Differend* Marxism has no privileged status in Lyotard's work: it is one of many defeated metanarratives, each one with its names which signal failure, exposed by events that cannot be fitted into its version of history. Yet Marxism does in a sense retain a special place, for it is through his relation to Marxism, through the 'crisis' of his apostasy, that Lyotard develops this key theme: resistance to the subsumption of events under some grand theoretical schema. It is a theme that recurs in some of Lyotard's last works. In a short piece from 1992, Lyotard distinguishes his own 'postmodern fable' from the great modern narratives: the latter are eschatological, offering redemption of some sort for humankind, whereas the former tells of the contingent development of material systems, with no thought of emancipation or redemption. Eschatology 'recounts the experience of a subject affected by a lack, and prophesies that this experience will finish at the end of time with the remission of evil'. The great narrative of modernity '*promises* at the end to reconcile the subject with itself and the overcoming of its separation' (Lyotard, 1997: 96–7). Marxism is one of the great narratives mentioned. Notwithstanding the deliberate simplicity of Lyotard's formulations here, they offer confirmation that despite his changing relation to Marx, his adoption of different positions and strategies in dealing with Marx, there is an identifiable consistency in his basic stance on Marx, first established in the essays written after the break with *Socialisme ou barbarie*. In his postmodern fable, Lyotard characterizes the great narratives of modernity in this way: 'An immemorial past is always what turns out to be promised by way of an ultimate end' (97). This is not a new, 'postmodern' position, but rather echoes what he had formulated more than twenty years before when accusing Marx of writing in nostalgia for some exteriority that needed rescuing, in piety for some wrong that needed redressing. So it is not so much that Marx is gradually left behind or forgotten as Lyotard becomes interested in new themes and develops new positions – for these themes and positions are the fruit of an exhaustive reassessment of Marx, emerging only out of an intense struggle with the Marxism that dominated Lyotard's life for over a decade. Marx *is* eventually sidelined, but only as the victim of a process that could not have started without him: he is swept up in a generalized dismissal of metanarratives that was only initiated in the first place by reflection on his work and legacy.

Missing Marx

Lyotard never simply conflates Marx and Marxism in *The Differend*: a role for Marx is kept, as witness to a differend (the duty of the philosopher). With Marxism identified as one of those defunct philosophies of history, however, Marx can do little better than adopt this task of the philosopher in general. Although Marx was more vigorously mocked in *Libidinal Economy*, he was put to greater use there than in *The Differend*. As Marx becomes marginalized, so too does Lyotard's analysis of capitalism. There is a critical edge in Lyotard's approach to capitalism in *The Differend* that is missing from *Libidinal Economy*, but this critical edge, although explicitly calling on Marx, is gained at the expense of depth of analysis: the richness of the descriptions in *Libidinal Economy*, the attention to the rhythm and movement of capitalism (which brought to mind *The Communist Manifesto*) are lost. Although named as one of the book's 'adversaries', little space is given to any comment on capitalism in *The Differend*. The last few pages are spent on an explication of the stakes of the economic genre as gaining time – time stored in commodities (though distinguished from Marx's socially necessary labour time, which is dismissed as reliant on a metaphysic of production). Williams claims that the value of Lyotard's criticism of capitalism in these pages 'is that it shows the political potential of Lyotard's later work in terms of an opposition to the extension of the demand for profitability and economic growth to all domains of life' (Williams, 1998: 126). But this critique has been performed elsewhere – by the Frankfurt School, by Marx himself, even by that 'bourgeois Marx' Max Weber – and in Lyotard's hands it becomes so thinned out that it loses its value. His comments are so brief that they read like a kind of degree zero analysis, reduced to a skeleton form. At the risk of slipping into a teleological chronology of Lyotard's work, it might be said that in a strange way *The Differend* is both a regression from and the culmination of the work done in *Libidinal Economy*. The analysis of capitalism becomes much weaker and thinner – yet in a way this analysis has simply been pushed to its limits, until it reaches its barest formula: a respect for the event. When Marx demonstrates that the exchange between worker and capitalist is just and equal, he does not simply conclude that the worker is the victim of a differend: the demonstration is a prelude to an explanation of how this state of affairs emerged, as Marx delineates the development of its necessary conditions, showing how labour-power became a commodity in the first place. In contrast, Lyotard (as in *Libidinal Economy*) tends to annul the specificity of capitalism, effacing the historicity of the conflict between worker and capitalist and reducing it to just another example of the differend.

The use of Marx that would have been beneficial here is not an option for Lyotard, in whose hands Marx has become a reduced figure, swept away in a broader dismissal of the philosophies of history and accused of falling into speculative traps. Yet Marx is far less the 'prisoner of the logic of result' than Lyotard thinks. His work does not presuppose a self (be it collective: the proletariat) that demands or prescribes communism; nor does it postulate some all-consuming system which annuls events or allows only those events which have already been announced in advance. To say that Marx confuses the Idea of the proletariat and the real working class, as Lyotard does, is to misunderstand the role of class in Marx's work. A class, even the proletariat, is neither an Idea nor simply an empirical referent. It is not really a 'thing' at all; rather than defining an entity, the concept of class performs a function: to talk of class indicates a new and different way of thinking, in terms of antagonistic social relations – antagonisms, moreover, that have their own historical specificity and are not just examples of the conflictual nature of Being.[9] Some of Marx's work may be open to Lyotard's criticism: it is the early critique of the *Philosophy of Right* that Lyotard cites, and here Marx does mix a philosophical ideal with a concrete reality, presenting the proletariat as 'a class with radical chains, a class in civil society that is not of civil society, a class that is the dissolution of all classes, a sphere of society having a universal character because of its universal suffering' (Marx, 1970: 141; cited in Lyotard, 1988*a*: 171).[10] But as Daniel Bensaïd argues, while 'the young Marx initially sought a solution [to the impasse of German idealism] in a speculative alliance between philosophy and the proletariat', his later work introduces a far more complex conception of class (Bensaïd, 2002: 193–4). This later conception of the proletariat is neither an Ideal subject demanding communism, nor simply an empirical reality – nor finally some confused mixture of the two. Class analysis in the mature Marx does not imply reliance on a universal subject, but means analysis of existing social relations.

Pace Lyotard, the proletariat neither prescribes communism nor acts as the goal for some project of history. History does not have a goal for Marx. Lyotard wants to keep things open: not to follow pre-determined criteria but to search for rules still unknown; not to submit everything to a final judgement or end but to judge in humour and anxiety, in the knowledge that there are only judged judgements. This is what signals the failure of the great narratives of modernity: the recognition that 'history does not necessarily have a universal finality' (Lyotard, 1992: 64). (And this is not announced by a further grand narrative, a metanarrative of the end of metanarratives; it is indicated by the signs of history, the names that testify to the bankruptcy of grand schemas past.[11]) Yet Lyotard is too hasty in dismissing Marxism as another metanarrative – and at times too careless in confusing Marx and Marxism. Certain Marxisms may have presented a philosophy of history, but in Marx himself there is a much more open analysis, and explicit rejection of speculative distortions whereby 'later history is made the goal of earlier history' (Marx and Engels, 1976: 50). There can be found in Marx something which breaks with all philosophies of history and is (to borrow Althusser's words) 'open to a future that is uncertain, unforeseeable, not yet accomplished' (Althusser, 2006: 264). Lyotard often writes as if a philosophy of history is the dominant theme in Marx, and so having knocked all philosophies of history to the floor, he finds little left in Marx's work, with Marx now fit only to play a part in Lyotard's own philosophy of the differend.

The basic objection to Marx offered in *The Differend* remains that elaborated in *Libidinal Economy*: where Marx seeks some firm ontological ground to establish his critique, Lyotard wants to remain open to intensities and events. For Lyotard, capitalism cannot be resisted in terms of some ontologically essential unity, however it is characterized: 'Not Being, but one being, one time' (Lyotard, 1988a: 70) – or, rather, several beings: events. It is the event that ultimately resists the hegemony of capitalism:

> The only insurmountable obstacle that the hegemony of the economic genre comes up against is the heterogeneity of phrase regimens and of genres of discourse. This is because there is not 'language' and 'Being', but occurrences. The obstacle does not depend upon the 'will' of human beings in one sense or in another, but upon the differend. (Lyotard, 1988a: 181)

The difficulty is that in seeking to present a thoroughly non-metaphysical philosophy, drained of all humanism or of anything that might be considered an ontological foundation, Lyotard falls back into nothing more than a defence of the event in which it is heterogeneity itself which resists. Like Lyotard's concept of desire, the event cannot be represented: as such, as a concept it can do little to throw light on existing circumstances.

This is not to insist that Lyotard should have returned to his Marxism, or to chastise him for failing to discuss capitalism in the correct terms, or failing to discuss it at all. But it is Lyotard himself who presents capitalism in terms of a differend, and who names the economic genre of discourse as one of his central targets. Yet having done so, in *The Differend* he offers only meagre resources with which to understand it. Of course, Lyotard does not claim that the modern world can only be understood in terms of differends; as he says, 'not all oppressions signal differends' (Lyotard, 1984a: 20). But in that case it might be said that Lyotard is reduced to something like the status that he reduces Marx to: a reminder or a disruptive voice. Lyotard acts as a counter to the Habermasian view of language as transparent communication aimed at consensus. More importantly, he acts as a useful counter to a certain idealist Marx. But this leaves much more in Marx that has been missed.

Conclusion

After *The Differend* Lyotard no longer talks much of capitalism but rather, in a series of remarkable, sometimes enigmatic essays, of processes of complexification, or more broadly the system of development.[12] Like capitalism's economic genre of discourse, '[d]evelopment imposes the saving of time' (Lyotard, 1991a: 2). But while capitalism is part of development, the latter cannot be reduced to the former: 'Capital must be seen not only as a major figure of human history, but also as the effect, observable on the earth, of a cosmic process of complexification' (Lyotard, 1991a: 67). Lyotard talks of resistance to development, though such resistance plays an ambiguous role, for the system 'has need of such obstacles to improve its performance' (Lyotard, 1997: 73). (Lyotard admits the possibility that this is a profoundly pessimistic analysis [Lyotard, 1994: 124].) What resists the system of development is not humanity but the 'inhuman' (carefully distinguished from the 'inhumanity' of the system): 'the debt each soul has contracted with the miserable and admirable indetermination from which it was born and does not cease to be born' (Lyotard, 1991a: 7). As before, then, Lyotard refuses any ontology: resistance cannot be rooted in some determinate given, but rather in what is indeterminate – that which defies knowledge.

Marx is invoked as someone who might aid understanding of these trends (cf. Lyotard, 1993a: 21), but he does not feature much in Lyotard's work after *The Differend*. He speaks more often of Marxism, and then usually to dismiss it as an example of a deceased metanarrative: Marxism 'had been a mistake. It had to be reclassified as another of the great metaphysical systems of the West, of Europe in particular. It had been their last episode' (Lyotard and Larochelle, 1992: 403). This rather sombre, even portentous, conclusion should not detract from the fecundity of Lyotard's long engagement with Marx, stretched over more than forty years; nor should it lead us to think that Lyotard ever repudiates Marx, for he defends the relevance of Marx until the end. Despite the numerous different stances he takes up, from the late 1960s there is a stable element in Lyotard's mutating positions on Marx. The central charge is never retracted: Marx writes in nostalgia for a lost unity, hoping for the return of immediacy and transparency. Undertaken most extensively by Lyotard in *Libidinal Economy*, this attack on Marx's ontology and teleology adds flesh to the bones of Althusser's critique of idealism, and puts Marx's own idealism into sharper and more detailed focus. Lyotard's pursuit of Marx's idealism is more rigorous than Althusser's in two senses: both in its clarification and exploration of Marx's idealist elements, and in its rejection of those elements. Lyotard refuses all ontology; there is no equivalent to a determination in the last instance in his work. This raises a problem (reflected in Althusser's later work): how to maintain critical analysis without relying on a reified ontology that proffers some definitive conception of Being, but without also collapsing into nothing more than a defence of the event or desire whereby we lose any capacity to orient ourselves. But it also opens up new possibilities in Marx. More rigorously anti-idealist, Lyotard is more suspicious of Hegel and, unlike Althusser, emphatically rejects dialectical thinking. This allows him to present a non-dialectical analysis of capitalism, one that is still nevertheless heavily indebted to Marx – indeed, one that is even more indebted to Marx, with Hegel exorcized. Lyotard also adds something to Marx's analysis: his emphasis on desire has its problems, but it also allows Lyotard to introduce a level of analysis neglected by Marx. Yet although Lyotard never wholly repudiates Marx, insisting to the end that Marx retains a role, he does tend to push Marx to the sidelines: as capitalism is retranscribed first into the language of the differend and then that of development and complexity, so Marx fades into the background. The reaffirmation of his importance at the end of *The Differend* can feel like a pious, dutiful homage to an old friend. While Lyotard's engagement with Marx produces many valuable insights, he tends also to overlook alternative Marxes. In order to begin exploring some of those alternatives, we should now turn to Derrida.

Chapter 3

Messianic Without Messianism: Marx Through Derrida

There will be . . . no future without Marx, without the memory and the inheritance of Marx: in any case of a certain Marx, of his genius, of at least one of his spirits.
(Derrida, 1994: 13)

At first glance Derrida's relation to Marx appears to be much less complicated than that of Lyotard – for it seems to be centred around only one book. Lyotard's early work was dominated by Marxism and he continued to engage with Marx throughout his life. Until the publication of his *Specters of Marx* in 1993, however, Derrida wrote little about Marx. Where Lyotard seemed to follow a familiar trajectory from revolutionary activism to 1970s' apostasy, there was no militant past with Derrida and his intervention on Marx arrived in a context quite different to that of a book like *Libidinal Economy*. *Specters of Marx* came long after the first wave of anti-communist sentiment washed across France with the *nouveaux philosophes*; it was published at a time when a new, more complacent anti-Marxism was basking in the sunshine of global neo-liberal hegemony, and the recent collapse of the Soviet Union was being used as retrospective confirmation of the wisdom of those earlier attacks. Although Derrida took a very different path to that of Lyotard in reaching Marx, there are nonetheless similarities between the two engagements. Derrida, like Lyotard, is suspicious of Marx's ontology and emphasizes the need to retain an openness to the event. But while Lyotard sometimes disparages Marx's contribution, in *Specters of Marx* Derrida does not stop reaffirming Marx's importance, and he finds in Marx that very openness to the event that he and Lyotard wish to defend.

It would be wrong to think that before 1993 Derrida simply had nothing to do with Marx, and it would be facile to divide Derrida's work into pre- and post-Marx periods. Nonetheless, Derrida had already produced an enormous body of work before offering a detailed reading of Marx and he himself has addressed the question of his hesitant approach to Marx. Thus in the first section of this chapter I look at Derrida's work before *Specters of Marx*, both to see how it feeds into the later reading of Marx and to examine the few early comments on Marx. In the next two sections I assess the two key aspects of the book: its effort to complicate and challenge Marx's ontology through the figure of the spectre, and its defence of an emancipatory eschatology in Marx against all teleology. I argue that *Specters of Marx* in many ways marks an improvement on Lyotard's reading and use of Marx, in particular in its insistence that something other than a philosophy of history can be found in Marx. In depicting this something as a messianic eschatology, however, Derrida relies on a philosophy of the event similar to that found in Lyotard, with all its attendant flaws when compared to Marx.

Deconstruction and Marx

Derrida's comments on Marx prior to *Specters of Marx* had been scattered and fragmentary, usually in response to questions from others; certainly he had offered no deconstructive reading of Marx comparable to his work on Plato, Rousseau, Hegel, and others. Yet this silence on Marx served only to inflame interest in Derrida's views on this subject – interest from both critics and enthusiasts, Marxists and non-Marxists. Derrida only added fuel to the fire by hinting that some work on Marx was forthcoming. In an interview from 1971 he insists – albeit in response to persistent questioning from some Marxists – on the necessity of an encounter between deconstruction and Marxism, claiming that this 'theoretical elaboration' is '*still to come*' (Derrida, 1981: 62). Hence the excitement that greeted Derrida's book-length study in 1993.[1] In this section, I shall trace Derrida's long path to Marx, beginning with a brief overview of his deconstructive strategies. Given the sophistication and intricacy of Derrida's work, this does not aim to be a comprehensive introduction, but only to touch on certain issues that are significant for his reading of Marx.

What is deconstruction?

If there is no satisfactory answer to the question 'what is deconstruction?', this is probably because it is not a very well-formed or useful question. This is partly because deconstruction itself renders the question unanswerable. 'Deconstruction is first and foremost a suspicion directed against just that kind of thinking – "what is . . .?" "what is the essence of . . .?" and so on' (Derrida, 1989: 73). But it is also because deconstruction (in Derrida's work at least) has never been a strict method or theory; it is rather a kind of strategic approach, 'an unclosed, unenclosable, not wholly formalizable ensemble of rules for reading, interpretation and writing' (Derrida, 1983: 40). The prevalence of the term 'deconstruction' in the secondary literature has perhaps less to do with the frequency with which it appears in Derrida's own writings and more to do with the demands of polemical criticism (Derrida becomes an easier target if his work is reduced to a series of simplified formulas) and marketability (it is easier to write and sell books on Derrida if he can be channelled through a few key terms). (These demands are not necessarily incompatible, and it would be hasty to assume that Derrida has not been complicit in them.) Rather than a single method of deconstruction, there are deconstructions of different texts, readings of works by various authors that are marked not only by their incredible rigour but also by their respect: Derrida's aim is neither to refute authors on the basis of inconsistencies in their work nor to smooth over any tensions in order to reconstruct a coherent argument or narrative. When he comes to read Marx, Derrida will offer neither straightforward endorsement nor outright rejection. If he finds difficulties in Marx's work then these are as likely to stem from the tradition of Western metaphysics in general as they are from any deficiencies peculiar to Marx, and these difficulties are not going to form the basis of a wholesale dismissal of Marx.

Deconstruction's challenge to the philosophical canon does not amount to a rejection. 'There is no sense in doing without the concepts of metaphysics in order to shake metaphysics. We have no language – no syntax and no lexicon – which is foreign to this history' (Derrida, 1978: 280). The distinctions characteristic of metaphysics – between the normal and the marginal, essential and accidental, pure and impure, good and evil – cannot simply be abandoned but must instead be undermined. This can be done through the introduction of a third term which will be both the condition of possibility of any binary opposition, accounting for the operation of axiological distinction, and its condition of impossibility, demonstrating that the supposedly primary term can never attain full presence. For example, *différance* is the play of differences that gives rise to the possibility of signification and conceptualization, yet is at the same time that which renders it impossible that any element of signification can be fully present, because each element is constituted only through its differential relations to something else. Given that *différance* 'is the play which makes possible nominal effects' (Derrida, 1982: 26), it is itself technically unnameable – but for Derrida the appropriate response here is not one of reverence for the ineffable or nostalgia for what cannot be presented, but an affirmation of this unnameability, achieved by offering a proliferation of names: *pharmakon*, which is both poison and antidote; *hymen*, which is both inside and outside; *supplement*, which is both extraneous and essential. This is a list that 'can never be closed' (Derrida, 1991: 275), and to which can be added the non-concept of 'deconstruction' itself. The deconstructive logic of both/and, in place of a logic of either/or, contaminates that which seems to be pure and self-sufficient, highlighting how that which is excluded as 'marginal' or 'parasitic' is in fact structurally necessary to that which is identified as 'normal' or 'ideal'. We shall see in more detail later how this logic operates, as Derrida uses the non-concept of the spectre to destabilize Marx's distinction between use-value and exchange-value.

A number of commentators have noted a slight change in Derrida's later works (from around the mid-1980s onwards): a 'shift from deconstructive quasi-concept to experience of aporia' as John Protevi puts it (Protevi, 2003: 184). As Protevi notes, this change should not be overstated, for there remains a continuity in Derrida's work. There is something like a shift of strategy, however. The earlier essays usually proceeded via a close analysis of some work by a particular writer, from whom a certain term is taken (supplement from Rousseau, for example) which then unravels the logic governing that writer's work. The later work heads straight for a particular concept (albeit often approached via analysis of different thinkers) that is common to the entire Western tradition, and locates some aporetic paradox in this concept. Perhaps the paradigmatic instance – if there can be such a thing in this case – of this later logic is the *decision*. Any true decision, claims Derrida, must be undecidable. Here 'undecidable' does not mean an equivocation between two determinate possibilities, but points to the fact that a decision is not really a decision if it is determined by existing rules: 'it cannot be deduced from a form of knowledge of which it would simply be the effect, conclusion, or explicitation' (Derrida, 1995a: 77). It must rather be undecidable, incalculable, *unconditional*, a sort of leap of faith unattached to knowledge – yet at the same time a determinate decision must be taken, in concrete, *conditional* socio-political circumstances. The condition of possibility of a decision – that it be made undetermined by existing rules – is simultaneously its condition of impossibility – because any decision must necessarily be determinate and have some reference to existing rules. Using this kind of analysis, Derrida has examined various different concepts: hospitality, responsibility, duty, gift, promise.[2] In each case, Derrida tries to think through a concept in its most rigorous form: to be worthy of its name, this concept (e.g. decision, forgiveness, belief) must go through the ordeal of what appears to be its opposite (the undecidable, unforgivable, unbelievable). Yet this rigorous, unconditional yet paradoxical and aporetic form of the concept is always tied to a conditional form, to which it is irreducible but from which it is inseparable. There is a constant negotiation between the two poles, which are distinct but indissociable. Like Derrida's early work, this strategy pits itself against an unmixed, pure logic of either/or that can designate uncomplicated, uncontaminated concepts without trouble.

This later strategy is developed by Derrida in 'Force of Law' (first given as a lecture in 1989) in relation to the notion of justice. This thinking will play an important role in *Specters of Marx*. In 'Force of Law', Derrida states that *justice* is *unconditional*, incalculable, infinite, irreducible to any rule or programme; yet justice must always be exercised through *law*, which is *conditional*, calculable, regulated, coded. Justice and law are absolutely heterogeneous yet also absolutely indissociable: for 'law claims to exercise itself in the name of justice and . . . justice demands for itself that it be established in the name of a law' (Derrida, 2002a: 251). While the law is deconstructible (because it has been constructed, it has a certain textual history), justice cannot be deconstructed: it is undeconstructible. Indeed, Derrida claims that deconstruction *is* justice (243). This undeconstructible justice is never fully present; it always remains 'to come'. A just decision cannot simply follow existing rules, because it must be a decision made freely, and a decision which simply followed rules would not be a free decision but only 'the programmable application or the continuous unfolding of a calculable process' (252). Yet at the same time it is not enough that a decision is free to confirm that it is just: the decision *must also* have reference to some rule or law, some encoded form of justice, for it to be recognized as just, even if the decision invents or reinvents this rule. But then this only defers the question of how one knows that this rule is just. Hence justice is never present because no decision is presently just:

> [E]ither it has not yet been made according to a rule, and nothing allows one to call it just, or it has already followed a rule – whether given, received, confirmed, preserved, or reinvented – which, in its turn, nothing guarantees absolutely; and, moreover, if it were guaranteed, the decision would have turned back into calculation and one could not call it just. (Derrida, 2002a: 253)

So justice is always to come. Derrida calls it an 'idea of justice', while distinguishing it from the notion of a Kantian regulatory idea. But despite this reluctance to call on Kant, Derrida here is much like Lyotard in seeking to keep judgement open, positing a form of judgement and action that does not simply confirm existing criteria, yet does not fall into a sterile relativism or pragmatism. There is no last judgement, no end: 'One is never sure of making the just choice; one never knows, one will never know with what is called knowledge' (Derrida, 2001: 56). This is what is expressed by Derrida's notion of a 'future-to-come' [*l'à-venir*]: a future that cannot be read off from the present, an 'overflowing of the unpresentable over the determinable' (Derrida, 2002a: 257). In places this logic is formulated in terms of a 'democracy-to-come': democracy as an opening to the event, to the coming of the other, as a respect for the singular, the incalculable, the impossible – yet this democracy that will never arrive is also, and necessarily, tied to democracy as it exists today, its present, determinate forms. There is 'a perpetually indispensable negotiation between the singular opening to the impossible, which must be safeguarded, and the method, the right, the technique, the democratic calculation; between democracy to come and the limited present of democratic reality' (Derrida, 2002b: 195). Democracy must respect singularity, alterity, yet must also count, calculate, identify, represent (Derrida, 1997b: 22). It has a conditional form as it must exist today and an impossible, unconditional form that is always to come.

Specters of Marx is interesting not only because it offers Derrida's first comprehensive engagement with Marx, but also because it follows both threads or strategies in Derrida's work. To the list of non- or quasi-concepts can be added the figure of the spectre: neither living nor dead, neither present nor absent, 'neither soul nor body, and both one and the other' (Derrida, 1994: 6). In addition, the book champions a notion of justice that is irreducible to the law: justice as the undeconstructible, as democracy-to-come. Indeed, *Specters of Marx* demonstrates that these are only two different strategies, and together signal a continuity in Derrida's work. 'The question of the ghost is also the question of the future as a question of justice' (Derrida, 2002*b*: 107). Neither is fully present, and neither can be accounted for in a dialectical or oppositional logic. Hence this focus on justice as opening to the event connects to Derrida's earliest work: 'différance is a thinking that tries to respond to the imminence of what comes or will come, to the event' (Derrida, 2002*b*: 93). But whereas Lyotard distanced himself from Marxism in favour of an openness to the event, Derrida in contrast finds this very theme within Marx, attributing to Marxism what he calls a 'messianic eschatology' (Derrida, 1994: 59).

Marx's metaphysics

Though Derrida proceeds largely by analysing philosophical texts, this does not mean he is an idealist. In Chapter 1, we followed Althusser to offer a preliminary definition of idealism as a philosophy of Origins and Ends. It is clear that Derrida is not an idealist in this sense: deconstruction undermines both *arkhe* and *telos*, for both imply the presence of something – the presence of an origin or an end, even if it is a presence temporarily absent: a lost origin or an end yet to be attained. *Différance* is not an originary difference, but precisely that which shows that there is no pure origin, because everything carries within it the trace of something other than itself. Even in a more conventional sense it is difficult to term Derrida an idealist, for it is in his work that language and writing are rethought in material terms: 'writing' for Derrida refers to any material system of marks or traces. To be idealist would be to imagine that meaning pre-existed writing in the form of an originary Idea, whereas for Derrida 'writing is *inaugural*'. It is partly the very materiality of writing, its inscription on 'a surface whose essential characteristic is to be infinitely transmissible' that means the play of signification can never be arrested once and for all (Derrida, 1978: 12).

Because the idealist-materialist distinction is one of the most persistent oppositions within the history of Western metaphysics that Derrida deconstructs, it is better to say that he wishes to disrupt this opposition rather than choosing one side over the other. Far from distancing him from Marx, this places Derrida firmly in Marx's footsteps: both thinkers seek a new concept of materialism that displaces the traditional opposition between idealism and materialism. Derrida has both suggested that his work can be understood as a 'critique of idealism' and warned against the dangers of a 'metaphysical materialism' that is 'reinvested with "logocentric" values' – a materialism that would merely be idealism turned on its head (Derrida, 1981: 62–5). It is partly for this reason that Derrida values the work of his friend and former colleague Althusser, who had similarly warned of materialisms that are only disguised idealism, with Matter in place of Mind. Before *Specters of Marx*, Derrida had welcomed Althusser's 'critique of the "Hegelian" concept of history', encouraging us to 'be wary of . . . the metaphysical concept of history. This is the concept of history as . . . the history of meaning developing itself, producing itself, fulfilling itself' (56–8). Derrida emphasizes that when he says an encounter between deconstruction and Marxism is ' *"still to come"*, I am still, and above all, thinking of the relationship of Marx to Hegel' (63). Hence the importance of Althusser's attempt to forge a non-Hegelian Marx. Nonetheless, this is not an uncritical reception of Althusser. Though appreciative of Althusser's critique of Hegelian historicism, Derrida echoes his warning to Lévi-Strauss that there is a risk of effacing history altogether (Derrida, 2002b: 157). Althusser's notion of overdetermination provides a welcome correction to rigid determinism and simplistic dialectical formulas – but it is simultaneously compromised and limited by the proviso 'determination in the last instance', which Derrida calls 'the metaphysical anchoring of the whole enterprise' (Derrida, 2002b: 170).

It is in an interview from 1989 in which Derrida discusses his relationship with Althusser that the former directly addresses the question of why he took so long to produce any thorough analysis of Marx. In earlier interviews Derrida had claimed that questions on the relation between Marxism and deconstruction are 'necessary, vast, and fundamental' (Derrida, 1995c: 71), stressing that an 'encounter' between deconstruction and Marx's materialism seemed 'absolutely necessary' (Derrida, 1981: 62). The need carefully to establish the conditions of this encounter can in part account for Derrida's hesitancy in dealing with Marx, but in the Althusser interview he details further reasons: personal, political, and philosophical. In the 1960s, Derrida says, his chief interests were Husserl and Heidegger – so on an intellectual level he found he was operating in a different problematic from his Althusserian contemporaries: the kinds of issues and questions he was working on were ignored by his Marxist colleagues (Althusser, Balibar et al.). Moreover, he says, he felt unable to raise these issues, he even felt 'intimidated': 'to formulate questions in a style that appeared, shall we say, phenomenological, transcendental, or ontological was immediately considered suspicious, backward, idealistic, even reactionary'. Wary of structuralism's reaction against phenomenology, Derrida saw something valuable in the latter (though emphatically not in the idealist form it took in Sartre). Feeling unable to introduce questions of Heideggerian ontology or Husserlian transcendental phenomenology – 'questions that then seemed to me to be necessary – even necessary against Husserl and Heidegger, but in any case *through* them' – into the discussions about Marx and Marxism, Derrida instead kept quiet (Derrida, 2002b: 151–3). Not only did he feel unable to raise these points, he felt that to do so might leave him branded as a political conservative: 'I didn't want to raise objections that would have appeared anti-Marxist' (156). Appreciating that Althusser's work was a positive force within Marxism as part of a struggle against the sterile dogma of the French Communist Party, Derrida did not want to raise criticisms that might undermine this good work and 'be taken for [the] crude and self-serving criticisms' that the Communist Party itself could form in opposition to Althusser (152).

It is possible that there is an element of retrospective revisionism in these comments from 1989: Derrida can present his silence on Marx as a consequence of an astute judgement of contemporary issues, when the real motivations may have been quite different.[3] But whatever his motivations for staying silent on Marx, the important thing is that Derrida had never been prepared to dismiss Marx outright. Nonetheless, he exhibits an uneasiness or dissatisfaction with certain themes not simply in Althusser and contemporary Marxism but in Marx too. It was not just that he was scared to raise his voice: Derrida also found something in Marx's work itself that unsettled him. 'I had the impression', he says, 'that it was still largely a metaphysical text' (Derrida, 2002*b*: 160). Against existing readings of Marx, Derrida wanted to find a different way of tackling Marx, a way that dealt with questions that Derrida was keen to address but which had been excluded from the agenda: 'I tried, discreetly, not to give in to the intimidation – by deciphering . . . the metaphysics still at work in Marxism' (Derrida, 1995*c*: 81). So when Derrida agreed with his questioners in a 1971 interview that the lacunae in his work with respect to Marx 'are indeed lacunae, not objections' (Derrida, 1981: 62), this does not mean that Derrida had no objections to make and that he was so happy with what he found in Marx that he felt no need to add any comments. Rather, it suggests that Derrida had no objections to Marx's works and project as such, no objections to the 'encounter' between deconstruction and Marxism that his interviewers raised. But in spite, or rather precisely because of the necessity of this encounter, Derrida wanted to take his time to challenge Marx and reveal his weaknesses.

Spirits of Marx

Beyond this targeting of certain elements in Marx's work – too metaphysical, too logocentric, too Hegelian, too *idealist* – Derrida finds something else there. When *Specters of Marx* arrives, Derrida makes it clear that he thinks Marx still has a place in our world, claiming that there will be no future without him. He argues that if deconstruction has so far 'been prudent and sparing but rarely negative in the strategy of its references to Marx', it is because Marx seemed to have been '*taken over*', 'welded to an orthodoxy'. But not only are there no objections to an encounter between Marxism and deconstruction, Derrida also goes so far as to place his own work '*in the tradition* of a certain Marxism', and even talks of 'this attempted radicalization of Marxism called deconstruction' (Derrida, 1994: 92). He affirms this in the face of a contemporary discourse – of politicians, academics, journalists – which declares the 'death' of Marx and Marxism and the triumph of political and economic liberalism. Derrida probably overplays the oppositional status of his book: there is always someone somewhere announcing the death of Marx and always someone else resurrecting him or calling on his ghost – and as he himself admits, his intervention comes after a longstanding demand to write about Marx. Nevertheless, the background to both Derrida's book and the conference which gave birth to it was marked by a conspicuously self-congratulatory tone on the part of Western liberals following the collapse of the Soviet Union, a celebration epitomized by Francis Fukuyama's (1992) *The End of History and the Last Man* (which Derrida submits to a brief but amusing and effective critique). Yet this liberal triumphalism is at once jubilant and anxious, manic and troubled: desperate to announce the benign and auspicious victory of liberal capitalism despite overwhelming evidence to the contrary. Against this anxious triumphalism, Derrida throws the spotlight on that which it would hide, detailing the suffering, exclusion, oppression, and violence that exist in the world, despite – or because of – the triumph of neo-liberal virtues, offering a list of ten 'plagues' of the 'new world order', including inter-ethnic conflict, developing-world debt, and the spread of nuclear weapons:

> Instead of singing the advent of the ideal of liberal democracy and of the capitalist market in the euphoria of the end of history, instead of celebrating 'the end of ideologies' and the end of the great emancipatory discourses, let us never neglect this obvious macroscopic fact, made up of innumerable singular sites of suffering: no degree of progress allows one to ignore that never before, in absolute figures, never have so many men, women, and children been subjugated, starved, or exterminated on the earth. (Derrida, 1994: 85)

This stirring indictment of global injustice is made in the name of a new, radicalized critique 'inspired by at least one of the spirits of Marx or of Marxism' (Derrida, 1994: 86). The *spirits* of Marx or Marxism: it is a central hypothesis of *Specters of Marx* that there is more than one 'spirit' of Marx. Like all texts, Marx's writings are radically heterogeneous: his work offers a number of alternatives, many Marxes.

Like Lyotard, Derrida is not interested in Marx's work as a unified system. As inheritors of the spirits of Marx, we must distinguish between them, 'filter, sift, criticize . . . sort out several different possibles', in order to reaffirm this inheritance (Derrida, 1994: 16). Derrida goes even further: for while all 'inheritance is always . . . a critical, selective, and filtering reaffirmation' (91–2), there is something in Marx's work which calls for its own reinvention:

> To continue to take inspiration from a certain spirit of Marxism would be to keep faith with what has always made of Marxism in principle and first of

all a *radical* critique, namely a procedure ready to undertake its self-critique. This critique *wants itself* to be in principle and explicitly open to its own transformation, re-evaluation, self-reinterpretation. (Derrida, 1994: 88)

Not only does Marx offer numerous possibilities to choose from, '[w]e do not have to solicit the agreement of Marx' for the choices we make. 'And we do not have to suppose that Marx was in agreement with himself' (Derrida, 1994: 34). This does not mean that Marx is simply a blank canvas on which we can sketch our own theory: Derrida often points to Marx's unique value in providing resources for the analysis of contemporary relations between nation-states, the market, international law, technological innovations, and capital. Yet Derrida does not provide these analyses himself: 'what I am putting forward here . . . corresponds more to a *position-taking* than to the work such a position calls for, presupposes, or prefigures' (53). In fact he is clearer about those spirits of Marx he wants to reject. We have already seen Derrida suspicious of the metaphysics in Marx. In *Specters of Marx* he expands on this identification of the unwelcome spirits of Marx, Marxisms that should be left to one side:

> We would be tempted to distinguish this *spirit* of the Marxist critique [as critique of liberal capitalism and its ills], which seems to be more indispensable than ever today, at once from Marxism as ontology, philosophical or metaphysical system, as 'dialectical materialism,' from Marxism as historical materialism or method, and from Marxism incorporated in the apparatuses of party, State, or workers' International. (Derrida, 1994: 68)

The identification in this passage of Marxism *as ontology* is important: the interrogation of Marx's ontology is one of the most important themes of Derrida's book. It relates the reading of Marx strongly to Derrida's work hitherto, aligning it with his deconstruction of the onto-theological heritage of Western metaphysics from Plato onwards. Against Marx's ontology Derrida proposes a 'hauntology': the study of the spectral. For the 'spectres of Marx' refer not only to the ghosts of Marx that haunt *us* today, but also to the spectres that haunted Marx himself.[4] It is using the figure of the spectre that Derrida deconstructs Marx.

Ontology and Hauntology

Though Lyotard continued to defend Marx's relevance, he tended to marginalize him in later works; Derrida, in contrast, though largely ignoring Marx for most of his career, is in *Specters of Marx* much more insistent than Lyotard in promoting Marx's significance. He is also, however, very critical of certain Marxisms, and certain aspects of Marx; as with Lyotard, these criticisms congregate around Marx's ontology. The two 'critiques' share various similarities (not the least of which is a suspicion of critique itself, hence the scare quotes), but Derrida's deconstruction of Marx's ontology requires its own extended analysis. While Derrida helps subvert certain ontological naiveties in Marx's work, he does not appreciate enough that Marx's turn to 'real relations' can also be read as a radical de-ontologization.

Chasing ghosts

We have seen that deconstruction has often proceeded by exposing metaphysical dualisms in a philosopher's work, in which one term is privileged over the other (considered secondary, derived, impure, etc.). Marx seems to have provided just such a dualism: that between use-value and exchange-value (in turn reflecting the dual character of human labour as useful, concrete labour and general, abstract labour). One way to proceed here might be to search for affinities between deconstruction and Marx, examining how both seek to undermine apparently natural and self-sufficient identities by demonstrating how such identities tend to suppress differential relations. Thus it might be argued that the law of value suppresses and homogenizes the heterogeneity of use-values. This is the path taken by Michael Ryan (1982) as part of his attempt to present deconstruction as a mode of Marxist criticism, offered some eleven years before *Specters of Marx*. Derrida, however, does not take this path. Instead – and like Lyotard before him – he seeks to question and complicate the relation between use-value and exchange-value. According to Derrida, Marx posits a use-value identical to itself, 'purified of everything that makes for exchange-value and the commodity-form'. For Derrida, '[i]t is not a matter . . . of negating a use-value or the necessity of referring to it. But of doubting its strict purity' (Derrida, 1994: 159–60).

This deconstruction of use-value/exchange-value is part of a wider reading of Marx's work, focused around the figure of the spectre. This figure, like *hymen* and *pharmakon*, comes from the very texts Derrida reads. Spectres haunt Marx's writings, to the extent that Derrida claims Marx was obsessed with ghosts, possessed by them, in intense, ambivalent fascination: Marx at once loved and hated ghosts. He pursued them across the landscape of his work, a man in a double pursuit of spectres, chasing after them in order to chase them away, conjuring them in order to exorcize them. Marx seeks to bind the ghost to an ontology, struggling against the ghost 'in the name of living presence as material actuality' (Derrida, 1994: 105). For the ghost is that which cannot be accounted for by classical ontology: both dead and alive, visible and invisible, sensuous and non-sensuous, present and absent, it disrupts the conventional distinctions of classical metaphysics. A spectre is not simply a spirit. If a spirit is an autonomized idea or thought, 'torn loose' from some material body, a spectre is then a 'paradoxical *incorporation*' of the spirit in a new body – but a strange, '*a-physical* body', a ghostly body: a 'second incarnation conferred on an initial idealization' (Derrida, 1994: 126–7). It is spectres that Marx wants to do away with, even as he calls them: he uses ghosts, but at the moment he turns to a spectral logic he then 're-philosophizes', 're-ontologizes', in a 'desire to conjure away any and all spectrality so as to recover the *full, concrete reality* of the process of genesis hidden *behind the specter's mask*' (Derrida, 1999b: 258).

Derrida finds ghosts throughout Marx's work: the constant reappearance of the term 'spectre'. For Derrida, this recurring motif cannot be explained away as a mere rhetorical strategy, a habit of writing.[5] The ghosts are too persistent: Marx keeps returning to ghosts, keeps chasing them, because he cannot banish them from his philosophy. He wants to be rid of spectres in the name of actual, living reality, but actual living reality remains haunted. Marx can never quite escape the spectral realm for the firm ground of ontology. The most famous spectre, of course, is that found in the opening lines of *The Communist Manifesto*: the spectre of communism haunting Europe. Even here, claims Derrida, Marx wants to do away with the ghost: he wants the spectre of communism to become the *living reality* of communism, hence exorcizing its spectrality. Similarly, in *The Eighteenth Brumaire* Marx praises those revolutions that sought 'to recover the spirit of revolution, not to relaunch its spectre'. The farcical period of 1848–51, in contrast, 'saw only the spectre of the old revolution on the move' (Marx, 1996a: 33). But it is with *The German Ideology* and *Capital* that Derrida undertakes his most extensive analyses of Marx's ghosts, as he seeks to demonstrate that the theories of ideology and fetishism, though different in other ways, both rely on this logic of the ghost: on Marx's attempt to distinguish spirit and spectre so he can chase away the latter.

From *The German Ideology* he takes Marx's lengthy assault on Max Stirner – an attack often dismissed by other commentators as a tedious diatribe, and usually cut from abridged versions of the book (thus perhaps reaffirming Derrida's claims that deconstruction takes place in the margins of philosophy). For Derrida, Marx pursues Stirner because Marx is obsessed with spectres and recognizes in Stirner a fellow obsessive, a kind of brother (both sons of Hegel), a brother-in-arms fighting ghosts. Stirner's mission is to combat the spectres of thought: to show that the abstract notions of idealism – God, Man, and so on – are not external powers over me but are nothing more than abstractions that I have created myself. The goal is to reappropriate these creations into oneself, to recognize these 'spooks' as one's own rather than subordinating oneself to them as if they were real powers. Describing this self-discovery, Stirner writes: 'The thoughts [that I created and owned] had become *corporeal* on their own account, were ghosts, such as God, emperor, Pope, fatherland, etc. If I destroy their corporeity, then I take them back into mine, and say: "I alone am corporeal"' (Stirner, 1995: 17). But for Marx, Stirner's reincorporation of these spectres does not re-establish the corporeality of the ego at all – quite the opposite, it merely creates a kind of superspectre, an entire body made of nothing but spectres. For Marx it is not enough to recognize the spectral forms of the abstraction that are Man, God, Pope, and so on and make a personal decision to banish them; one still has to deal with their 'real' earthly forms,

> to think of the practical interrelations of the world. . . . By destroying the *fantastic* corporeality which the world had for him, he finds its real corporeality outside his fantasy. With the disappearance of the *spectral* corporeality of the Emperor [for example], what disappears for him is not the corporeality, but the *spectral character* of the Emperor, the actual power of whom he can now at last appreciate in all its scope. (Marx and Engels, 1976: 126)

Having banished the spectres, Marx claims, one must then deal with the actual, real social relations.

In effect, Derrida argues, Marx and Stirner both want the same thing: to exorcize the spectres. '[A] common stake incites the polemic. It is called the specter. And Marx and Stirner want to be done with it. . . . The disagreement is over the means to this end, and over the best solution' (Derrida, 1994: 132). Marx thinks that Stirner's 'reappropriation' does nothing more than create a superspectre, 'the ghost of all ghosts'. 'Marx', writes Derrida, 'seems to be warning Stirner: If you want to conjure away these ghosts, then believe me, I beg you, the egological conversion [i.e. Stirner's solution] is not enough': one needs to go further and take account of the practical structure of the world, the living Pope, the real power of the emperor, the actual relations that make up the fatherland, and so on. *That* is the way to achieve 'reappropriation of life in a body proper', which is what both Marx and Stirner want (129–31). This shared goal is the reason why Marx pursues Stirner across more than three hundred pages of *The German Ideology*.

Real relations

Yet it might just as well be said (and in modest homage to Marx's fondness for chiastic formulations) that Marx does not chase Stirner for so long because he is obsessed with spectres; rather he chases spectres for so long because he is obsessed with Stirner. 'Spectre' is Stirner's own term – and in fact Marx more often attacks what Stirner calls 'the holy'. The attack on Stirner is part of a wider assault on the Young Hegelians, also covering Feuerbach and Bauer. But Feuerbach and Bauer have already been dealt with: it is Stirner who must be finished off. What can be seen in *The German Ideology* is not so much Marx's obsession with ghosts as his inability to stop writing (that trait identified by Lyotard), combined with his desire to have the last word. One can question whether Marx shares a common enemy with Stirner at all. Does he not instead think that Stirner has misidentified the enemy? Stirner has made the mistake common to other Young Hegelians, in that he has taken (a crude, uncritical version of) Hegel at his word: Stirner believes ideas really do rule the world – and hence he only has to combat these ideas in order to achieve liberation. He is able to declare these ideas 'spectres' and then announce that he is not scared of them and knows how to banish them. For Marx, spectres are not the enemy: there is no point chasing them, when one could be dealing with real relations.

Derrida might respond that this confirms his charge against Marx: that Marx does not want to believe in ghosts. In attempting to show that Stirner has picked the wrong enemy, Derrida can claim, Marx wants to convince Stirner that ghosts do not exist, that he is chasing something that is not really there. Marx certainly lends himself to this deconstructive reading in *The German Ideology*: he is constantly contrasting the real existing world with thoughts and ideas; life with thought; reality with the illusions of philosophy; empirical relations with speculative relations; the actual world with meagre categories; content itself with names and phrases; the material life processes of individuals with the phantoms formed in their brains. The spectre for Derrida is precisely that which would complicate these neat divisions. In this sense Derrida's aim is accurate, for Marx is often found trying to bring things back to 'real relations'.

But what are these real relations, repeatedly opposed to ideas, thoughts, illusions? As Callinicos argues,

> the distinctive feature of capitalist relations, as Althusser and his collaborators sought to show in *Reading Capital*, is precisely that they are *not* present. The capitalist mode of production is a structure which can be discerned only in its effects, and whose nature and operations must therefore be reconstructed through a process of theoretical labour. (Callinicos, 1996: 39–40)

Class relations are not a 'living presence as material actuality' but are relational: no single element of a mode of production can ever be fully present to itself because each is only composed in relation to other elements. Derrida's deconstruction does have some force when it comes to *The German Ideology*, for the 'real world' of this book is not yet composed of the relations of production: this key category has not yet been developed by Marx. There is a danger in Marx's work, highlighted by Lyotard as well as Derrida: in seeking to draw too easy a contrast between the real and the ideal, the risk is that Marx relies on a notion of pure, uncomplicated material actuality as that which is simply given. If this danger is particularly evident in *The German Ideology*, that is because it is a polemical, transitional work, although it is true that Marx does not always escape the temptation elsewhere. It is, however, only a danger: not an unbreachable impasse governing everything that Marx wrote, but only one possible way of reading him, one potential inheritance among many. There is another way to read Marx that brings him much closer to Derrida than to

Stirner. Whereas Stirner seeks to fight established powers by raging against the abstract forms of idealism, for Marx

> the point is no longer to *denounce* the abstraction of 'universals', of 'generalities', of 'idealities', by showing that that abstraction substitutes itself for real individuals; it now becomes possible to *study* the genesis of those abstractions, their production by individuals, as a function of the collective or social conditions in which they think and relate to one another. (Balibar, 1995: 36)

Marx does this not by reducing the ideal or the spectral figures of thought to the real presence of 'full, concrete reality', but by showing how ideas and real, material relations are interconnected, so that one may talk of a 'materiality of the idea' and an 'ideality of matter' (Macherey, 1999: 20). Rather than seeking a pure distinction between the material and the ideal, for the mature Marx the relations of production are both material and ideal. His terms and arguments are more hauntological than Derrida appreciates.

Dancing tables

According to Derrida, it is not only in ideology that Marx chases spectres: the fetish also relies on this logic of reincorporation into an a-physical body (Derrida, 1994: 127). Through a reading of *Capital*, Derrida extends his analysis of Marx's spectres, and like Lyotard, he takes the first chapter on the commodity. The commodity 'retains that bodiless body which we have recognized as making the difference between specter and spirit' (151). Derrida is much taken with the image Marx uses to introduce 'the mystical character of the commodity' – that of a dancing table. As soon as it emerges as a commodity, Marx writes, the table

> not only stands with its feet on the ground, but, in relation to all other commodities, it stands on its head, and evolves out of its wooden brain grotesque ideas, far more wonderful than if it were to begin dancing of its own free will.

The table as a commodity – as a use-value produced for exchange – is a sensuous thing which is at the same time suprasensible, a sensuously suprasensible thing (Marx, 1976a: 163–5). Hence in Derrida's terms, the commodity is a spectre: 'neither dead nor alive, it is dead and alive at the same time'; an autonomous automaton, mechanically free, sensuous non-sensuous (Derrida, 1994: 150–3). As Marx says, in '[s]o far as it is a use-value [that is, a thing we find useful], there is nothing mysterious about it'; it is when it 'emerges as a commodity' that it becomes mysterious. 'The mystical character of the commodity does not therefore arise from its use-value' (Marx, 1976a: 163–4). And so for Derrida: 'The commodity thus haunts the thing, its specter is at work in use-value' (Derrida, 1994: 151).

Derrida claims that, just as in *The German Ideology* Marx wanted to show Stirner the best way to exorcize ghosts, so in *Capital* he wishes to exorcize the spectre of exchange-value from use-value by purifying use-value of commodification: 'Marx wants to know and make known *where, at what precise moment*, at what *instant* the ghost comes on stage, and this is a manner of exorcism, a way of keeping it at bay'. But for Derrida this is an impossible endeavour: use-values are haunted from the beginning. There is no pure use-value unaffected by the spectre of exchange-value: use-value 'is in advance contaminated, that is, pre-occupied, inhabited, haunted by its other, namely . . . the commodity-form, and its ghost dance'. There is no pure use-value 'identical to itself', 'no *use-value* which the possibility of exchange and commerce . . . has not in advance inscribed in an *out-of-use* – an excessive signification that cannot be reduced to the useless'. Even the *concept* of use-value makes no sense without this haunting, without the possibility of exchange, substitution, repetition, of use by another at another time (Derrida, 1994: 160–1).[6] Here we see the familiar logic of deconstruction at work: that which is excluded as secondary or parasitic (exchange-value) in fact is always a necessary structural possibility of that which is supposedly originary and self-sufficient (use-value). The ineradicable possibility of exchange – use by another – is both what makes it possible to conceive of an object as a use-value and what makes it impossible to conceive of a pure use-value fully present to itself. 'Spectre' is the term used by Derrida to account for this operation: the spectre is both the condition of possibility of the axiological distinction between use and exchange and its condition of impossibility. There is an echo of Lyotard here: Marx is accused of setting up a metaphysical opposition between use-value and exchange-value, in which the latter is a derivative corruption of the pure naturality of the former.

In reviewing *Specters of Marx*, Jameson points out that use-value for Marx is not a lost purity, the way things once were before contamination by the market, when objects were valued purely for their use. For there was fetishism in the past as well, though of a more directly religious or political nature. 'Use-value lies thus also in the future, before us and not behind us' (Jameson, 1999: 55–6). This objection is correct as far as it goes: Derrida, like Lyotard, would be wrong to think that Marx looks back in nostalgia to a time uncorrupted by the market. (It is a shame Derrida does not address this objection in his response to Jameson in 'Marx & Sons'.) Yet it leaves some of Derrida's questions unanswered: for even if Marx does not look back to an uncontaminated use-value, he may still use it as a conceptual distinction, in which use-value is uncorrupted by exchange, somehow pure. Derrida concedes that the concept of use-value has analytical power, even that the distinction between use and exchange is a necessary one, but he wants to challenge the purity of the concept and complicate the distinction. Moreover, Jameson implies that Marx looks forward to a time when use-value *will be* uncontaminated by exchange – and Derrida does not accept this. This is not to say, however, that Derrida's analysis is correct – only that Jameson's response does not quite hit its target. Jameson himself concedes that 'an uncertainty may well persist as to whether even its [i.e. use-value's] residuality betrays a secret ontological longing at the heart of Marxism, or at least at the centre of Marx's own writing' (Jameson, 1999: 46). In order to try to clear up some of that uncertainty, I want now to look at what Marx says about value in *Capital* and elsewhere.

Naturalization and spectralization

What Marx aims at with his analysis of value is a kind of 'denaturalization': the main point of his distinctions is not to exorcize exchange-value in the name of a natural use-value purified of exchange (whether in the past or the future) – but, on the contrary, to demonstrate that what seems natural and essential is really social, historical, and contingent. He wants to show how and why it is that under capitalism value and use-value become confused. For Marx, use-value is the property of a thing and value is human labour objectified. Under capitalism, however, it appears the reverse is true: value is naturalized as a property of things and use-value comes to be seen as a property of men. The social characteristics of man's labour are reflected as objective characteristics of the products of labour: social relations between producers are displaced by a fantastic relation between things that seems to exist independently of the producers. This is because it is only when products are exchanged, when they come into contact with each other, that their value comes into play (hence the value of products seems to be their own property), while the worker only considers the use-value of his product insofar as it must be useful to others (hence the use-value of products seems only to concern men) (Marx, 1976a: 164–6). Derrida acknowledges that Marx pursues this critique of the way in which what is social is naturalized, yet argues that this naturalization is targeted as the other side of a simultaneous spectralization: social relations have been naturalized at the same time as and for the same reasons that simple, solid use-values have been denaturalized or spectralized. It is through this substitution, whereby social relations are reflected as natural relations between things, that the product of labour becomes 'suprasensible'; this is the 'mystical' or 'fantastic' form. Hence Derrida can claim that

> this phantasmagoria of a *commerce* between market things . . . corresponds *at the same time* to a naturalization of the human *socius*, of labor objectified in things, and to a denaturing, a denaturalization, and a dematerialization of the thing become commodity, of the wooden table when it comes on stage as exchange-value and no longer as use-value. (Derrida, 1994: 157)

Thus Marx, argues Derrida, not only wants to denaturalize that which is really social – to reaffirm value as the result of social labour between men and not of commodities themselves – but also to naturalize, or despectralize, that which appears to be social – to reassert the familiar solidity of real objects that seem to have taken on a fantastic, ghostly life of their own.

It is true – as we have already seen in relation to Lyotard and Althusser – that Marx does tend to idealize a certain kind of naturality, with his favourable comparisons between pre- and post-capitalist societies in their transparency and immediacy. But there is another, more productive way of looking at this. For Althusser, the section on fetishism is an idealist residuum that distracts from the 'true heart' of *Capital*: the final part on primitive accumulation. But in fact the beats from this heart also resound in the section on fetishism: for here too Marx is dealing with a concrete analysis of specific historical forms. For Marx use-value and exchange-value are not simply abstract concepts, but distinctions that are necessarily made every day; indeed, it is *because* they are abstract concepts that it is necessary to study their genesis in relation to everyday activities and relations. To understand what Marx is doing, his work needs to be viewed within the context of the material practices and institutions to which it is connected, instead of seeing it as nothing more than an exercise in philosophy.

Marx is always clear about the need to distinguish between value and exchange-value, something Derrida is not careful to do. Exchange-value is 'the necessary mode of expression, or form of appearance, of value' (Marx, 1976*a*: 128). Value is the objectification of abstract human labour: the value of a commodity is measured by the labour-time socially necessary for its production. A thing has use-value because it has utility for man, and it has value because it contains human labour. Thus anything containing labour has value – even Robinson Crusoe's table and chair have value, because he has made them himself. But value does not appear except in relation to other commodities, except in exchange: 'the value of a commodity is independently expressed through its presentation as "exchange-value"' (152). Hence the exchange-value of a commodity is only a particular historical form of 'what exists in all other historical forms of society as well, even if *in another form, namely, the social character of labour,* so far as it exists as the *expenditure of "social" labour-power*' (Marx, 1996*b*: 249). Thus use-value is not a pure standard by which the corruptions of exchange can be measured. Value is always present in any use-value containing human labour; exchange-value is the particular form value takes in exchange – and Marx would agree with Derrida that use-values can always be given over to exchange, to an out-of-use (exchange is not unique to capitalism). Though of course Marx's distinctions between use-value and exchange-value, and between exchange-value and value, are couched in philosophical language and need to be understood in the context of the Western metaphysical tradition, their meaning, significance, and impact are not exhausted by philosophy: they are not merely logical oppositions between ontological categories but distinctions drawn from and necessarily connected to everyday activities:

> In fact in every price-list every single sort of commodity goes through this illogical process of distinguishing itself from the others as a *good*, a *use-value*, as cotton, yarn, iron, corn, etc., of presenting an '[economic] good' [as] qualitatively different in every respect from the others, but at the same time presenting its *price* as qualitatively the same, [i.e.] presenting a quantitatively different thing *of the same essence*. (Marx, 1996b: 247)

Moreover, for Marx the distinction between use-value and exchange-value is important primarily because it reflects the dual character of labour. In a letter to Engels in 1868, Marx boasts that the novelty of his work in *Capital* lies (at least in part) in his revelation that 'if the commodity has a double character – use value and exchange value – then the labour represented by the commodity must also have a two-fold character. . . . This is, in fact, the whole secret of the critical conception' (Marx and Engels, 1956: 238–9). This distinction between concrete and abstract labour is in turn not (simply) a metaphysical abstraction but, like that between use-value and value, one which is made each day and which takes on special significance under capitalism. Each act of labour is necessarily a specific, useful act (weaving, sewing, etc.) and a general expenditure of labour-power, 'a productive expenditure of human brains, muscles, nerves, hands etc.' (Marx, 1976a: 134). This latter takes on significance under capitalism because labour then becomes general in reality: the worker no longer possesses a skill, but only a universal labour-power to sell. These distinctions, then, and the analysis of commodities and value, cannot be separated from analysis of existing conditions and struggles – understood not as the ontological immediacy of the world, but as the historical specificity of any situation. Marx insists that he only considers the products of labour through analysis of specific economic forms, 'not from helter-skelter quibbling over the concepts or words "use-value" and "value"' (Marx, 1996b: 243). Polemical as this offhand remark might be, it can be said that Derrida's commentary often looks like helter-skelter quibbling: he reads *Capital* as if Marx is doing nothing but grappling with an inherited set of metaphysical problems; he does not discuss the way Marx relates concepts to determinate conditions, nor the circumstances within which Marx wrote (still less the circumstances within which Derrida himself writes).

This is a significant difference between Marx and Derrida. The former always pays attention to the particular situation, with its own historical specificity and complex composition of social forces and relations. This is the 'real world' whose links to philosophy Marx tries to establish. *Pace* Derrida, Marx does not ontologize the 'real' – whether expressed in terms of material actuality or use-value. On the contrary, as Bensaïd argues, Marx *de-ontologizes*:

> [T]he *Grundrisse* and *Capital* present themselves as a labour of mourning for ontology, a radical deontologization, after which no space remains for any 'world beyond' whatsoever ... There is no longer any founding contrast between Being and existence, nothing behind which there lies concealed some other thing that does not come to light. (Bensaïd, 2002: 116)

To analyse things in terms of material social relations, as Marx does, is not to depend on a metaphysical ontology, exorcizing the spectral in the name of the living presence of actuality; it is to free critical thought from a conception of Being, examining social relations as they exist and not in terms of some hidden essence. This is a spirit of Marx that Derrida could have called upon. But Derrida does not seem willing enough to take seriously his own claim that there are *many* Marxes to draw upon. In the following section, I want to show that he also seems unwilling to follow his claim that deconstruction is in the tradition of Marxism: too eager to find the metaphysics in Marx, Derrida then struggles to find the positive heritage gifted by him.

Teleology and Messianicity

Derrida's attitude towards Marx on the question of teleology is a little different from that of Lyotard: Derrida is far more disposed to find in Marx's work something other than a philosophy of history. But in a sense he is too keen, smothering Marx under his own deconstructive terminology. Calling on what he terms Marx's 'messianicity', Derrida loses sight of Marx's own demand for revolutionary intervention.

Thinking the event

Rather like Lyotard, in his later works Derrida becomes more and more interested in the notions of the event and justice. As the groundless ground of deconstruction, the spectre is undeconstructible. When considered in terms of the event, this undeconstructibility is understood as justice. The event must always remain 'to come': if it arrives and is recuperated within existing laws or programmes then it is no longer an event. For Derrida, the event must come as a surprise, as something unexpected: as Lyotard puts it, the event 'does not arrive where one expects it; even a non-expectation would be disappointed' (Lyotard, 2006: 46). Distinct from law, justice is an opening to the event and the arrival of the radically other, the unforeseeable. Justice here is thought in terms of dislocation, against concepts of Being and time as presence, unity, or harmony: it welcomes the singularity and alterity of the other. Like the ghost, it cannot be thought within a binary or dialectical logic that opposes what is present, actual, and empirical to what is absent, ideal, and regulatory. Justice here is irreducible to any existing institution or even concept, yet does not act as some Kantian regulatory idea: it forms part of a future that will never be present (neither present nor absent – like ghosts). As elsewhere in Derrida's work, in *Specters of Marx* this concept of justice is linked to the idea of democracy-to-come, but this time it is also aligned with what Derrida terms messianicity. While he argues that Marx wants to chase away ghosts, he claims that what remains undeconstructible in Marx is 'a certain emancipatory and *messianic* affirmation' (Derrida, 1994: 89).[7] Messianicity is 'what remains irreducible to any deconstruction, what remains as undeconstructible as the possibility itself of deconstruction'. It is a non-religious messianism, 'even a messianic without messianism, an idea of justice – which we distinguish from law or right and even from human rights – and an idea of democracy – which we distinguish from its current concept and from its determined predicates today' (Derrida, 1994: 59). Derrida writes of a 'messianic without messianism' in order to distinguish this messianicity from all determinate messianisms (religious or otherwise). This is a 'quasi-transcendental' messianism, 'a universal structure of relation to the event' (Derrida, 1999b: 249). It is an idea of the messianic as a 'waiting for the event *as* justice' (Derrida, 1994: 168). Distinct from all determinate, conditional messianisms, there is also this indeterminate, unconditional messianicity, irreducible to any religious or political messianicity – yet the two poles, conditional and unconditional, are indissociable: it is *quasi*-transcendental because there can be no pure unconditional messianicity uncontaminated by conditional messianisms.

There are clear similarities to Lyotard's work here. Derrida presents messianicity as 'a way of thinking the event "before" or independently of all ontology' (Derrida, 1999b: 249), which would make an appropriate summary of much of Lyotard's work. Like Lyotard, Derrida wishes to challenge all teleology by formulating a concept of justice that cannot be reduced to the law, as an affirmation of a future that cannot simply be read off from the present: to anticipate some determinate future would 'cancel the eventness of the event' (Derrida, 1997a: 2). But what is significant here is where Lyotard and Derrida place Marx. As we saw in the last chapter, while Lyotard retains a place for Marx, he renounces Marxism as one of those modern, *eschatological* theories which annuls the event and forecloses the possibility of the unexpected – indeed, his critique of modern, eschatological theories is developed primarily via his renunciation of Marxism, which along with Hegelianism stands as the central example of such a theory. Up to a point Derrida is in agreement with Lyotard: he also wants to retain a sensitivity to the event, and he also finds in Marxism – and in Marx – an eschatology. Beyond any ontology, Marxism '*also itself carries with it and must carry with it, necessarily*, despite so many modern or post-modern denials, a messianic eschatology' (Derrida, 1994: 59). But the difference is that for Derrida this eschatology is not something that needs to be purged, as an embarrassing or dangerous relic: it is not that which forecloses the event but precisely that which welcomes it. Derrida insists on distinguishing between teleology and eschatology – in order to retain the latter while abandoning the former. Teleology annuls the future by trapping it within a predictable sequence or programme of results, while eschatology (in Derrida's terms) opens itself to a 'future that cannot be anticipated' (168). Derrida thinks that both currents run through Marx's work. In *Specters of Marx* he reiterates his opposition to 'the metaphysical concept of history and the end of history' that can be found in both Marx and Hegel, that 'onto-theo-archeo-teleology [which] locks up, neutralizes, and finally cancels historicity' (70, 74). But against these currents, against this onto-teleology, Derrida calls on another spirit of Marx, on Marx's messianic eschatology: an anticipation of justice as an 'absolute rift in the foreseeable concatenation of historical time' (Derrida, 2002*b*: 95).

In doing this Derrida certainly distinguishes himself from other readers of Marx: not only from those orthodox Marxists who would insist on Marx's teleological vision, but also from those who (like Althusser) wish to strengthen Marx by dissociating him from all teleology and eschatology, as well as those who (like Lyotard) are tempted to turn away from Marx because he is tainted by both. But Derrida does find a precedent: in 1940 Walter Benjamin wrote of 'a *weak* messianic power' as he sought to contrast Marx's 'historical materialism' with a historicism that charts the progression of mankind through 'a homogeneous, empty time' (Benjamin, 2003: 390, 395). Like Derrida, Benjamin opposes a dislocated time to a homogeneous temporal continuum, and an active anticipation to a passive faith in a predetermined *telos* that would be the fulfilment of some distant origin. Benjamin talks of redemption, but not in the sense of the grand narratives identified by Lyotard, which posit redemption as the realization of a promised finality. Rather, Benjamin offers solidarity with history's victims, in contrast to historicism's sympathy with the victor; he calls on a working class which is 'nourished by the image of enslaved ancestors rather than by the ideal of liberated grandchildren' (394). For this redemption the working class cannot simply sit back and wait, comfortable that it is 'moving with the current', resting in 'an anteroom . . . in which one could wait for the emergence of the revolutionary situation with more or less equanimity' (393, 402). For Benjamin, messianism calls for intervention; not watching time flow by until the messiah arrives as predicted, but the seizure of a moment: 'a messianic arrest of happening, or (to put it differently) a revolutionary chance in the fight for the oppressed past', a chance 'to blast open the continuum of history' (396). 'Messianic anticipation', explains Bensaïd in reference to Benjamin and Marx, 'is never the passive certainty of an advent foretold, but akin to the concentration of a hunter on the lookout for the sudden emergence of what is possible' (Bensaïd, 2002: 85).

Not really Marx

While acknowledging possible similarities between his own 'messianic without messianism' and Benjamin's 'weak messianic power', Derrida is also careful to dissociate the two: his own thinking of messianicity, he claims, does not 'belong – not really, not essentially – to the Benjaminian tradition . . . . I do not believe . . . that the continuity between the Benjaminian motif and what I am attempting to do is determinant – or, above all, that it is sufficient to account for what is going on here' (Derrida, 1999*b*: 249). Although Benjamin presents Marx's idea of a classless society as a secularization of the idea of messianic time (Benjamin, 2003: 401), Derrida thinks that Benjamin's messianism remains determined by Judaism; moreover, he thinks that Benjamin links 'the privileged moments of this "*weak* messianic power" . . . to determinate historico-political phases, or, indeed, crises' (253). It is doubly determined, religiously and politically: on the one hand by Judaism and on the other by a concrete historical context. For Derrida, in contrast, 'the universal, quasi-transcendental structure that I call messianicity without messianism is not bound up with any particular moment of (political or general) history or culture (Abrahamic or any other)' (254).

I shall leave aside the question of Benjamin's Judaism and its relation to his Marxism, interesting as it may be.[8] But Derrida is surely right that Benjamin's messianism is bound up with a particular political moment. This does not mean that Benjamin's comments have relevance only to his specific context – the spread of fascism across Europe, the Nazi-Soviet pact, and so on – and are now to be treated only as an insight into a past world. Rather, what he calls weak messianic power must always be tied to existing political circumstances. A weak messianic power is precisely a power, our power to act, and hence no longer simply waiting for a messiah: it is always an intervention at a moment of crisis. This connects the present with the future: Benjamin is not calling for an openness to the future in general, but for a future that can redeem the past. This does not mean that he predicts the future or offers a *telos* but it does mean that his 'messiah' does not come as a complete surprise. Benjamin calls for a fight in the name of an oppressed past, and in the hope of a better future. He demands intervention in the name of the victims of history: at once a break with the past, out of history and with an uncertain end, and in the name of the past, of the oppressed.

Where Benjamin talks of an active power, Derrida suggests that his own version of messianicity is a power*less*ness, a giving of oneself to the event. It is a waiting, albeit a 'waiting without waiting': a waiting without expectation, 'waiting for an event, for someone or something that, in order to happen or "arrive", must exceed and surprise every determinant anticipation' (Derrida, 1999b: 251). There is here a kind of passivity not wholly unlike that which accompanies a teleological philosophy of history: with a philosophy of history we sit back and wait for what we already know will happen; with a philosophy of the event, such as that found in both *Specters of Marx* and *The Differend*, we sit back and wait to welcome what we cannot expect. It is true that '[t]eleology is, at bottom, the negation of the future, a way of knowing beforehand the form that will have to be taken by what is still to come' (Derrida and Ferraris, 2001: 20). But whereas teleology cannot account for unexpected contingencies, Lyotard and Derrida seem unable to account for anything else. Benjamin's demand for active intervention in the name of the past requires a sharp socio-historical analysis that can identify specific connections between the past, the present, and possible futures. Derrida's messianicity, on the other hand, is linked to specific, determinate circumstances only as formal conditions of possibility. In contrast to Derrida, Benjamin situates himself between the past and the future, waiting for a moment in which the latter can avenge – not fulfil – the former. What distances Derrida from Benjamin here surely also distances Derrida from Marx: it looks as if Derrida's thinking of messianicity does not belong to the Marxian tradition – not really, not essentially. Marx does not know, or claim to know, exactly what the future will look like, but he believes it will develop immanently from the present via processes that can be analysed rather than simply coming as a surprise.

There is no doubt something of Derrida's messianicity in Marx's work. But this is not surprising: indeed, it seems unavoidable if, as Derrida says, this messianicity is a universal structure of experience, if 'we are by nature messianic. We cannot *not* be, because we exist in a state of expecting something to happen' (Derrida, 2002c). It is difficult to see, then, how Marx could not be messianic. It may be that Marx affirms this messianic outlook while others try to repress, displace, or ignore it. Yet this affirmation is surely not unique to Marx, and it is not clear that it tells us anything other than that Marx was a radical thinker who looked to a future different from the present. The motif of messianicity has not emerged from a reading of Marx's writings, but from Derrida's own writings – from that encounter with justice first explicated in 'Force of Law'.[9] So what Derrida ends up praising is not so much Marx's work but the work of Derrida himself. Derrida seems both unwilling to distinguish Marx's own 'eschatology' – instead subsuming Marx under his own figure of messianicity – and unable to link his messianicity to Marx, beyond mere assertion of this link. His deconstruction of Marx follows the texts in minute detail – but this adherence to the texts has evaporated when Derrida presents his messianic theme. The danger is that Marx gets absorbed into deconstruction, his irreducible specificity lost. We saw that Lyotard faced a similar problem. Retranscribed into their respective philosophical languages, Marx's unique contribution risks being pushed into the background when he encounters

Lyotard and Derrida. This never quite happens – both Lyotard and Derrida manage to illuminate Marx in numerous ways – but it is a constant threat.

An interesting light is shed on this by Derrida himself, in some comments made in his interview on Althusser, four years before the publication of *Specters of Marx*. Discussing the Althusserians, Derrida says that although he thinks the onto-theo-teleology in Marx is 'ineradicable', he finds their attempts to do away with it very interesting. Of this manoeuvre, he says:

> Now *that* is interesting! I will always be ready to subscribe to that gesture. But when they do this, there's no point in citing Marx any more or in pretending that Marx *meant-to-say-this* – there's no point, in any case, in lending privilege to that reference and excluding all others. They could perform that gesture without Marx or else with so many others. . . . (Derrida, 2002*b*: 190.)

That, of course, is exactly what Derrida has done: performed this (deconstructive) 'gesture' with so many others. These comments certainly do not exclude the possibility of doing the same with Marx – and even in this interview Derrida stresses the importance of reading Marx[10] – but they do suggest that one needs to provide good reasons for using Marx: to demonstrate what it is in Marx that demands attention. Otherwise there really is 'no point in citing Marx'.

Philosophy and actuality

It cannot be doubted that Derrida values Marx's work very highly, and he insists on Marx's contemporary relevance. But the force of this insistence is undermined because it is not always clear why Derrida thinks Marx is necessary. Derrida demands that a depoliticized, 'philosophico-philological' Marx should not prevail, that a Marx muffled by academic philosophers should not win out over a radical, political Marx (Derrida, 1994: 31–2). But the risk is that the Marx who emerges from deconstruction is precisely a philosophico-philological one. This would not meet Derrida's own demands, and it would call into question his placement of deconstruction in the tradition of Marxist critique (because it would imply that deconstruction itself was merely philosophico-philological).

Marx himself comments in *The German Ideology*:

> One has to 'leave philosophy aside', one has to leap out of it and devote oneself like an ordinary man to the study of actuality, for which there exists also an enormous amount of literary material, unknown, of course, to the philosophers. . . . Philosophy and the study of the actual world have the same relation to one another as onanism and sexual love. (Marx and Engels, 1976: 236)

While this remark may appear both flippant and polemical, it can usefully dramatize a key difference between Marx and Derrida: this concern the former has for the actual world. It is very tempting to extend the analogy and contrast Marx the energetic, promiscuous love-maker with Derrida the habitual, compulsive onanist. But then one could always deconstruct the opposition between onanism and sexual love that Marx proposes – indeed, Derrida has already done so in relation to Rousseau, for whom 'masturbation was to be added to so-called normal sexual experience', just as 'writing comes to be added to living self-present speech' (Derrida, 1976: 167). One could note that this deconstruction is already underway even in this little extract from Marx, who suggests that one access the 'actual world' through 'literary material', thereby unravelling any clean distinction between the real world in all its actuality and a philosophy that would be distant, abstract, and purely literary. One could note, finally, that deconstruction itself is not simply concerned with philosophical or literary texts: Derrida argues that 'a deconstructive practice that had no bearing on "institutional apparatuses and historical processes" ..., which was satisfied to work on philosophemes or conceptual signifieds, and so forth, would not be deconstructive' (Derrida, 1995c: 72). 'I have', he claims elsewhere, 'only ever been occupied with problems of actuality, of institutional politics, or simply of politics' (Derrida, 2002b: 91). Deconstruction, he says, 'is not *neutral*. It *intervenes*' (Derrida, 1981: 93). Philosophy as (political) intervention: this is an idea from Marx, and as such Derrida is not wrong to situate deconstruction in the tradition of Marxism.

But is the deconstructive intervention of the same order as Marx's interventions? In Derrida one does not find the kind of historico-political analysis that Marx provided. Derrida presents his messianicity as 'an active preparation', a 'commitment without delay' (Derrida, 1999b: 249), but it is something very different from Marx's agitation for revolutionary change. Arguing that Marx's relevance lies in large part in his potential insights into the relations between capital, law, states, and so on, Derrida does not develop these insights himself, instead restricting himself to a preliminary 'position-taking'. But it often seems as if this preliminary position-taking is all deconstruction ever does: it does not go on to provide the kind of specific, historically sensitive analyses of existing situations that Marx provides. The reason for this may be that deconstruction simply cannot provide these kinds of analyses – which may be why Derrida insists on the continued importance of Marx, as a thinker who clearly can. This claim need not be read as a denigration of deconstruction, but rather recognition of its limits and reassertion of Derrida's own comments on Marx.[11] Nor does it mean that deconstruction has no political relevance. It may be tempting to agree with Rorty's assertion that deconstruction has helped create 'a self-involved academic left which has become increasingly irrelevant to substantive political discussion' (Rorty, 1996: 69), but in fact deconstruction helps problematize and rethink the notion of 'politics' itself, and all its associated concepts and terms.[12] Indeed, it is precisely this problematization of 'politics' that complicates Marx's demand to 'leave philosophy aside'. The demand for philosophy to be replaced by or reduced to some other thing – whether it be politics, history, society, economics, real life, or whatever – is complicated by deconstruction's demonstration that politics, history, society, and so on are themselves deeply philosophical and metaphysical concepts. In Bennington's words, 'the very concept supposed to reduce the transcendental claims of philosophy itself comes to occupy a transcendental position'. Thus 'the attempt at a *political* reduction of philosophy' amounts to 'the demand for the concept "politics" to be placed in the very transcendental position it is self-righteously supposed to reduce and explain, but to which it remains blind' (Bennington, 2000: 20). This argument is eloquently summarized by Martin McQuillan (2007a: 9): 'philosophy cannot be held accountable to politics because politics itself is a philosophical concept'.

But while it is true that 'politics' is a philosophical concept, politics is not exhausted by its philosophical conceptuality. This does not just mean that, as Derrida would argue, there can be no purely philosophical conception of politics because that which is supposedly pure, unconditional, and transcendental is always contaminated by the impure, conditional, and empirical, and hence politics will always necessarily be tied to actual socio-political circumstances. It means that politics is always generated at the intersection of a number of practices, both discursive and non-discursive, and it is this which Derrida does not seem to acknowledge. In effect, this is the critique of Derrida that is made by Foucault, in the latter's response to Derrida's reading of *The History of Madness*. Foucault argues that Derrida has privileged philosophy at the expense of other practices, at once reducing philosophy to a textual set of propositions (and thus effacing the extent to which philosophy is also an exercise that modifies the subject) and excluding the material relations of power within which philosophy is embedded. As Foucault states: 'The stakes of the debate [between Foucault and Derrida] are clearly indicated: Could there be anything anterior or exterior to philosophical discourse?' (Foucault, 1998: 395). For Foucault and Marx, the answer to this question is *Yes*. This is not to say that somehow Foucault is a 'better' Marxist, or that we can pit Foucault and Marx against Derrida. It does, however, suggest that Foucault may tell us something about Marx that Derrida can not.

Conclusion

We can conclude by saying that Derrida only deconstructs Marx. This is not to disparage Derrida's reading of Marx, however: the great strength of that reading is precisely that it is a deconstruction – but this is also its great weakness. In many ways Derrida's engagement with Marx is an advance on that of Lyotard, which in itself had much to offer. Like Lyotard, Derrida highlights certain dangers and difficulties in Marx's work, undermining the faith that the future can be pre-programmed or that critique can be grounded in the pure essence of some natural given. Lyotard never rejected Marx, and always maintained that there was more in Marx than these dangers, but he did tend to marginalize Marx, allowing his onto-teleology to overshadow alternative perspectives in his work. Derrida not only extends and deepens the subversion of Marx's ontology, he also champions Marx's contemporary relevance with greater force than Lyotard, insisting that alongside a teleological philosophy of history, there is in Marx a respect for the event and an open future. But in formulating this respect in terms of messianicity, Derrida tends to lose sight of Marx's own work. Derrida is insistent that '[w]hether they wish it or know it or not, all men and women, all over the earth, are today to a certain extent the heirs of Marx and Marxism' (Derrida, 1994: 91). But given this, something more is needed to affirm this inheritance. The basic faults and merits that Derrida identifies in Marx's work – his reliance on ontology and his affirmation of messianicity – are not unique to Marx. Moreover, Derrida does little to acknowledge Marx's own strategies for undermining metaphysics. While Derrida turns to a quasi-transcendental philosophy of the event, Marx leaves philosophy aside. This does not mean rendering philosophy irrelevant, but recognizing that philosophy is not everything. In turn, it does not mean resorting to some unthought notion of the concrete or a naïve 'ontology of presence as actual reality' (Derrida, 1994: 170) – or, at least, it does not have to mean this, as we shall see if we examine Foucault's reading of Marx.

Chapter 4

The History of the Present: Marx Through Foucault

I don't wish to protect my work by a visa which would validate it as Marxist . . . . It's up to you to decide whether it is Marxist or not and whether or not that is relevant.
(Foucault, 2005b: 18)

Lyotard had dedicated his early life to the propagation of Marxism, and continued to write on Marx even after the loss of that revolutionary fervour. For a long time Derrida said very little about Marx unless prompted, but then produced a careful, book-length study. Foucault, in contrast, never wrote very much about Marx: there is no equivalent to *Specters of Marx* among his books, no late celebration after a long silence. There are only a few remarks spread here and there across various books and interviews; comments that are often inconsistent, sometimes contradictory. Although Foucault had once been drawn to Marxism, he left the French Communist Party (PCF) after around only three years as a member and, unlike Lyotard, it seems he 'was not an ardent militant' (Eribon, 1991: 54). His first book, 1954's *Maladie mentale et personnalité* was strongly influenced by Marxism, emphasizing the importance of economic contradictions and class struggle. But the book's second edition edited out this Marxist influence, and from that point on Foucault rarely spoke of Marx: when he did, it was often in order to define his work against Marxism. In places Foucault explicitly criticizes Marx, while many of his writings read like a coded assault on Marxism. This position with respect to Marx and Marxism – a studied silence punctuated by critical assaults – led many to accuse Foucault of a deep hostility towards both.[1]

Despite these accusations, and despite Foucault's occasional complicity in their formulation, Foucault's work in fact has much in common with that of Marx. Certainly his work feels closer to Marx than that of either Lyotard or Derrida, despite the greater willingness of those two authors to discuss Marx. Foucault produces histories that 'are studies of "history" by reason of the domain they deal with and the references they appeal to; but they are not the work of a "historian"' (Foucault, 1992: 9). This would not be a bad summary of

Marx's own project. In this chapter I shall examine that project in more detail than I have so far. In part this is because Foucault himself says so little directly about Marx: there is no great text on Marx to analyse. But more importantly, it is because Foucault, while offering no grand analysis, reveals more of Marx. Foucault is just as suspicious of Marx's idealism as Lyotard and Derrida – but Foucault's way of combating this idealism is not to propose a messianic philosophy of the event: rather, he offers the kind of detailed historical analysis that Marx himself offers. In this chapter I want to develop a firmer idea of what that kind of analysis entails. Yet as well as revealing Marx in a clearer light, Foucault's work also helps highlight some of the difficulties that materialist philosophy faces. The first thing we should do, however, is to examine Foucault's scattered comments on Marx in order to assess his own judgement of Marx.

The Latest Barrier of the Bourgeoisie

Discussing Foucault's 1966 work *The Order of Things* in the year of its publication, Sartre (still in his Marxist phase) lambasted the author for his 'denial of history', going on to claim of the book: 'Behind history, of course, it is Marxism which is attacked. The task is to come up with a new ideology: the latest barrier that the bourgeoisie once again can erect against Marx' (Sartre, 1971: 110). The limits of Sartre's judgement become evident once the complexity of Foucault's relation to Marx is explored.[2] Later in the chapter we shall examine Foucault's specific affinities, advances, and shortfalls with respect to Marx, but first it is important to establish a broader picture of what he has to say about Marx and Marxism. We can begin by looking at Foucault's characterization of humanism in *The Order of Things*, before moving on to his broader subversion of Marxism, and his use of and praise for Marx.

Marx's humanism

Although Sartre's accusations against Foucault are ultimately fallacious, even puerile, it is not difficult to understand why he found a certain anti-Marxism in *The Order of Things*. Sartre mentions the book's supposed suspension of history, but his comments were probably spurred by its explicit discussions of Marx. Although Marx does not have a starring role in *The Order of Things*, it is one of the few places where Foucault comments directly on Marx's work, and his remarks – even allowing for their deliberately provocative nature – are not especially complimentary or encouraging. 'At the deepest level of Western knowledge', Foucault claims, 'Marxism introduced no real discontinuity; it found its place without difficulty . . . . Marxism exists in nineteenth-century thought like a fish in water: that is, unable to breathe anywhere else' (Foucault,

1970: 261–2). (Foucault here is referring to the ideas introduced by Marx rather than a Marx*ism* separate from Marx.)

At the 'deepest level' of knowledge, the archaeological level that Foucault is exploring, Marx's work shares a platform with Ricardo's as part of the new form of knowledge called economics. In the mutation that saw the classical age's analysis of wealth superseded by nineteenth-century economics, Foucault identifies two phases: the first marked by Adam Smith's introduction of a concept of labour irreducible to the representation of something else (need, goods, value), as an ordering principle in its own right; the second marked by Ricardo's location of the source of all value in labour as a producing activity. On top of this, Marx's work is a minor modification: in opposition to conventional bourgeois economics, perhaps, but still situated firmly within the same epistemological boundaries: 'Their controversies may have stirred up a few waves and caused a few surface ripples; but they are no more than storms in a children's paddling pool.' Ricardo may link History to an anthropology of finitude by positing a slow erosion towards a final stabilization of development, while Marx posits a violent eruption and a restoration of what had been suppressed, but both look to a denouement that 'will cause man's anthropological truth to spring forth in its stony immobility'; hence, 'the alternatives offered by Ricardo's "pessimism" and Marx's revolutionary promise are probably of little importance' (Foucault, 1970: 261–2).

A denouement that is the realization of an original truth: already comparisons can be made with the critical readings of Marx offered by Lyotard and Derrida.[3] What makes Foucault's reading interesting is the way he carefully situates Marx's onto-teleology within a wider humanist discourse. For Foucault does not restrict himself to commenting on Marx's relation to classical political economy. Questioned about his comments in *The Order of Things* a year after they were published, Foucault appeared to backtrack a little:

> What I said about Marx concerns the specific domain of political economy. Whatever the importance of Marx's modifications of Ricardo's analyses, I don't think his economic analyses escape from the epistemological space that Ricardo established. On the other hand, we can assume that Marx inserted a radical break in people's historical and political consciousness, and that the Marxist theory of society did inaugurate an entirely new epistemological field. (Foucault, 1998: 281–2)

But this does not seem quite to fit with what Foucault says in *The Order of Things* itself. Having situated Marx alongside Ricardo within nineteenth-century economics, Foucault then places Marx within a much wider epistemological arrangement: Marx is in the thick of the modern, humanist episteme. As the classical age gives way to the modern, Foucault explains, an analysis based on representation gives way to what he calls 'the analytic of finitude', and 'man appears in his ambiguous position as an object of knowledge and as a subject that knows' (Foucault, 1970: 312). Man recognizes that he is limited by things outside himself, he is revealed as a finite being: yet this very limitation, this finitude, is at once the condition of possibility of man's knowledge. There is a strange double-movement in which positive facts provide the possibility for man's finite knowledge, but man's finite knowledge provides a foundation for the possibility of knowing positive facts. Man is both constituted and constitutive, object and subject. It is Kant who first articulates this way of thinking, but Marx too is tied to this humanist discourse.

Foucault identifies three different ways in which modern thought has operated within the analytic of finitude. First, man becomes 'a strange empirico-transcendental doublet' (Foucault, 1970: 318), both an object to be studied and the condition of all knowledge: here there is a fluctuation between a positivist analysis which grounds knowledge in man's nature or history, in the empirical facts studied, and an eschatological analysis which grounds knowledge in the discourse used, in the promise of a truth foretold. Second, man appears as a cogito both embedded in an unthought, obscure density, and capable of apprehending this unthought: here knowledge is established by thinking the unthought, in an act that simultaneously transforms man by illuminating the darkness in which he finds himself. Third, man is both always already in history and set back from history as the source of historical time itself: here knowledge anticipates the return of an elusive origin. Foucault suggests that each of these aspects linking positivity and foundations – empirical and transcendental, cogito and unthought, retreat and return of origin – can be found in Marx's work. Marx searches for a discourse both positivist and eschatological, empirical and critical, in which 'man appears . . . as a truth both reduced and promised' (320). He also seeks to throw light on the dim space in which man has developed, on 'the inexhaustible double that presents itself to reflection as the blurred projection of what man is in his truth', so dreaming 'of ending man's alienation by reconciling him with his own essence' (327). Finally, Marx offers the recovery of our origin as 'a promise of fulfilment and perfect plenitude' (334). His name offered by Foucault as a representative example in each domain of the analytic of finitude, it might even be said that Marx's work stands as the epitome of the modern, humanist discourse, deep in that 'anthropological sleep' from which we may only now be waking.

The Order of Things is concerned with the rules of discursive practices, not individual thinkers, and it offers an archaeology of the human sciences, not a critical history of ideas. Nonetheless, as brief as its comments on Marx are, it offers some of Foucault's most extended and explicit remarks on Marx's philosophy. While he does not aim to assess the worth of particular thinkers, by placing Marx very firmly in the modern episteme Foucault does little to suggest that Marx has much to offer any kind of post-humanist thought. Not only is he denied any significant innovatory contribution to modern economics,

Marx also seems stuck in an anthropologism whose time is up. Foucault leaves it to Nietzsche to herald the possibility of a knowledge with neither God nor man, to rouse us from our long sleep.

Foucault's critical discussion of Marx has much in common with the reflections made by Lyotard and Derrida. In particular, by tying Marx to the empirico-transcendental doublet that is man, Foucault essentially argues that Marx remains wedded to an ontology and an eschatology – with eschatology here mirroring Lyotard's use of the term (referring to the achievement of a promised finality) rather than Derrida's more positive use (referring to an open, indeterminate future). For Foucault's Marx, man is at once reduced to the purity of an ontological given and promised to a predicted future – precisely why Marx is criticized by Lyotard and Derrida (who, while reformulating eschatology in more positive terms, still criticizes Marx for retaining a teleology).[4] Like Lyotard and Derrida, Foucault finds something else, something more favourable in Marx – yet at the same time his critical remarks are not restricted to those on Marx's humanism.

Subverting Marxism

If his explicit comments on Marx in *The Order of Things* can seem intended to belittle the significance of Marx's impact, a critical subversion of Marx and Marxism can also be found in Foucault's method. *The Archaeology of Knowledge*, which sets out Foucault's archaeological methodology in laborious detail, mentions Marx only a couple of times. As we shall see later, in these explicit references Foucault now appears much more positive about Marx's contribution. But aside from these brief comments, and in common with much of Foucault's other work, at various points in the book there surfaces an implicit critique of Marxism. This critique is in places conducted via Althusser, although Althusser's name is not heard: there is a kind of silent dialogue between Foucault and Althusser in the 1960s and 1970s through which the former often seems keen to distance himself from Marx and Marxism.

As Foucault tries to distinguish his own archaeological method from a more conventional history of ideas, many of his comments appear to be surreptitious criticisms of Marxism. Foucault says he is looking for systems of formation: the complex groups of relations functioning as rules governing discursive practices. These systems are internal to the practices themselves: they are not 'imposed on discourse from the outside', as 'determinations which, formed at the level of institutions, or social or economic relations, transcribe themselves by force on the surface of discourses' (Foucault, 1977a: 73–4). Archaeology, says Foucault, is concerned with the non-discursive as well as the discursive: with institutions, events, practices, political and economic processes. But he is not looking 'to isolate mechanisms of causality' (162), to explain how economic processes, for instance, have determined the emergence and development of discursive formations. Rather, he is interested in the particular relations between discursive practices and non-discursive domains: the ways in which the former are articulated in the latter, and the manner in which discourse itself organizes and transforms institutions and practices. Similarly, he does not reject the concept of contradiction, but emphasizes that he wants to describe the different types, levels, and functions of contradictions within a particular discursive practice as 'a space of multiple dissensions' (155). He does not seek to uncover the dominant, central contradiction that gives rise to discourse, 'the founding, secret law that accounts for all minor contradictions and gives them a firm foundation', a foundation in 'the economic and political conflict that opposes a society to itself' (150–1). Lastly, Foucault claims that he analyses discursive strategies in terms of the conditions of their existence, not in terms of the particular interests of a speaking subject: 'though membership of a social group can always explain why such and such a person chose one system of thought rather than another, the condition enabling that system to be thought never resides in the existence of the group' (Foucault, 1970: 200).[5]

Foucault here positions himself against idealist attempts to explain everything in terms of some essential core or unifying principle. Yet the most obvious target of his comments is Marxism: though he does not name either Marx or Marxism, he hardly needs to. It is clear that he is trying to distance his work from analyses of a Marxist type: certainly he will not have pleased those who hope to explain things by reference to the determining force of the economy, the central contradiction of capitalism, or the dominance of the bourgeoisie. If Marx is the object of hostile derision in *The Order of Things*, it can seem as if he remains a target in *The Archaeology of Knowledge*, albeit this time one whose face is hidden from view, with his name left unspoken. So in the explicit comments in *The Order of Things* and in the theoretical elaboration of *The Archaeology of Knowledge*, at the very least a certain suspicion of Marxism and a challenge to Marx can be detected.

After this latter book Foucault develops his methodology. Dreyfus and Rabinow (1982) suggest that Foucault's earlier work is subject to the problems it identifies in the human sciences: it too is both empirical and transcendental, with Foucault at once necessarily involved in the discourses he studies and offering himself as nothing more than a detached observer. For Dreyfus and Rabinow, Foucault moves beyond this impasse by consciously situating his own discourse, and reversing the primacy of theory over practice: the aim is no longer to uncover the autonomous theoretical rules which organize social practices, but to situate theoretical discourse as one practice among many. The archaeology of knowledge is supplemented by and subordinated to a genealogy of practices. But Foucault's renewed interest in material practices is not matched by a new declaration of solidarity with Marx. If anything, Marx makes even fewer direct appearances in Foucault's work after 1970; yet as before, Foucault often seems to be positioning himself against Marxism. We shall look more closely at Foucault's new conceptualization of power later, but for now it is enough to note that it offers a challenge to Marx. Whereas Marx claimed that '[p]olitical power, properly so called, is merely the organized power of one class for oppressing another' (Marx and Engels, 1998: 26), for Foucault power is strategic, ubiquitous, and productive: it is not a property belonging to a single individual or group, it is not located in a particular institution or class, and it is not exercised simply through prohibition and repression.

It is partly for these reasons that Foucault is suspicious of the Marxist notion of ideology. In *The Archaeology of Knowledge*, in comments apparently directed at Althusser, Foucault questioned the division between science and ideology, announcing that '[i]deology is not exclusive of scientificity' (Foucault, 1977a: 186). His subordination of theory to practice does not lead Foucault to a new appreciation of the concept of ideology, but rather entrenches his suspicions. 'In traditional Marxist analyses', he writes elsewhere,

> ideology is a sort of negative element through which the fact is conveyed that the subject's relation to truth, or simply the knowledge relation, is clouded, obscured, violated by conditions of existence, social relations, or the political forms imposed on the subject of knowledge from the outside. (Foucault, 2001: 15)

In contrast, Foucault claims that in his own analyses 'the political and economic conditions of existence are not a veil or an obstacle for the subject of knowledge but the means by which subjects of knowledge are formed, and hence are truth relations' (15). For Foucault, the concept of ideology – with its humanist and idealist undertones – simply cannot account for the complexity of the relationship between knowledge and power that he wishes to analyse.

The somewhat clandestine critiques of Marxism that Foucault makes in developing his own 'analytics of power' become more explicit in volume one of *The History of Sexuality*, which challenges the Freudo-Marxism of Reich and Marcuse. And once again, Foucault's pronouncements – rejecting an idea of power as a centralized system of domination – seem to come into conflict with Marxism even where it is not named. For many, the suspicion that Foucault is some kind of anti-Marxist is confirmed by his association with the *nouveaux philosophes*, who claimed to draw on Foucault's insights. Foucault returned the compliment, heaping praise on Glucksmann et al., and at times expressing sentiments that seemed to align him with their crude anti-Marxism.[6]

Praising Marx

So if Sartre and others saw in Foucault's work an attack on Marx and Marxism, it is not too difficult to see why. There can be found in Foucault's work – in his direct references, his methodology, and his intellectual alliances – a mixture of hostility, suspicion, and derision: sometimes a careful distancing from Marxism, sometimes an obvious subversion of Marx. Nonetheless, this should not prevent further examination of the relation between Foucault and Marx. There are two important reasons why this investigation should proceed, despite Foucault's apparent misgivings when it comes to Marx. First, Foucault does not simply 'attack' Marxism: he offers considered, rigorous – albeit often implicit – criticisms of various aspects of Marx's work, criticisms which cannot be brushed off as 'bourgeois'. As with Lyotard and Derrida, Foucault can help highlight particular shortcomings and blind spots in Marx's work. Second, for every offhand taunt directed at Marx, there is in Foucault's work some respectful homage; for every conflict of method, some productive use of Marx. In no way can Foucault's attitude be labelled 'anti-Marx': he is clearly influenced by Marx and in many places explicitly praises him. There is certainly an ambiguity in Foucault's attitude towards Marx – but this tension discloses the complexity of the relationship rather than revealing a fundamental hostility.

The relation is not only complex but also somewhat playful. 'I quote Marx without saying so', Foucault says, 'without quotation marks, and because people are incapable of recognising Marx's texts I am thought to be someone who doesn't quote Marx' (Foucault, 1980: 52). Foucault calls this a 'sort of game', and although it may seem irritating to those who do not know the rules, it is possible to discern good reasons for playing it. First, Foucault does not want to have to label himself Marxist or non-Marxist, and thus to treat Marx's work as some grand system that one must either subscribe to or renounce. To the contrary, he treats Marx as the producer of a box of tools which will prove useful only if Marxism's 'theoretical unity' is 'in some sense put in abeyance, or at least curtailed, divided, overthrown, caricatured, theatricalised, or what you will' (81).[7] Moreover, Marx's tools do not have to be used in the way in which Marx intended: Foucault makes inventive use of Marx; he produces his own Marx, so to speak. What he says of Nietzsche can also, I think, be applied to Marx:

> The only valid tribute to thought such as Nietzsche's is precisely to use it, to deform it, to make it groan and protest. And if commentators then say that I am being faithful or unfaithful to Nietzsche, that is of absolutely no interest. (Foucault, 1980: 53–4)

A second reason for playing this elusive game, in which Foucault uses Marx without acknowledgement, can be found in the contextual situation. Foucault's background is much like that of Lyotard: his very earliest works attest to the influence of the dominant threads of postwar philosophy in France – phenomenology and Marxism – but he develops a distinctive position in reaction against these trends. He has spoken of belonging to a generation limited by the horizon of Marxism, phenomenology, and existentialism, and of feeling 'stifled' by this horizon (Foucault, 1986: 174). It was not that Foucault felt that

Marxism was too tangled up in phenomenology and so, like Althusser, looked for a new Marxism, or a return to Marx: Marxism itself was for Foucault stifling, something that he felt he needed to escape. At the very least he seems to have been bored by Marxism, and at worst found it oppressive and constraining. Given the rigidity of the postwar PCF, this sense of oppression is not surprising. But Foucault's aim was not to return to an original Marx unaffected by party politics: 'not so much the defalsification and restitution of a true Marx but the unburdening and liberation of Marx in relation to party dogma' (Foucault, 1998: 458). It was not simply the official Marxism of party dogma that Foucault wanted to break away from, but also an academicized Marxology which reads Marx as any other philosopher, presenting 'Marx as a professor and not as a militant' (to borrow a phrase from Negri [1984: xv]).

In general, Foucault attacks not Marx but 'certain conception[s] currently held to be Marxist' (Foucault, 1980: 88). For example, he criticizes the notion of ideology not in order to undermine Marx, but to push Marx's materialism even further: to show 'how power relations can materially penetrate the body in depth, without depending even on the mediation of the subject's own representations' (Foucault, 1980: 186). (And in doing so he comes close to Marx's own theory of fetishism, as discussed in Chapter 1.) Marx is certainly not spared criticism, but it is balanced, even outweighed, by praise. In line with the game Foucault plays, comments on Marx are few and sometimes contradictory, but explicit homage is not wholly absent. We have already seen that Foucault later qualifies his comments made about Marx in *The Order of Things*. In that book, Marx was embedded in the modern discourse of man; a year later he was the engineer of a radical break. This latter verdict is reinforced in Foucault's 1969 essay 'What is an Author?', where Marx is offered alongside Freud as one of those 'founders of discursivity' who 'established an endless possibility of discourse' (Foucault, 1998: 217). This apparent contradiction, between two different positions on Marx, does not reveal a hopeless incoherence in Foucault's thought. Rather like Lyotard, Foucault does not look for consistency. 'Do not ask me who I am', he says, 'and do not ask me to remain the same' (Foucault, 1977a: 17). But Foucault's somewhat elusive position on Marx is not simply testament to this general desire to avoid simple categorization. More specifically, it demonstrates that Foucault (again like Lyotard) does not have a single, uniform position on Marx and Marxism. Indeed, Foucault proceeds on the basis that not only is Marx distinct from Marxism, but also that there is no single Marx: he is a plural and diverse resource. As Foucault says, 'As far as I'm concerned, Marx doesn't exist' (Foucault, 1980: 76).[8]

Although *The Archaeology of Knowledge* offers an implicit critique of various Marxist orthodoxies, it also praises Marx himself. Marx is still presented as operating to a large extent according to the same rules as Ricardo, but their differences appear to be more than storms in a paddling pool: Foucault now says that Marx 'revealed[ed] an entirely new discursive practice on the basis of political economy' (Foucault, 1977a: 188). More interestingly, Marx no longer seems to be tied to that wider humanist episteme to which he was tethered in *The Order of Things*. He is now placed alongside Nietzsche as an inaugurator of that 'decentring' operation which introduced a new form of history: 'general history' in place of 'total history', searching for discontinuous ruptures in a dispersed space of relations and series, instead of grouping everything around a single principle in a search for continuous patterns and totalities. Far from being locked in humanism from the start, it was later historians who transformed Marx into a defender of the sovereignty of the human subject. 'One is led . . . to anthropologize Marx, to make of him a historian of totalities, and to rediscover in him the message of humanism' (Foucault, 1977a: 13). Foucault traces his own methodology back to Marx, going so far in an interview from 1975 to claim that 'Marxist history' is basically a pleonasm, so great is Marx's influence: 'One might even wonder what difference there could ultimately be between being a historian and being a Marxist' (Foucault, 1980: 53).

Marx clearly has value in Foucault's eyes, then, as a thinker who introduced a break in history, and in the writing of history. Foucault would agree with Derrida that we are all, necessarily, heirs of Marx. But Foucault's strategy is in a sense the opposite of Derrida's: where the latter loudly pronounced his affiliation with Marx but often seemed to do little with him, the former constantly draws on Marx but without speaking his name. Nonetheless, there are places where Foucault consciously aligns himself with Marx – and also with certain streams of Marxist thought. For example, while drawing some sharp contrasts with his own work, he praises the Frankfurt School, claiming that if he had read them earlier, 'there are many things I wouldn't have needed to say, and I would have avoided some mistakes' (Foucault, 2001: 274).

Hence there can also be found in Foucault – in his direct references, his methodology, and his intellectual alliances – a mixture of praise, emulation, and respect: a subtle use of Marx and a conscious recognition of his contribution, albeit often in combination with a critique of Marxism as a unified, systematic theory. Étienne Balibar expresses this tension well, mapping in Foucault's work 'a movement . . . from a *break* to a tactical *alliance*, the first involving a global *critique* of Marxism as a "theory"; the second a partial *usage* of Marxist tenets or affirmations compatible with Marxism'. For Balibar, 'the opposition to Marxist "theory" grows deeper and deeper whilst the convergence of the analyses and concepts taken from Marx becomes more and more significant' (Balibar, 1992: 53). Balibar nicely presents a key aspect of Foucault's work: its rejection of Marxist theory, whether sanctified by the party or the university, and simultaneous reliance on Marx's concepts. However, it is important to avoid setting up a false alternative here: it is not that Foucault opposes Marx to Marxism, lauding the former while denigrating the latter. As we have seen, for Foucault 'Marx' does not exist: not only is Foucault uninterested in a systematic theory called Marxism, he is also uninterested in a coherent oeuvre named Marx. The rejection of Marxism does not leave a 'truer' Marx standing; it opens up the possibility of a more inventive and productive use of Marx.

So although Foucault offers no study of Marx comparable to those undertaken by Lyotard and Derrida, it is possible to draw out a number of common elements in their respective attitudes towards Marx. Like Lyotard and Derrida, Foucault calls on Marx's work not as a unified system but as a box of tools, and he calls for a radical, political Marx, while warning against Marx's onto-teleology, his simultaneous reduction and projection of man to a truth given and promised. But whereas Lyotard and Derrida turn to a messianic philosophy of the event in place of a Hegelian teleology, Foucault pursues a different path.

History and Genealogy

Foucault's studies pursue what might be called a deanthropologized history. In *The Archaeology of Knowledge*, Foucault traces this type of history back to Marx's decentring: his 'historical analysis of the relations of production, economic determinations, and the class struggle' (Foucault, 1977a: 13). In this section, I want to take seriously Foucault's acknowledgement of Marx's influence and further explore possible affinities between Marx and Foucault on the question of history. Despite the fact that he stays largely silent on Marx, Foucault is in fact a better guide to Marx's historical work than either Lyotard or Derrida. In particular, Foucault's genealogies, though most obviously influenced by Nietzsche, offer a form of history very like Marx's own historical analyses – a form that avoids the teleology that Lyotard and Derrida set themselves against, but without having to resort to a philosophy of the event. Before drawing comparisons with Marx's work, it will be useful to delineate Foucault's own historical methods, archaeological and genealogical.

From archaeology to genealogy

The first thing to note is that Foucault does not offer any general historiographical theory. Even the methodological prescriptions of *The Archaeology of Knowledge* only provide guidelines for a restricted area of research – and these guidelines have emerged not from abstract, generalized reflection but from the specific work Foucault has already done. 'I have tried', he writes, 'to draw up a survey . . . of the work that I had done in certain fields of concrete research, rather than produce plans for some future building' (Foucault, 1977a: 206). With the injection of Nietzschean genealogy around 1970, Foucault's historical work changes direction somewhat – but this is a development rather than a repudiation of the earlier work, so let us proceed by examining Foucault's work from the 1960s.

Perhaps the primary theme that arises from this work – certainly as it crystallizes in *The Archaeology of Knowledge* and associated essays – is that of *discontinuity*. Foucault does not pretend to have invented this notion, or to have been the first to have introduced it into the study of history, but situates his writings in the context of historical work already taking place (Bachelard, Canguilhem, Serres, Braudel, and Furet are all mentioned). To emphasize discontinuity is to target more traditional forms of history which seek to place everything in some vast continuous totality: some grand evolutionary schema in which all ideas can be explained in terms of tradition and influence and all events in terms of development and teleology. For Foucault and like-minded historians, discontinuity is not something that needs to be explained away, eliminated before the real work of establishing patterns and systems can begin. Rather, it becomes both something the historian finds in his investigations and an interpretative tool: 'both instrument and object of the investigation, since it delimits the field of an analysis of which it is itself an effect' (Foucault, 1998: 300). Discontinuity does not simply replace continuity, with the notions of break, rupture, and mutation substituted for those of evolution, teleology, and development. The notion of discontinuity has itself been transformed: 'no longer a pure and uniform void interposing a single blank between two positive patterns; it has a different form and function, according to the domain and level to which it is assigned' (300). The historian no longer makes use of totalizing models, but implements specific and multiple levels of analysis. Historical time itself is splintered. 'History . . . is not a single time span: it is a multiplicity of time spans that entangle and envelop one another' (430).

There is another, related target alongside continuity. 'Continuous history', writes Foucault, 'is the correlate of consciousness: the guarantee that what escapes from it can be restored to it; the promise that it will some day be able to appropriate outright all those things which surround it and weigh down on it' (Foucault, 1998: 301). There are clear echoes here of *The Order of Things*: the key theme of the humanist episteme which that book analysed was man's attempt to apprehend and master the dense exteriority in which he finds himself enclosed. Traditional history, then, with its search for continuity and its promise of appropriation, is for Foucault simultaneously a form of humanism: 'the last bastion of philosophical anthropology' (302). It is a history which establishes and celebrates the sovereignty of the human subject, with individuals swept up in a developing totality of which, it is finally revealed, they are also the authors: history as 'both an individual project and a totality' (280).

In this presentation of a non-teleological, ahumanist history which constructs a multitude of different historical times, the echo of another thinker can also be heard: Althusser's critique of historicism, in the early pages of *Reading Capital* in particular, has many parallels with Foucault's pronouncements on historical method. The difference, perhaps, is that whereas Althusser draws a somewhat abstract, theoretical critique of traditional history, Foucault *practises* this critique in his work by implementing his alternative method to study actual events. In this sense at least it is Foucault rather than Althusser who is closest to Marx, for Marx's methodology emerged from the kind of concrete engagements that Foucault undertakes. Foucault himself praises 'the quite remarkable critique and analysis of the notion of history developed by Louis Althusser' (Foucault, 1998: 281), thus further confirming that he does not see a necessary, fundamental incompatibility between his own approach to history and certain Marxist approaches. Foucault sometimes criticizes Marxist historiography, but is often careful to distinguish this from Marx's own work. Questioned, for example, about 'the privilege of history as a harmonic science of totality, as the Marxist tradition presents it to us', Foucault replies: 'As far as I can tell, that idea, which is widespread, is not actually found in Marx' (Foucault, 1998: 282).

Moreover, Foucault suggests that the traditional history he seeks to undermine is in a sense anti-Marxist: by drawing on an evolutionary model and tracing the seeds of current society back to 'the dawn of time', this traditional method of history neutered the possibility of revolutionary change, concluding that human history 'can never harbor within itself anything more than imperceptible changes' (Foucault, 1998: 423, 431). For Foucault, on the other hand, historical study has the opposite aim: 'to demonstrate how things which appear most evident are in fact fragile, and . . . rest upon particular circumstances . . . . [T]he goal is to render us free to effect possible transformations' (Foucault, 2005*b*: 19). This project, of opening the way to new forms of thought and life by showing that what appears necessary may be contingent, becomes more explicit in Foucault's later work on ethical practices of freedom, but it is a dominant theme in all his work, and can even be seen as a kind of unifying thread in his writings.

It is certainly a key element of genealogy as Foucault presents it. The genealogist discovers that what had seemed necessary and essential is accidental and contingent: 'he finds there is "something altogether different" behind things: not a timeless and essential secret but the secret that they have no essence, or that their essence was fabricated in a piecemeal fashion from alien forms' (Foucault, 1998: 371). These words are from Foucault's 1971 essay 'Nietzsche, Genealogy, History': published between *The Archaeology of Knowledge* and *Discipline and Punish*, the essay marks something of a shift in Foucault's work. With genealogy, Foucault turns more explicitly to the social institutions, political practices, and economic processes with which discursive practices are entwined. The emphasis is no longer primarily on sudden, discontinuous breaks and ruptures, but on the intricate, tangled emergence and dispersion of events and ideas. There is no repudiation of earlier methodological commitments, however. The targets are familiar: 'The traditional devices for constructing a comprehensive view of history and for retracing the past as a patient and continuous development must be systematically dismantled'

(380). Genealogy like archaeology opposes all teleology: 'it must record the singularity of events outside of any monotonous finality' (369). Following Nietzsche, it questions the form of 'history whose function is to compose the finally reduced diversity of time into a totality fully closed upon itself'; it rejects historical study 'whose perspective on all that precedes it implies the end of time, a completed development' (379). Likewise, it rejects the possibility of tracing events back to a unique origin or cause. Questions of material power come to the fore: genealogy records the conflict of forces, 'the hazardous play of dominations' and their hold upon the body (376).

Using this modified methodology, Foucault offers what he calls in *Discipline and Punish* 'the history of the present' (Foucault, 1977*b*: 31). This does not mean that Foucault is guilty of the 'involuntary *presentism*' of which he is accused by Habermas (1987: 276). Foucault does not seek to impose present meanings upon the past, any more than he seeks to demonstrate how our present is the necessary development of the past. Rather, he tries to show how we got to where we are: to show how accidental, how contingent our present is by uncovering the conflicts, detours, struggles, and deviations that have dragged us here. Foucault does not do this as a detached spectator, offering a metadiscourse which floats above the phenomena it observes or uncovers its underlying laws: he affirms that he wants to produce 'historical work that has political meaning, utility and effectiveness' and hence has chosen areas in which he has already been involved in political and personal struggles (Foucault, 1980: 64). His demonstrations of how things might be different are not idle, speculative fancies, but interventions that advocate concrete change.

It is thus possible to identify a number of features of Foucault's historical work, in both its archaeological and genealogical forms. First, it is anti-teleological and non-totalizing: it studies the past in order to ask how things have happened, not to demonstrate their necessary finality, and it records events by relating them to a multiplicity of specific historical times, not by containing them in a system of continuous development. Second, it is politically committed, acknowledging its own place in history and actively engaging in present struggles: it does this by demonstrating the fragility and contingency of existing customs and institutions and by 'an insurrection of subjugated knowledges', a recovery of buried struggles and local memories against 'the tyranny of globalising discourses' (Foucault, 1980: 81–3). Finally, it abandons the sovereignty of consciousness: not in order to dissolve the individual subject but 'to arrive at an analysis which can account for the constitution of the subject within a historical framework' (117).

A Nietzschean Marx?

None of this fits with a certain caricature of Marx: the Marx who sought to establish a grand interpretative and analytical system that would lay down objective, scientific laws ensuring the development towards communism of the proletariat as the universal subject. Moreover, it could be claimed, Foucault turns to Nietzsche and not Marx for inspiration and guidance for his historical studies. In what follows I want to vindicate Foucault's alignment of his methodology with that of Marx by elucidating points of convergence between the two thinkers, highlighting common interests and methods. In part I shall do this by arguing that Foucault is in many ways closer to Marx than to Nietzsche – but first I want to shake off the clichés that cling to Marx and reveal a different figure, separate from his caricature, by showing that Marx is not so very different from Nietzsche in the first place. This can be done by following some allusive suggestions from Foucault, who offers an alternative to any opposition between Marx and Nietzsche by raising the possibility of a kind of Nietzschean Marx.

In his 1964 essay 'Nietzsche, Freud, Marx' Foucault discusses these three 'masters of suspicion' – but not, as Ricouer would have it, in terms of a suspicion of surface, plunging into the depths to recover latent meaning; on the contrary, in terms of a suspicion of depth, aiming to show 'that depth was only a game and a surface fold'. Hence, claims Foucault,

> at the beginning of *Capital*, [Marx] explains how, unlike Perseus, he must plunge into the fog to show that, in fact, there are no monsters or profound enigmas, because everything profound in the conception that the bourgeoisie has of money, capital, value, and so on, is in reality nothing but platitude. (Foucault, 1998: 273)

This Marx would be much like Foucault, revealing that what presents itself as profound and essential, is nothing of the sort. Three more features distinguish this Nietzschean Marx. First, he refuses to return to absolute origins: see, for example, his '[r]efusal of the "Robinsonade"' (Foucault, 1998: 274). Idealization of origins is a game for classical political economy, not Marx. Next, he interprets not some passive, primary object, but only other interpretations: 'not the history of the relations of production but a relation already offering itself as an interpretation, since it appears as nature' (276). Marx (according to Foucault) seeks to disrupt bourgeois certainties about what is 'essential' or 'natural', not to establish his own sacred truths. Finally, Marx knows that any interpretation is infinite and must always turn back on itself. These comments from Foucault – tentative suggestions rather than a rigorous analysis – are interesting because they evoke a Marx close to Foucault, and one quite different from the figure sometimes raised by Lyotard and Derrida (and, in fact, by Foucault himself elsewhere). This Marx does not look forward to the return of some natural origin; rather, like Foucault he seeks to disrupt existing certainties, in an endless task that reflexively situates itself and perpetually turns back on itself.

In this essay, Foucault presents Marx and Nietzsche as interpreters of interpretations, but what he perhaps underplays here (though not elsewhere) is the material nature of their respective critiques. Both Marx and Nietzsche examine the brutality of history, with its physical violence and conflicts of forces. Whilst Nietzsche discovers 'how much blood and horror is at the bottom of all "good things"' (Nietzsche, 1998: 44), Marx states that 'capital comes [into the world] dripping from head to toe, from every pore, with blood and dirt' (Marx, 1976a: 926). Both men seek not only to reveal the violence behind 'good' or 'natural' things, but in doing so to disrupt the easy narratives of peaceful progress. For Nietzsche, '[t]he "development" of a thing, a custom, an organ does not in the least resemble a *progressus* towards a goal' (Nietzsche, 1998: 58). Things do not have a natural end which is marked on their bodies at birth: 'there is a world of difference between the reason for something coming into existence in the first place and the ultimate use to which it is put, its actual application and integration into a system of goals' (Nietzsche, 1998: 57). Having somehow come into the world, often in a haphazard and random way, all things – customs, practices, institutions – can then be reinterpreted, repossessed, modified, and transformed to serve different powers and strategies.

Marx offers a similar insight: his aim in detailing the violence that accompanied the birth of capitalism is not only to show that capitalism is historical – and not an eternal necessity that stretches back to the dawn of time – but also to show that there was no smooth, natural progression from feudalism to capitalism. There is undoubtedly a teleological strain in some of Marx's work, but there is also something much like what Nietzsche – and after him Foucault – offers: an account of the way in which different elements can be manipulated, combined, transformed, and submitted to some end quite different from their previous use and significance. As we saw in Chapter 1, Althusser brings out this aspect of Marx in helpful fashion, emphasizing the aleatory nature of the encounter that establishes capitalism, 'the idea that every mode of production comprises *elements that are independent of each other*, each resulting from its own specific history, in the absence of any organic, teleological relation between those diverse histories' (Althusser, 2006: 199). 'Aleatory' is Althusser's term, but the theme is found clearly in Marx. In *Capital* he claims that a fundamental condition of capitalism is the existence of a class of workers with only their labour to sell, and that these workers were divorced from the means of production in a number of different ways: feudal lords chased the peasantry from their estates and stole common lands; the dissolution of the monasteries drove tenants from church estates; clan chiefs seized land that really belonged to the clan as a whole; the Highlands were cleared first for sheep farming and then for deer preserves opened for sport. None of these actions were carried out with the aim of creating a propertyless mass to serve capitalism – but such a mass of people, having come into being for quite different reasons, could *then* be put to work in a capitalist system which needed them as a precondition.

This is how capitalism supplanted feudalism: not through a plan that deliberately created its own conditions, but through the confrontation of elements that had already come into existence as the result of quite separate events. 'The knights of industry . . . only succeeded in supplanting the knights of the sword by making use of events in which they had played no part whatsoever' (Marx, 1976a: 875).

It is true that teleological or evolutionist tendencies can be found in Marx – even (and this is something Althusser does not admit) in *Capital*'s section on primitive accumulation. So, for example, Marx claims that '[f]orce is the midwife of every old society which is pregnant with a new one' (Marx, 1976a: 916), a phrase which suggests a simple and linear, even necessary, succession rather than an uneven and haphazard history made up of complex encounters of random events. But that there are different possible histories in Marx, sometimes even in the same chapter of a single book, should not dissuade the reader from drawing comparisons with Foucault. As Balibar (1995: 116, 110) has shown, Marx does not really have a single model of history: so, for example, the simple evolutionism offered by the '1859 Preface' is quite different from the temporal dialectic found in *Capital*, itself distinct from the notion of 'singular historicities' Marx proposes in some of his later letters. This variety arises at least in part because Marx is not interested in providing a general historical methodology: like Foucault, his methodologies arise from specific studies of concrete situations. Because Marx's work is (again like Foucault's) politically committed, it changes along with actual historical events, altering its focus and even its concepts and procedures in response to setbacks and advances. This, remember, is an aspect of Marx's work which is largely overlooked by Derrida, who, while championing Marx as a radical political figure, tends to present Marx's philosophy as another development within the metaphysical tradition rather than as a response to the circumstances in which Marx found himself.

Marx's histories

There is much else in Marx that resembles Foucault's take on history, beyond this political commitment. In fact, in many ways the resemblance between Foucault and Marx is greater than that between Foucault and Nietzsche. Having drawn comparisons between Marx and Nietzsche, thus eliminating certain caricatures of Marx and bringing him closer to Foucault, it is now possible to take Marx even closer to Foucault by releasing Nietzsche from our grasp: having taken us this far, it is time to change alliances and pit Marx and Foucault against Nietzsche. When read side by side, Nietzsche can seem somewhat naïve in comparison to Marx. Both Marx and Nietzsche challenge 'universal' and 'eternal' ideas and values by bringing to light the material interests and violent struggles that are intertwined with the growth, development, and entrenchment of those ideas and values. To take one example: in the *Genealogy of Morality* Nietzsche traces the concept of guilt back to the relation between buyer and seller. But having done so, he does not then question this relationship: indeed, he calls it 'the earliest and most primordial relationship between men', claiming that '[b]uying and selling, together with the psychology which accompanies them, are older than even the beginnings of any social form of organization and association' (Nietzsche, 1998: 51). Rather than refusing a return to origin, Nietzsche seems here to be doing just that – and, moreover, in a fairly conventional (even liberal) way. Marx starts from little more than the assumption that people live, and hence feed and clothe themselves: '[i]ndividuals producing in society' (Marx, 1973: 83). Nietzsche, on the other hand, does not seem to question his 'primordial relationship', and even suggests that it is older than society itself – as if people can exchange goods *before* they enter society, as if exchange is not itself a social act, or as if the notion of a time before any social association makes any sense.

Nietzsche has a tendency to relate values and concepts back to individual motivations and actions, as if history can be rewritten as psychology. At the same time, however, he uses great, broad brush strokes in tracing the movement of (for example) entire religions. This combination – reduction to individual psychology and extrapolation to global currents – pushes Nietzsche close to exactly the kind of history that Foucault rejects: that is, history as both an individual project and a totality. Nietzsche's sweeping, speculative musings are very far from Foucault's laborious, detailed investigations – investigations which, in fact, resemble those of Marx more than Nietzsche. It is Marx who pored over dozens of factory reports in a labour that was, to use Foucault's characterization of genealogy, 'gray, meticulous, and patiently documentary' (Foucault, 1998: 369). Although Foucault is clearly influenced by Nietzsche, his genealogical method is not identical to Nietzsche's. 'Nietzsche, Genealogy, History' should not be taken as a straightforward presentation of Foucault's own methodology (yet nor as an impartial recreation of Nietzsche's methods). While Foucault clearly concurs with many of Nietzsche's proscriptions and instructions, there are also significant differences between their two approaches to history, and it is often in these areas that Foucault is closest to Marx. It might even be said, in the light of Foucault, that Marx offers a genealogy of capitalism. He provides a 'profane history' that rejects faith in the notion of a 'providential end' that can explain 'the progress of history' (Marx, 1995: 125, 129–30). For Marx the role of historical study is to explain how we have arrived where we are – but not to posit the present (or even some predicted future) as the fulfilment of a natural progression. As we saw in Chapter 2, *The German Ideology* dismisses that speculative distortion whereby later history becomes the goal of earlier history.

Perhaps Marx's most direct remarks on historical method are found in the *Grundrisse*, which reinforces his anti-teleological approach. He proposes that bourgeois society provides the key to understanding all previous societies, providing the categories with which they can be examined. Here the famous analogy is found: 'Human anatomy contains a key to the anatomy of the ape. The intimations of higher development among the subordinate animal species, however, can be understood only after the higher development is already known' (Marx, 1973: 105). But this is not a teleological outlook. Human anatomy can help us understand apes because humans have developed from apes – not because apes are destined to become humans. Likewise, bourgeois social relations are not predestined. No more than Foucault is Marx guilty of presentism, of seeing in the past only an identity with the present or the necessary stages of development towards the present. Marx explicitly rejects these options, mocking 'those economists who smudge over all historical differences and see bourgeois relations in all forms of society', and dismissing the 'so-called historical presentation of development [which] is founded, as a rule, on the fact that the latest form regards the previous ones as steps leading up to itself' (105–6). What Marx seeks to demonstrate is that both bourgeois society and our knowledge of it are historical: 'even the most abstract categories, despite their validity – precisely because of their abstractness – for all epochs, are nevertheless, in the specific character of this abstraction, themselves likewise a product of historic relations' (105). That these categories can shed light on the past does not mean that either the categories themselves or the relations they illuminate are eternal. On the contrary, Marx's interest lies in showing that that which seems natural and eternal is historical and impermanent. He does this in explicit opposition to those classical economists who see in bourgeois society a natural and eternal necessity, who believe that 'there has been history, but there is no longer any' (Marx, 1995: 131). In denaturalizing the present, and in showing that history is not subject to a patient and predictable evolution, Marx hopes also to demonstrate the possibility of revolution: to show that societies are open to change – change which is often sudden and violent. Marx's own work, profoundly politicized as it is, hopes to play a part in breeding this revolution.

Given that there are no predestined ends or uniform evolutionary framework for Marx, there can be no universally valid supra-historical model: 'history cannot be made with formulas' (Marx, 1995: 148). It must be understood in its specific complexity. He chastises those who would use his theory as a 'master key' and thereby 'metamorphose my historical sketch of the genesis of capitalism in Western Europe into an historico-philosophic theory of the general path every people is fated to tread, whatever the historical circumstances in which it finds itself' (Marx and Engels, 1956: 379). But it is not just that there can be no question of producing some suprahistorical system that can explain the development of all societies: even given the restricted aim of explaining the emergence of a single society, there is no single historical time that can be applied. There is no uniform rhythm but (as Althusser has helped show) a plurality of different temporalities. The empty, homogeneous time that Derrida and Benjamin reject is likewise rejected by Marx, for whom there is no abstract, linear time but rather a conflict both in and for time – the time used to measure value and fought over in the struggle for the normal working day. 'Time is no longer a sort of supposedly uniform standard of reference, but a social relation that is determined in production, exchange and conflict' (Bensaïd, 2002: 250). Just as for Foucault, for Marx there are specific levels of analysis which, rather than slipping everything into a broad narrative stream, must bring out the uneven and differentiated character of historical change. In contrast to the attachment to stadial progression sometimes attributed to a certain clichéd Marx, in fact he details the complex development of different forms of production, not as a smooth progression but a difficult, intricate tangle, with different forms coexisting – so that he could write of Germany in the preface to *Capital*: 'Alongside the modern evils, we are oppressed by a whole series of inherited evils, arising from the passive survival of archaic and outmoded modes of production, with their accompanying train of anachronistic social and political relations' (Marx, 1976a: 91). As late as 1875 he needed to write of European capitalist societies 'more or less free of admixtures of medievalism' (Marx, 1996b: 221).

This Marx, then, is very different from that sometimes presented by Lyotard: he does not look forward to the future recovery of a lost origin, anticipating a preordained redemption. He is perhaps closer to the Marx found in Derrida: he sometimes relies on teleology, but this theme does not dominate his work and he welcomes an unpredictable future that will in part come as a break in the chain of history. Yet, as argued in the last chapter, clear differences exist between Derrida's messianicity and Marx's revolutionary perspective. It is, in fact, when Marx is read alongside Foucault that Marx's strengths really emerge. There is something satisfying, even amusing, about this fact, given that while Lyotard and Derrida have both written dense studies on Marx, Foucault has restricted himself to a few enigmatic comments. Foucault's Marx exists between the lines; he is brought to us in secret, unexpectedly. This Marx neither announces a predicted finality nor simply opens himself to an entirely unexpected event. He starts from the present, not in order to show how necessary or eternal our familiar institutions are, but how strange and accidental – and how open the future is. This Marx is no more the 'true' Marx than that of Lyotard and Derrida – but it does throw light on areas that Lyotard and Derrida miss. There is no single Marx – so a teleological evolutionism can be found alongside a genealogical critique – but some aspects of his work are more original than others, and it is Foucault rather than Lyotard or Derrida who best highlights this novelty. There is found in Marx a historiographical project very similar to Foucault's. Marx too puts forward an anti-teleological and non-totalizing history attendant to the specific situation. It is politically committed, recognizing the historicity of its categories, and developed in order to activate change. It remains to be seen, finally, how it renounces the sovereignty of consciousness and demonstrates how the individual subject has been historically constituted. Here we must turn to the concepts of power and subjectivity as they are put forward by both Marx and Foucault in their specific historical studies. This will reveal further similarities, and shed more light on forgotten or ignored parts of Marx; yet it will also in turn put Foucault under the spotlight, and reveal potential weaknesses in his own work.

Power and Subjectivity

In the previous section, I argued that of the three post-structuralists we have so far examined, it is Foucault who throws most light on Marx's approach to history. All three reject the Marx who relies on a philosophy of history, yet all three also find something else in Marx. But rather than Lyotard's differend or Derrida's messianicity, it is Foucault's genealogy that best illuminates this alternative. In this section, I want to do something similar by showing that it is Foucault again who best illuminates potential alternatives in Marx to the ontology of humanism. This will be done by looking at the issues of power and subjectivity. Lyotard and Derrida both reject the Marx who depends upon an anthropological ontology which posits a natural human subject whose powers and capacities, now repressed or alienated, will one day be liberated or restored. But both also acknowledge – and follow – something very different in Marx, namely his decentring of the subject. Foucault goes further: he not only follows this decentring, he also looks at the concrete material practices that *produce* subjects within a complex network of social relations. Because for Foucault the question of subjectivity is always linked to the question of power – the individualizing techniques that produce different subjectivities are techniques of power – it will be useful to begin by reconstructing Foucault's analytics of power.

Rethinking power

What I want to do here is not to provide a comprehensive account of Foucault's thoughts on power, but to draw out some contrasts and comparisons with Marx. Foucault introduces a genuinely novel way of looking at power, one that rejects traditional approaches to the topic. Conventionally, power is thought of as a thing which one person or group possesses and uses to oppress or control another person or group. Instead of thinking of power as a possession in this way, Foucault thinks of it in terms of strategies or tactics: power is not a thing but a relation. In this sense, power is everywhere – but not because it radiates from some fundamental centre: 'I do not have in mind a general system of domination exerted by one group over another, a system whose effects, through successive derivations, pervade the entire social body' (Foucault, 1979: 92). Power is ubiquitous because everyone is involved in power relations.

Each of these relations involves particular mechanisms and techniques of power which must be studied in their specificity: there is no uniform apparatus of power. There may well be wider patterns of domination in society – of one class or gender over another, for example – but these must be investigated in relation to local and immediate power relations, rather than assuming that one system of domination provides the model for all power relations. If it can be said that power 'is not that which makes the difference between those who exclusively possess and retain it, and those who do not have it and submit to it' (Foucault, 1980: 98), then this is not only because power does not reside in one place and is not a possession: it is also because power is not something which is simply employed upon an existing subject who then submits or obeys. Power does not act upon a given subject or element: it 'determines the elements to which it is applied' (Foucault, 2003: 45). Power is therefore not – or at least not wholly – repressive: it is primarily productive. The individual for Foucault is not so much the target of power – as a collection of forces and capacities to be repressed – as both its point of application and its effect: a set of capacities generated and coordinated by power. 'The individual is the product of power' (Foucault, 2001: 109). Thus against theories of power as proprietary, centralized, uniform, and repressive, Foucault advances an analysis of power relations as strategic, ubiquitous, multiple, and productive. This analysis is not without its confusions: Poulantzas (1978: 150–1) is correct to argue that there is an ambiguity, with Foucault using 'power' sometimes to refer to a set of relations and sometimes to one static and essentialized pole of the power-resistance relation. Nonetheless, Foucault's analysis is far from incoherent, and in its novelty and insight acts as a challenge to all hitherto existing theories of power. It can be characterized as a materialist analysis not only because it examines the ways in which power invests the forces and energies of the body, but also because it stands opposed to the idealism of Origins and Ends: for Foucault the study of power cannot be submitted to a single explanatory grid oriented by a core underlying principle, and there is no originary force or energy which power acts upon and is in need of liberation.

Foucault himself tends to contrast his analytics of power with what he calls the juridical theory of power, in which the key question is that of legitimacy. For the juridical theory, power is exercised by the sovereign upon the subject (who is prohibited from certain actions) but beyond a certain limit – to be established by philosophical enquiry – power becomes illegitimate and tyrannical. For Foucault, Marxism shares with this juridical view a number of assumptions – in particular the idea that power is a possession held by one group, operating through oppression. It can even be argued that Marxism shares an emphasis on legitimacy. In *The History of Sexuality* Foucault states:

> Another type of criticism of political institutions [distinct from liberal juridicalism] appeared in the nineteenth century, a much more radical criticism

in that it was concerned to show not only that real power escaped the rules of jurisprudence, but that the legal system itself was merely a way of exerting violence, of appropriating that violence for the benefit of the few, and of exploiting the dissymmetries and injustices of domination under cover of general law. But this critique of law is still carried out on the assumption that, ideally and by nature, power must be exercised in accordance with a fundamental lawfulness. (Foucault, 1979: 88)

Given that Marxism is not actually named here, we cannot be certain that it is Foucault's target – but we have already seen that criticism of an unnamed Marxism is one of Foucault's favourite tactics. The implication here is that Marxism's attack on existing society is still undertaken in terms of a distinction between legitimacy and illegitimacy: it is illegitimate, even unlawful, for the proletariat to be oppressed in the way that they are. In places Foucault (1980: 88) links Marxism with the juridical theory in terms of a common 'economism': for the liberal-juridical view power is a commodity that can be exchanged via a contract; for Marxism the role of power is to serve the economy. This economism reduces power in two ways: it makes it secondary to the economy, and annuls the specificity of different power relations by interpreting them all according to the same logic.

It is above all the reductive nature of this analysis that Foucault objects to. He thus rejects what Lyotard would call the metanarrative of Marxism, or what Foucault himself calls total history: the attempt to unite all events around a single, dominant theme. But as I have so far argued in this chapter, Foucault's critical subversion of Marxism does not entail or depend upon a rejection of Marx; nor does it preclude the use of certain Marxist concepts and categories. In *The History of Madness* one can find this simultaneous use and subversion of Marxism in Foucault's analysis of the birth of the asylum. Foucault claims that one factor that made possible the isolation of madness in the asylum was a new wish to free the poor from confinement and reintegrate them into the economy: to restore the poor to the circuits of production, to *use* them in the drive to create wealth. 'As they were now essential to wealth, the poor had to be liberated from confinement and placed at its disposal' (Foucault, 2006: 412). But as the need for confinement of the poor diminished – as the idle, vagabonds, migrants, beggars, and so on, were allotted their place in the labour market – there arose the difficulty of what to do with the mad, previously placed within the same system of confinement as the poor. Thus economic factors played a vital role, and Foucault analyses these processes within the context of the rise of capitalism. But he does not claim that the bourgeoisie, as the dominant power in society, set out from the beginning to inter the insane as part of some grand plan, or even according to some necessary, underlying logic. There is a complex interplay between changing social and economic conditions and the uses to which new discourses and apparatuses are put by dominant forces and classes. A developing desire to free the poor from confinement (this desire itself arising from a combination of factors, including the development of different forms of thinking within political economy) created new conditions for the possibility of thinking about madness; in turn, changing methods of categorizing madness led to certain methods of normalization and techniques of exclusion that could be used effectively by the bourgeoisie. 'We need to see how these mechanisms of power, at a given moment, in a precise conjuncture and by means of a certain number of transformations, have begun to become economically advantageous and politically useful' (Foucault, 1980: 101). Alongside a critique of Marxism (dismissed as complicit with the juridical view of power), Foucault undertakes a quiet, subtle use of Marx's conceptual apparatus.

Discussing his view of power, Foucault has said:

> There is a sort of schematism that needs to be avoided here – and which incidentally is not to be found in Marx – that consists of locating power in the State apparatus, making this into the major, privileged, capital and almost unique instrument of the power of one class over another. (Foucault, 1980: 72)

This 'incidental' qualification is in fact highly significant, for it again demonstrates that Foucault is careful to reprieve Marx from what otherwise appear to be attacks on Marxism. This is fully appropriate, as Marx's own investigations into power are far closer to Foucault's work than to the juridical theory that Foucault outlines – closer than Foucault himself admits. Marx's aim is not to establish the legitimate distribution of power but to map existing relations of domination. He demonstrates that the economy – a realm of natural and spontaneous order and harmony according to classical political economy – is deeply invested by these relations of domination: in other words, the aim is not to establish power's secondary status with respect to the economy, but to expand the scope of power so that it permeates relations previously thought to be outside power.

Clearly Marx does in places present power in terms that Foucault would reject: as we saw earlier, he claims in the *Manifesto* that political power is simply the organized power of one class for oppressing another. But even a claim like this must be treated with caution. In the first place, Marx is here distancing himself from the liberal juridical view: the claim is that state power is not something whose legitimate boundaries can be established, but a form of domination. Moreover, political power is not exhaustive of society's power relations: to the contrary, political power depends upon and is embedded in a wider set of relations. In *The Eighteenth Brumaire* Marx makes this distinction clear, arguing that Louis Napoleon was able to seize and consolidate his position because the bourgeoisie recognized 'that to retain its power in society intact its political power would have to be broken' (Marx, 1996a: 71). Power is something that operates in different ways and at different levels, and is irreducible to the repressive power of the state. 'Power' designates a much wider social antagonism, a broad battlefield of which the state is only a part: it is not a thing but a field of relations. Even where Marx talks of power as a possession he is careful to qualify things: in a discussion of capital as 'the governing power' over labour, Marx writes that the 'capitalist possesses this power, not on account of his personal or human qualities, but inasmuch as he is an *owner* of capital' (Marx, 1988: 36). Power can only be understood within the context of a field of relations in which individuals take up different subject positions. Rather than delineating the manner in which a centre of power represses a natural, originary energy or force, Marx investigates the productive capacity of power as it is applied at a local level.

Producing subjects

Perhaps unsurprisingly for two thinkers whose conceptual tools emerge only from their concrete studies, it is in their specific analyses of the operation of power that the affinities between Foucault and Marx are made manifest. This is especially evident in *Discipline and Punish*, which sees Foucault drawing on Marxist concepts and themes, and in places explicitly acknowledging Marx as a precursor.[9] Foucault argues that the development of disciplinary power is intimately linked to the rise of capitalism: late-eighteenth century calls for reform of the penal system were not simply a result of repugnance at the inhumanity of existing punishments or outrage at the excessive abuses of the sovereign. They were the start of 'an effort to adjust the mechanisms of power' (Foucault, 1977*b*: 77), to restructure the economy of punishment, and must be viewed within their socio-economic context. The desire to achieve greater regularity and efficacy of penal intervention, 'to insert the power to punish more deeply into the social body' (82), cannot be dissociated from the need to protect the wealth and property of the emerging bourgeoisie. As the bourgeoisie acquired property rights, new techniques of punishment were used to stamp out illegalities that had formerly been tolerated but were now inimical to their interests, while at the same time enclosing and controlling those infringements that could not be eradicated, rendering them politically harmless and economically negligible, or even using them as sources of profit. In a distinction Foucault calls 'a class opposition', the bourgeoisie punished illegalities of property while it 'reserved to itself the fruitful domain of the illegality of rights' (fraud, tax evasion, etc.) (87).

But more than simply a method of control, a way to protect property, disciplinary power *creates* a certain kind of subject: it 'produces subjected and practised bodies, "docile" bodies' augmented in economic force but diminished in political force (Foucault, 1977*b*: 138). These are the bodies capitalism needs as part of its productive machinery. On the one hand, discipline acted as a technique for maximizing the utility of expanding productive forces and an increasing population; on the other hand, it was a counterpart to the juridical norms that established the dominance of the bourgeoisie, 'the other, dark side of these processes' (222). None of this is to claim that disciplinary techniques were invented by the bourgeoisie with the original aim of increasing production and profit – rather that these techniques emerged against the background of the rise of capitalism and were adopted and used by the bourgeoisie to facilitate a certain management of society.

It is obvious enough that Foucault – with his talk of class oppositions and the dominance of the bourgeoisie – has drawn upon Marx for his analysis of the birth of the prison. But for this reason, Foucault's work can in turn throw light on Marx's project. In describing all the techniques which create a certain kind of subject – the application of timetables and examinations, the enclosure and arrangement of people and things, the control of postures and gestures, the division and management of time – Foucault claims that '[d]iscipline "makes" individuals' (Foucault, 1977*b*: 170). And this is what Marx is interested in: the creation, required by capitalism, of the individual as a subject position. Just as it was possible to read Marx through Foucault in order to bring out a non-teleological Marx, so it is possible to read Marx through Foucault in order to bring out a de-ontologized Marx: one who details the creation of different subjectivities rather than relying on a notion of human essence. Anticipating Foucault, Marx states that 'human beings become individuals only through the process of history' (Marx, 1973: 496). Capitalism needs a certain sort of subject, and so must produce more than simply commodities: the 'production of capitalists and wage labourers is ... a chief product of capital's realization process' (Marx, 1973: 512;). Political economy has its ideal subjects: 'the *ascetic* but *extortionate* miser and the *ascetic* but *productive* slave' (Marx, 1988: 118). But capitalism does not merely require ideals, and the individual is not merely a myth of bourgeois ideology, nor even simply a result of the process of commodity exchange.[10] The individual is produced for and in the production process itself, as a material reality, with each individualized worker a necessary part of the collective machinery of production. It is not enough that, expropriated from the land and separated from the means of production, the proletariat is tied to capitalism by 'the silent compulsion of economic relations': capitalism needs 'a working class which by education, tradition and habit looks upon the requirements of that mode of production as self-evident natural laws' (Marx, 1976*a*: 899). There develops in each factory an 'industrial army of workers under the command of a capitalist' (450). The label – 'industrial army' – is no mere rhetorical flourish of the pen: Marx specifies, in an analysis as detailed as Foucault's, the 'barrack-like discipline' to which workers are submitted in order to increase and assure 'the regularity, uniformity, order, continuity and energy of labour' (549, 535).

It is no coincidence, nor playful or pious homage, that Foucault refers to Marx in *Discipline and Punish*. Although it is an exaggeration to claim that Foucault's notion of disciplinary power is 'virtually derived from Marx' (Read, 2003: 195n80), their respective projects converge at a number of points and levels – not least because Foucault has borrowed heavily from Marx. This convergence uncovers a certain Marx: this Marx does not rely on an idealist conception of some natural given (transparency of social relations, unalienated essence of human nature), or an unthought notion of concrete actuality opposed to abstract or illusory speculation. Rather, he employs a materialist analysis of existing social relations, examining the ways in which individual subjects are created within specific material practices and processes. This is what concrete analysis is in Marx. This does not mean, of course, that there are no differences between Marx and Foucault. In his analysis of specific relations, the latter is always resistant to any unifying logic. In *Discipline and Punish*, for example, he makes it clear that he is interested not simply in the reproduction of capitalist production, 'but also the production of knowledge and skills in the school, the production of health in the hospitals, the production of destructive force in the army' and so on – and he is interested in these other relations in themselves, not merely because they in turn contribute to the reproduction of the conditions of production in the strict sense (Foucault, 1977b: 219). There is a multiplicity of power relations in society and they must be studied in their individual specificity rather than being submitted to a central logic.

Foucault's insistence on recognizing the plurality of power relations can act as a check to a reductionist Marxism that would interpret every act and relation purely in class terms. Yet this does not mean abandoning reference to class or capitalism: Foucault himself speaks of both. As Deleuze says, Foucault 'certainly does not deny the existence of class and class-struggle but illustrates it in a totally different way' (Deleuze, 1988b: 25). There is a danger of critical analysis becoming too reductionist – with everything related back to a single explanatory cause – but there is also a danger (which Foucault does not always escape) that it becomes too diffuse – unable to account for the connections between different relations. One can avoid the metaphysical anchoring of an analysis that tries to explain everything in terms of the capitalist economy, while still recognizing the importance of beginning with capitalism as the dominant social form. Marx foregrounds capitalism not in order to contrast it with the prior existence of an uncorrupted Eden, nor to use it as a master key which can open all mysteries – but, rather, because it is the dominant mode of organizing human life: of producing and reproducing the conditions of life.

Material bodies

One might argue that Marx and Foucault both start from the same place: they offer materialist analyses that begin with human bodies – bodies that must eat, sleep, clothe themselves, and so on, but which are malleable rather than just given, and can be managed, trained, and transformed. But here a difference between Marx and Foucault emerges, one which foregrounds the issues surrounding the pursuit of materialist philosophy. Balibar suggests that Foucault might claim that he is the better materialist than Marx, because there is no chance of Foucault's nominalism lapsing into metaphysical idealism.[11] Making this case for Foucault, Balibar writes:

> Not only does the practice of 'historical nominalism' make idealised notions like 'sex', 'reason', 'power' or 'contradiction' impossible, but it also *forbids* one to pass directly from the material nature of bodies to the ideal nature of life, whilst others are unable to desist from moving from the material nature of social relations to the ideal nature of dialectics. (Balibar, 1992: 55)

But Balibar argues that Marx could in turn reverse the objection, countering the accusation that he must slide into idealist dialectics. Marx agrees with Foucault 'that historical *individuals* are *bodies* subjected to disciplines' – but the difference is that Marx, unlike Foucault, has already thought bodies '*in relational terms*. Therefore', Balibar has Marx say, 'it is I who am the most thoroughgoing nominalist, the least metaphysical, of the two of us' (Balibar, 1992: 56). It is Foucault, rather than Marx, who is most in danger of lapsing into metaphysical idealism, because Marx's bodies are always thought historically and relationally. Foucault, in contrast, offers 'bodies and pleasures' as the basis for a 'counterattack' against power (Foucault, 1979: 157), as if they are an unmediated site of resistance. He thus tends to slide into what Balibar (1992: 55) terms 'vitalism'. Balibar is not the only thinker to pick up on this theme in Foucault's writings. Judith Butler (1990: 96) refers to it as an 'unresolved tension' in his work. On the one hand, there is an attempt to show that what is given as 'natural' or 'essential' is really historical, contingent, and cultural; on the other hand, however, there is a reliance on 'an unacknowledged emancipatory ideal', a notion of 'a *natural* heterogeneity' that demands liberation (Butler, 1990: 94, 101). The body in Marx is thought in relation to others and to its own historical circumstances; in Foucault, according to Butler, it becomes a source of resistance as the site of a 'prediscursive libidinal multiplicity' (97). The charge of vitalism cannot simply be dismissed as an attempt by critics to discredit Foucault's work. For one thing, both Balibar and Butler praise and draw upon that work before they criticize it. But in addition, there are some commentators who cite this vitalism as an asset of Foucault's work. Negri, for example, writes approvingly:

> In Foucault, humanity appears as a set of resistances that release (outside any finalism that is not an expression of life itself and its reproduction) an absolute capacity for liberation. Life is liberated in humanity and opposes anything that encloses it and imprisons it. (Negri, 1999: 27)

We should be careful here, for this dehistoricized vitalism is a risk in Foucault's work rather than its ineluctable conclusion. Far from casually relying on an idealized notion of life, for example, Foucault explicitly identifies such a notion as part of the power-knowledge complex that he seeks to undermine – and, furthermore, implicitly aligns it with Marxism. In volume one of *The History of Sexuality*, he argues that in the nineteenth century the forces of resistance unwittingly colluded with new forms of power. What Foucault calls 'bio-power' operated not by using death as the ultimate sanction but by optimizing life; yet resistant discourses also championed life, not questioning this notion but implicitly affirming its presuppositions, demanding the '"right" to life, to one's body, to health, to happiness, to the satisfaction of needs, and beyond all the oppressions or "alienations", the "right" to rediscover what one is and all that one can be' (Foucault, 1979: 145).[12] As usual, Marxism is not mentioned here, but it is not difficult to see that it is one possible target of Foucault's critique. Yet things are complicated because Foucault himself seems to rely on this very notion of 'life' as a resistant power. Eager to repel suggestions that he is claiming that life has become completely administered, entirely dominated by power, he writes: 'It is not that life has been totally integrated into techniques that govern and administer it; it constantly escapes them' (143). It is not surprising that readers like Negri have taken from Foucault the idea of life as naturally resistant force.

This problem is not Foucault's alone: indeed, it is similar to that faced by Lyotard. We saw that, having abandoned the firm ground of idealist ontology, *Libidinal Economy* equivocated between tacit reliance on a kind of libidinal vitalism which can ground critical judgement and complete abandonment of critique altogether. If that vitalism is also a danger in Foucault, then so is the risk of forsaking any critical standpoint. Foucault never goes as far as *Libidinal Economy*, but in his work it can often be difficult to see any way out of our present circumstances: there is little to inspire hope for change. While his genealogies demonstrate that our present circumstances are not natural or necessarily essential, Foucault does little to show a way out of these circumstances. In common with Lyotard, there is a refusal to posit alternatives. In one sense this is merely an admirable eagerness to avoid teleological determination of the future. 'I have absolutely no desire to play the role of a prescriber of solutions', Foucault says (Foucault, 2001: 288). But this can also suggest indifference towards the future. Certainly it does not much help those searching for an alternative to the present. 'I think', he says, 'that to imagine another system is to extend our participation in the present system' (Foucault, 1977c: 230). Whereas *Libidinal Economy* might conceivably be characterized as a celebration of what exists, at times Foucault seems to come close to the *nouveaux philosophes* by foreclosing the possibility of any radical change: in an interview from 1984, he asks his interlocutor to 'remember all the prophecies, promises, injunctions, and programs that intellectuals have managed to formulate over the last two centuries and whose effects we can now see' (Foucault, 1988: 265). This last comment is cited by David Owen, who, in response to possible criticisms of Foucault, correctly notes that '[t]he "failure" of Foucault's methodology to be able to provide *moral* reasons for resistance is . . . not an unfortunate unconscious lacunae within his thinking but a quite deliberate ethical stance' (Owen, 1994: 161). This is correct, but the criticism I am raising here is not the Habermasian accusation that Foucault has failed to provide *grounds* for resistance. Rather, it is that in too eagerly repudiating teleology, Foucault leaves little room for thinking about the future.

The 'unresolved tension' in Foucault's work, then, is not simply between an analysis that emphasizes contingency and one that naturalizes: it is also between a tacit naturalization and a renunciation of the possibility of radical change. Rudi Visker has picked up on this particular tension in Foucault. Like Butler, Visker (2003: 302, 311) argues that Foucault, in seeking to justify opposition to what exists, relies upon 'the dream of a sort of primordial spontaneity of a body' – or, rather, Foucault posits this notion of an originary self-sufficiency while simultaneously disavowing it. Without this 'dream', Visker suggests, Foucault's genealogies can do little other than demonstrate that things could be different from the way they presently are. But short of advocating a political decisionism – in which we oppose some things and not others on the basis of a whim – this demonstration merely begs the question of why we should not keep things as they are, or indeed of whether we can really change things at all given our present circumstances. Foucault thus seems to equivocate between the justification of resistance in the name of an authentic and spontaneous origin and the rueful observation that things might have been different. In the former case we have lapsed into idealism; in the latter we are required to do little but shrug our shoulders and acknowledge the contingency of a situation which we are nevertheless probably stuck in. In both cases the specificity of critique is lost: why oppose one particular system when they will all have crushed an original authenticity, or when they are all contingent and have always left other possibilities unrealized?

This tension in Foucault's work is real, but it need not become an impasse. There is no need to limit the choice to two options: that of finding normative grounds or that of relinquishing the possibility of change. Foucault's aim is not to ground resistance, or even to give people reasons to resist. It is not his task to tell people whether or not they should resist. 'Is one right to revolt, or not? Let us leave the question open. People do revolt; that is a fact' (Foucault, 2001: 452). Foucault here is not proposing a mystificatory 'will to be against' such as that proposed by Hardt and Negri (2000: 210). Rather, he is clarifying the role of the philosopher, whose job is not to tell us what to do but to alter our way of looking at the world in ways that may be useful for those who have already decided to resist. This attitude, I would argue, brings Foucault very close to Marx: both thinkers begin from existing struggles and create their thought in a kind of dialogue with these struggles, responding to the development of events and forging new tools to be used in future struggles. In the final chapter, we shall have reason to return to this relation between philosophy and existing struggles.

Conclusion

Despite the apparent modesty of Foucault's engagement with Marx – tending to comment on him only critically or when prompted – on the whole it is more productive than those of Lyotard and Derrida. Foucault's general approach to Marx has much in common with Lyotard and Derrida: not looking to uncover the truth in or of Marx, but treating him as a box of tools and praising his unique innovations. The targets of his critique are familiar as well, though in Foucault the attack on humanism is more explicit. Where Foucault really excels is in bringing out the materialist alternatives that already exist in Marx: in place of a philosophy of history there is a history of the present (and not a philosophy of the event); in place of an ontology of natural givens, there is an examination of the production of subjectivity. That these insights into Marx's work emerge as Foucault borrows from and even distorts Marx, rather than from any careful philosophical investigation, should not surprise us, for this fits with the aspiration of Foucault (and, in fact, of post-structuralism more generally): to use Marx as a political resource rather than to produce an academic analysis of his work. There are nonetheless difficult tensions in Foucault's work, and in a sense Foucault faces the same problem that Lyotard and Derrida faced: how does one retain the possibility of critique and of radical change once one can no longer draw upon an onto-teleology? While Derrida and the later Lyotard rely on a philosophy of the event, Foucault and the earlier Lyotard flirt both with a return to natural origins and with the preclusion of the possibility of social transformation. Foucault, however, suggests a way out of this potential impasse: he neither offers philosophy as an external standard by which to judge the world, nor uses philosophy to point to the event as the unattainable horizon of an open future. Rather, he situates philosophy as a discursive practice that interacts with other practices and that rather than assigning itself priority recognizes its own limits. As Deleuze puts it: 'philosophical theory is itself a practice . . . . It is no more abstract than its object. It is a practice of concepts, and it must be judged in the light of the other practices with which it interferes' (Deleuze, 1989: 280). It is to Deleuze that we now turn.

Chapter 5

Becoming Revolutionary: Marx Through Deleuze

[I]t is correct to retrospectively understand all history in the light of capitalism, provided that the rules formulated by Marx are followed exactly.
(Deleuze and Guattari, 1977: 140)

In 1995 Deleuze claimed that his next book – 'and it will be the last' – would be titled *Grandeur de Marx* (Deleuze, 1995a: 51). Unfortunately, Deleuze's death later that year meant that his book on the greatness of Marx was never published. Nonetheless, Marx has a strong presence elsewhere in Deleuze's work, especially in the two volumes of *Capitalism and Schizophrenia* written with Félix Guattari, and it is entirely appropriate that his final book would have been on Marx. The presence of Marx in Deleuze's work is often overlooked by commentators in favour of other influences on his philosophy (usually Spinoza, Nietzsche, and Bergson – though there are so many influences that it is easy for any one of them to be overlooked). This is unfortunate, because of all the post-structuralists, it is in Deleuze's work that Marx is most visible. While Marx plays an important role in the work of each post-structuralist, and while all champion his contemporary relevance, in Lyotard, Derrida, and Foucault he can at times become something of a shadowy or sidelined figure: a neglected friend in Lyotard, an awkward appendage in Derrida, a secret ally in Foucault. Deleuze, in contrast, is not shy in proclaiming his affiliation to Marx: he draws deeply, explicitly, and repeatedly from Marx's work, to the extent that Jacques Donzelot can refer to Deleuze's attempt to be 'more Marxist than Marx', his engagement with Marx producing a 'hyper-Marxism' (Donzelot, 1977: 35–6). As Donzelot recognizes, Deleuze's use of Marx is not orthodox or straightforward. Jean-Jacques Lecercle has spoken of Deleuze's ' "para-Marxism", which implies displacement through a form of translation or transfer' (Lecercle, 2005: 41).[1] In common with the other post-structuralists, Deleuze transforms Marx as he uses him.

One of the purposes of this chapter is to bring to light Deleuze's reliance on and use of Marx, drawing parallels with the readings of Marx we have already analysed. While Deleuze very rarely criticizes Marx, it will be seen that for Deleuze too the problematic aspects of Marx centre on his potential idealism. What Deleuze does is to show how one can still draw from the heart of Marx while avoiding this danger: Deleuze takes from him a historical analysis of capitalism which evades the troublesome aspects of his work identified by Lyotard, Derrida, and Foucault, and shows that one can follow Marx's rules without falling into Hegelianism.

In this chapter, I shall spend more time teasing out insights and relations (as I did with Foucault) than criticizing weaknesses and flaws (as I did with Lyotard and Derrida). This is not because Deleuze rarely comments on Marx, as is the case with Foucault: on the contrary, Marx is frequently directly cited in Deleuze's work. Rather, it is because – as is also the case with Foucault – Deleuze's use of Marx is so productive and instructive. This does not mean that we shall approach Deleuze uncritically, however. If parallels can be drawn between Deleuze's reading of Marx and those of the other three post-structuralists, then so too does Deleuze share some weaknesses with them: in particular, he shares some of the flaws found in Foucault's work. I shall begin this chapter by introducing Deleuze's reading of Marx, placing it within the context of his work overall, before going on to show how heavily Deleuze relies on Marx and yet how idiosyncratically he uses him, looking at his analysis of capitalism. The final section looks further at this analysis, before addressing some criticisms that have been made of his work, focusing on accusations of vitalism and dualism.

Difference, Dialectics, and Universal History

By this point, having looked at Lyotard, Derrida, and Foucault, it can be seen that there are a number of common elements in post-structuralist approaches to Marx. In many respects Deleuze's relation to Marx is typical of post-structuralism: he reads Marx critically and selectively, has little time for Hegelian teleology or idealist ontology, and calls on Marx as a radical, political figure. I want to relate this attitude towards Marx to Deleuze's broader philosophical project, especially his ontology of difference and his rejection of dialectics – but also to show how Deleuze's specific reading of Marx enhances the picture I have sketched so far. In particular, Deleuze's use of Marx's universal history builds on the portrait of Marx as a non-teleological historical critic that was developed in the previous chapter.

Remaining a Marxist

It is important to remember something that often seems forgotten: Deleuze thought of himself as a Marxist. 'I think Félix Guattari and I', he claimed, 'have remained Marxists, in our two different ways, perhaps, but both of us' (Deleuze, 1995b: 171). Of course, as Derrida has argued, we are all heirs of Marx and Marxism, and the question of who is or is not a Marxist has become largely redundant – not because Marx is now an old-fashioned irrelevance but, on the contrary, because Marx is too important to be reduced to such a simple question, as if 'one had to choose: to be "for" or "against" Marx, as in a polling booth!' (Derrida, 1999b: 231.) But by identifying himself as a Marxist, Deleuze does something more than simply acknowledge Marx's influence: he takes a certain position with respect to Marx, an affirmative stance which entails a definite use of Marx. It is *this* that is worth investigating – and yet of the many books on Deleuze, few even mention Marx, and fewer still look in detail at Deleuze's relation to Marx. In some ways this is understandable: Marx appears largely in the books co-authored by Guattari, especially *Anti-Oedipus*, and is mentioned relatively rarely in Deleuze's solo works. This has made it possible to attribute Deleuze's 'Marxism' (and much else) to what Slavoj Žižek calls the 'bad influence' of Guattari. Deleuze's own work, Žižek argues, is largely apolitical: 'It is crucial to note that *not a single one* of Deleuze's own texts is in any way directly political; Deleuze "in himself" is a highly elitist author, indifferent toward politics' (Žižek, 2004: 20). Žižek's position is complicated: he advocates another Marxist politics sympathetic to Deleuze's solo philosophy but distinct from the malign idealism he attributes to Guattari's bad influence. But what Žižek – and apparently many others – cannot countenance is that the Marxism already present in the work of Deleuze and Guattari is as much the product of Deleuze as of Guattari. When we start seeing Marx's name, these commentators seem to think, we can switch off: it is Guattari speaking.

We should be wary of trying to disentangle the respective contributions of the two authors of *Anti-Oedipus*: as Deleuze has said of their relationship: 'we do not work together, we work between the two' (Deleuze and Parnet, 2002: 17).[2] Yet there are little clues which, while they may not explain exactly who wrote what, do at least clarify things and undermine the idea that the Marxism of their work must have come from Guattari, with Deleuze's contribution purely philosophical and apolitical. Deleuze has suggested that many of the most innovative ideas came from Guattari. 'There is not one of these ideas which did not come from Félix, from Félix's side (black hole, micro-politics, deterritorialization, abstract machine, etc.)' (19). This does not mean that Deleuze was not involved in the creation of new concepts, but it seems that it was also left to him to systematize and order things, acting as what he calls a 'lightning rod' for Guattari's thoughts (Deleuze 2006: 239). The careful, methodical, rigorous analysis of capitalism that is provided by the Deleuze and Guattari books thus bears all the hallmarks of Deleuze – and it is deeply indebted to Marx. While they were writing *Anti-Oedipus*, Guattari wrote to Deleuze: 'I have the feeling of always wandering around alone, kind of alone, irresponsibly, while you're sweating over capitalism. How could I possibly help you?'

(Guattari, 2006: 137). It seems unlikely that an apolitical or 'elitist' thinker would have been sweating over capitalism, and Guattari's anxiety suggests that if anything it was Deleuze who was taking the lead in engaging with Marxist political thought. Deleuze should therefore be taken at his word: *both* he and Guattari were Marxists.

It is nonetheless also important to heed Derrida's argument: it is not enough simply to point at someone and name him a Marxist. Deleuze's precise connection to Marx needs to be established: how he uses Marx, what he rejects, what he defends. For like Derrida and the other post-structuralists, Deleuze does not simply 'remain' a Marxist, but reads him selectively. Deleuze has written of Freud:

> We refuse to play 'take it or leave it'. . . . As if every great doctrine were not a *combined formation*, constructed from bits and pieces, various intermingled codes and flux, partial elements and derivatives, that constitute its very life or its becoming. (Deleuze and Guattari, 1977: 117)

This applies not only to Freud, but to other writers as well, including Marx. Deleuze's attitude to the works of other thinkers reflects his attitude to his own work, well summarized when he claims that he and Guattari 'are not among those authors who think of what they write as a whole that must be coherent' (Deleuze, 2004: 278). But if Deleuze does not accept everything that Marx offers, it can be difficult to see what it is that he rejects, for he does not spend time criticizing Marx or exposing his weaknesses. This makes him a little different from the other post-structuralists. To avoid slipping into the logic of that which would be criticized, neither Derrida nor Lyotard (at least in his *Libidinal Economy* phase) tend to speak of critique, and, as we have seen, Foucault offers few direct comments on Marx at all. But in their own ways, all three identify difficulties, tensions, and flaws in Marx's work. In Deleuze's work, in contrast, it is very difficult to find anything other than praise for Marx. This, of course, reflects Deleuze's own manner of doing philosophy rather than complete agreement with everything Marx wrote. Michael Hardt is not wrong when he writes: 'If a philosopher presents arguments with which Deleuze might find fault, he does not critique them but simply leaves them [i.e. those arguments] out of his discussion' (Hardt, 1993: *xix*). Deleuze is interested in philosophers that he can *use*: like Foucault, he believes that a theory is 'exactly like a toolbox. . . . A theory has to be used, it has to work' (Deleuze, 2004: 208). And here in fact Deleuze realigns himself with the other post-structuralists: he does not try to establish the true Marx, or the truth in Marx, but sets him to work. Among all the post-structuralists Deleuze's use of Marx is perhaps the most idiosyncratic and inventive, yet it is Deleuze who expresses the greatest support for Marx and who unashamedly declares himself a Marxist. Far from offering a confusing paradox – the strictest Marxist does the most to contort Marx's theories – this well captures the post-structuralist attitude towards Marx: any inheritance must be critical and selective, and the most inventive use is the greatest praise.

Creating concepts

In seeking to employ Marx rather than establish the truth of his work, Deleuze is following his own conception of philosophical practice. It is worth looking at that conception to understand better what Deleuze will and will not use in Marx. 'Philosophy', Deleuze writes, 'does not consist in knowing and is not inspired by truth. Rather, it is categories like Interesting, Remarkable, or Important that determine success or failure' (Deleuze and Guattari, 1994: 82). Above all, philosophy creates concepts that can then be used: not to stabilize identities and create a better picture of the world, but on the contrary to disrupt those identities and produce new ways of seeing and being. 'If one concept is "better" than an earlier one, it is because it makes us aware of new variations and unknown resonances, it carries out unforeseen cuttings-out, it brings forth an Event that surveys us' (28). Philosophy struggles against *doxa* 'to tear open the firmament and plunge into the chaos' (202). This image of philosophy is opposed to what Deleuze calls the dogmatic image of thought. The dogmatic image proceeds via recognition and representation: a unified subject recognizes a given object, which is represented in terms of identity, resemblance, analogy, and opposition. Deleuze does not deny that acts of knowledge of this kind take place. Indeed, they take place every day – we could not do without representation – but this is the problem: they are too banal to tell us much about how thought really works and what it is able to do: the dogmatic image disguises the working of thought, presupposing what needs to be explained. For Deleuze, neither subject nor object are simply given: both are the outcomes of dynamic processes of genesis. Identity, resemblance, analogy, and opposition may be indispensable categories, but they are themselves effects of a more fundamental difference. Rather than beginning from secure identities which are then differentiated from each other, philosophy must begin with difference in itself: 'difference is behind everything, but behind difference there is nothing' (Deleuze, 1994: 57). The role of philosophy is not to discern relations between existing objects or forms, but to show how such objects are generated out of what, in reference to Bergson, Deleuze calls a 'primordial virtual totality' (Deleuze, 1988*a*: 99). In doing so, philosophy testifies that what exists is the result of processes of becoming without uniform or predictable outcomes. Hence the present is always overflowing with the potential to be different; something always escapes stable conformity: '[t]here is always something that flows or flees. . . .' (Deleuze and Guattari, 1988: 216). Philosophy is therefore not disinterested reflection on what exists; through the creation of concepts it frees up thinking and brings forth events: '[t]he concept is the contour, the configuration, the constellation of an event to come' (Deleuze and Guattari, 1994: 32–3.) This does not imply a retreat from the world, however: 'in the analysis of concepts, it is always better to begin with extremely simple, concrete situations, not with philosophical antecedents, *not even with problems* as such' (Deleuze, 2006: 362–3). Beginning from concrete situations, philosophy shows how things might be different.

Rather than being merely epistemological, this critique of representation is also ethical and political. Recognition is conferred not just on a supposedly given object but also on the values of that object. The dogmatic image of thought thus endorses a given set of established values, as well as the established political institutions of a society: 'thought "rediscovers" the State, rediscovers "the Church" and rediscovers all the current values that it subtly presented in the pure form of an eternally blessed unspecified eternal object' (Deleuze, 1994: 136). Dominant values and institutions, which are the product of a contingent arrangement of different forces, are presented as eternal necessities. Against the recognition of established values, Deleuze issues a call for the creation of new values which will disrupt the present order. While philosophy must start with concrete situations, it creates concepts to open up the future to something new and to welcome a future that cannot be read off from the present, configuring an event which 'escapes History' (Deleuze and Guattari, 1994: 110).

This critical image of philosophy is not far from the image of materialist philosophy that has already begun to emerge via the three readings of Marx that we have examined thus far. This is philosophy as intervention rather than reflection: but intervention not to facilitate the arrival of a future that is already known – rather to welcome a future that cannot be known. At this point we should pause, however, and consider a potential objection to my attempt to align Deleuze with the three post-structuralists we have so far looked at: for, in contrast to them, Deleuze approaches philosophy not by rejecting ontology but by embracing it. In their own different ways, Lyotard, Derrida, and Foucault are all interested in undermining ontology by exposing its limits: releasing the libidinal drives on which identity rests, exposing the tensions which ontological thought hides, demonstrating that supposed ontological certainties are in fact historical and contingent. In short, they can be said to reject onto-teleology and thus idealism as we defined it in Chapter 1. Deleuze, on the other hand, pushes ontology to its limits not to undermine it, but to create a new ontology. Badiou goes as far as to say that 'Deleuze purely and simply identifies philosophy with ontology' (Badiou, 2000: 20).[3] Yet the novelty of Deleuze's ontology in fact aligns him with the other post-structuralists. He does not propose an idealist ontology that seeks to ground all phenomena in a pure, original Being. For Deleuze, as we have suggested, beings are the results of processes of becoming; in this sense, Deleuze's is an ontology of becoming rather than being, or rather one that shows being *is* becoming. His philosophy of immanence refuses to submit life to some transcendent order above or outside what exists, to first principles or final causes that posit some ultimate goal: there cannot be anything outside this life, beyond or beneath it. Deleuze thinks in terms of virtuality precisely in order to reject all essentialism: the virtual differs from the possible in that whereas the latter assumes a preexisting set of models which are then limited by their realization, and which must resemble the real beings they become, the virtual is itself real and results in actual beings which are the outcome of divergent creative processes. The virtual is thus neither limited nor exhausted by actualization: the present can always be different. In this way, Deleuze firmly rejects idealism as I defined it in Chapter 1. I have argued that for the post-structuralists the most problematic elements of Marx revolve around ontology and teleology. Even though he very rarely criticizes Marx, for Deleuze too these are difficult aspects of Marx's thought, aspects that need to be rejected – even if, as Hardt suggests, he does this by ignoring them. Deleuze refuses to fit critical analysis into a totalizing philosophy of history or to ground it in some natural given. This does not mean, however, that we should overlook the differences between Deleuze and the other post-structuralists, or between any of them. As we shall see later, Deleuze's commitment to ontology does not come without its problems.

Nietzsche contra Hegel

As with the other post-structuralists, for Deleuze it is Hegel who personifies many of the worst currents of philosophy, and it is the Hegelian aspects of Marx which must be rejected: Althusser, claims Deleuze, deserves praise for his 'liberation of Marx from Hegel' (Deleuze, 2004: 145).[4] Indeed, of all the post-structuralists Deleuze is the most vociferously anti-Hegel. It is often the case that in Deleuze the typical characteristics of post-structuralism are boldest, most visible; as if, even though he presents a philosophy of immense subtlety and complexion, he traces his ideas with clearer, sharper lines. Hence just as the anti-Hegelianism is most acute in Deleuze, so the battle lines between Hegel and his foil are clearest: Deleuze explicitly pits Nietzsche against Hegel. We have already seen a strong Nietzscheanism in Deleuze's philosophy, with his call for the creation of new values. Deleuze does not seek a knowledge which 'gives itself the task of judging life, opposing it to supposedly higher values, measuring it against these values, restricting and condemning it' (Deleuze, 2001: 68). He rejects this idealist denial of life, which searches for a Reason behind and beyond what is given, and instead demands a 'thought that would *affirm* life instead of a knowledge that is opposed to life. . . . Thinking would then mean *discovering, inventing, new possibilities of life*' (Deleuze, 1983: 101). All this necessarily complicates Deleuze's relation to Marx, for while Marx can certainly be heard in this affirmative, practical philosophy, Nietzsche is the more obvious reference. Like Foucault (and to a lesser extent Lyotard and Derrida), Deleuze must juggle both Marx and Nietzsche.

Deleuze draws a sharp distinction between the Nietzschean form of philosophy he advocates and the dialectical thinking he detests, with the latter presented as a form of *ressentiment*. It is not quite that Deleuze *opposes* Nietzsche to the dialectic, for opposition is itself one of the concepts Deleuze calls into question: the dialectic 'thrives on oppositions because it is unaware of far more subtle and subterranean differential mechanisms'; Deleuze wants to reveal 'the differential relations of forces which are hidden beneath sham oppositions' (Deleuze, 1983: 157). Where Nietzsche examines the interplay of concrete forces, the dialectic remains abstract, and can only produce abstract results. In dialectics 'one begins with concepts that, like baggy clothes, are much too big' – concepts which will fit anything but which show us nothing (Deleuze, 1988a: 44).[5] Against Deleuze's Nietzschean philosophy of affirmation and creation, the dialectic marks a triumph of reactive forces: a force which denies all that it is not, in which difference becomes negation and affirmation becomes contradiction. The limit of dialectical thinking – personified, according to Deleuze, by Stirner – is a triumphant nihilism, a self-dissolution in which everything is denied. The dialectic, then, is at once abstract and reactive, lacking subtlety and creativity: in dialectics there is negation instead of affirmation, opposition and contradiction instead of difference, recognition of established values instead of creation of new values, labour instead of play. Deleuze is quite clear about situating his attack on the dialectic as part of a 'generalized anti-Hegelianism' (Deleuze, 1994: *xix*), presenting Nietzsche as the arch-enemy of Hegel: 'Anti-Hegelianism runs through Nietzsche's work as its cutting edge' (Deleuze, 1983: 8).

This raises the question of Deleuze's attitude to the thinker who, after all, did not claim to have refuted the Hegelian dialectic but to have stood it on its feet. Deleuze claims that both Nietzsche and Marx found their 'habitual targets' in 'the Hegelian movement, the different Hegelian factions' (Deleuze, 1983: 8). Yet he clearly recognizes that Marx's position is more complicated than that of Nietzsche, and he does not allot Marx a wholly unambiguous place. In *Nietzsche and Philosophy* Deleuze appears unsure of whether Marx is still bogged down in Hegelian labour or is ready to join the Nietzschean dance. Nietzsche does not want to stand the Hegelian dialectic on its feet, but to do away with it altogether. Nietzsche tried to invert Kant, not Hegel: to undertake a truly positive and immanent critique that does not – like Kant's, and like all idealism – fall back on an external transcendent principle; one that is not content merely to criticize forms of knowledge, truth, and morality, but goes on to criticize knowledge, truth, and morality themselves. If Deleuze asserts that Nietzsche escapes the dialectic, of Marx he asks: 'Has the dialectic found its point of equilibrium and rest or merely a final avatar, the socialist avatar before the nihilist conclusion? . . . Does Marx do anything else but mark the last stage before the end, the proletarian stage?' (Deleuze, 1983: 162). In *Nietzsche and Philosophy* this question is left unanswered: but Deleuze's later use and praise of Marx demonstrate clearly that he does not wish to bury Marx with Hegel. Yet it must be a certain kind of Marx that Deleuze retains: a non-dialectical Marx interested in the subtle, differential interplay of concrete forces rather than the resolution of abstract contradictions; a creative Marx who affirms the immanent potential of life rather than submitting it to the judgement of some transcendent order.

History of contingency

In places Deleuze echoes Foucault by aligning Marx with Nietzsche. Both Marx and Nietzsche, says Deleuze, offer 'a radical and total critique of society'. This critique is not a reactive, negative critique, but only the prelude for an equally radical moment of creation: 'a great destruction of the known, for the creation of the unknown' – exactly what Deleuze himself calls for (Deleuze, 2004: 136). Many of these issues surrounding Deleuze's attitude towards Marx – Deleuze's hatred of Hegel, his sympathy for Nietzsche, his rejection of idealism, his similarity to Foucault – come together around his approach to history. Like Foucault, Deleuze praises Marx's historical methodology while distancing himself from a Hegelian philosophy of history and advocating a genealogical-style study of breaks and discontinuities. Foucault sometimes directly cites Marx, but more often links his historiographical methodology to Nietzsche. Deleuze, on the other hand, is much more explicit in his praise of Marx, frequently reminding us of his *grandeur*. If Foucault coyly concedes Marx's influence, Deleuze loudly announces that one must follow Marx's rules: this means that history can be understood in the light of capitalism, as long as capitalism is understood from the perspective of universal history. For Deleuze this is not a totalizing, Hegelianized history in which capitalism is the culmination of a process of historical progression, the penultimate stage before all contradictions are reconciled. Rather, it is more like something Nietzsche might offer: 'universal history is the history of contingencies, and not the history of necessity. Ruptures and limits, and not continuity. For great accidents were necessary, and amazing encounters that could have happened elsewhere, or before, or might never have happened' (Deleuze and Guattari, 1977: 140). Deleuze is thinking of the encounter that Althusser raised: the contingent meeting of free workers and free money. 'Capitalism forms when the flow of unqualified wealth encounters the flow of unqualified labor and conjugates with it' (Deleuze and Guattari, 1988: 453). This is exactly what Marx says, and Deleuze reads him in Althusserian style: the conjugation is not necessary or predetermined, but contingent, aleatory; it might never have happened.[6]

As with Foucault, then, reading Deleuze shows that Marx is not so very far from Nietzsche. But in his greater willingness to draw on Marx, Deleuze goes a little further than Foucault and actively embraces a *universal* history. Reading Marx through Foucault offers a Marx who looks at the past in order to free up the present, to demonstrate that things have been – and can be – different. Deleuze's emphasis on universal history brings the reminder that the past and the present are linked in a further way in Marx's work. The past can free up what seems essential in the present partly because the present is made up of the accidents and encounters of the past. This also means that the past can be read in terms of the present – not in Habermas's 'presentistic' sense, whereby the meaning of the present is imposed on a reluctant past, but rather in Marx's sense: the key to the anatomy of the ape is contained in the anatomy of the human. Capitalism is universal not in the sense that it is necessary, nor that all social formations have 'really' been capitalist, but in the sense that it provides a privileged position from which to present a retrospective reading of history. For Deleuze, as we shall see, capitalism's generalized decoding of flows reveals the coding and overcoding strategies of previous societies. It is in this way that 'capitalism has haunted all forms of society': as a limit to repel (Deleuze and Guattari, 1977: 140). Capitalism is 'at the end of history' (153) not as at the end of a logical progression, but as the limit of all other social formations.

What Deleuze offers via Marx, then, is not a record of the smooth progression of definite social stages in a linear succession, but the revelation that although different social forms can be distinguished, their intermixture means that they cannot be definitively separated. As Deleuze puts it in *A Thousand Plateaus*, 'everything coexists, in perpetual interaction'. More accurately, even that which does not yet exist in a concrete form 'pre-exists' and acts upon other formations, even if only as a potential threshold to be warded off: 'what does not yet exist is already in action, in a different form than that of its existence' (Deleuze and Guattari, 1988: 430–1). Thus to say that elements of one social form can be seen in another is not to posit an identity or even resemblance, for those elements can be taken up and used in different ways. Remnants of past ages may reappear in capitalism, but for quite different purposes: 'the events that restore a thing to life are not the same as those that gave rise to it in the first place' (Deleuze and Guattari, 1977: 261). This, as we saw in the previous chapter, is Nietzsche: 'there is a world of difference between the reason for something coming into existence in the first place and the ultimate use to which it is put'. But as we have also seen, it is Marx as well: there is a world of difference between the reasons for a propertyless mass coming into existence in the first place and the ultimate use to which they were put. 'The knights of industry . . . only succeeded in supplanting the knights of the sword by making use of events in which they had played no part whatsoever.'

I have come to Deleuze last, then, because his work retrospectively enlightens the other post-structuralist engagements with Marx. Not in the sense that Deleuze marks the last stage in a chronological succession – as if each post-structuralist in his turn, beginning with Lyotard, attempted to tackle Marx, each one learning a little from the mistakes of the last – but because in its unashamed and committed use of Marx's concepts Deleuze's engagement with Marx throws light on the successes and failures of other, contemporary engagements. For instance, all four post-structuralists challenge Marx's teleology, whether implicitly or explicitly. Lyotard ended up rejecting much else in Marx for this reason. Derrida pointed to an alternative, non-teleological Marx, but his messianicity is offered as a quasi-transcendental structure of experience rather than something specific to Marx. It took Foucault to show how Marx really presents a non-teleological history – but Foucault keeps a certain distance from Marx. It is, finally, with Deleuze that a Marx without teleology is reached: a universal history that is the history of contingency. Here is a Marx closer to Nietzsche than to Hegel, but who also offers much more than Nietzsche. What Deleuze, by his own admission, really takes from Marx is an analysis of capitalism (which no one is going to find in Nietzsche): if history can be understood in terms of capitalism, then in turn an understanding of capitalism itself is needed. Deleuze takes this understanding directly from Marx, while simultaneously transforming it.

Capitalism and Desire

While drawing from the heart of Marx, Deleuze does not simply repeat what Marx says – if he did, there would be no point in reading him. As Lecercle suggests, he transcribes Marx into his own terms, and in so doing bends Marx in a new direction. Given Deleuze's antipathy towards Hegel, he cannot take from Marx a dialectical analysis of capitalism in which society is defined by contradictions later to be resolved. There is a subtler movement in capitalism for Deleuze – a movement that Marx records and Deleuze helps bring to light. Like Foucault, Deleuze also brings in the question of subjectivity, at once following Marx and inventing his own concepts in order to address this issue. In examining Deleuze's account of capitalism, we can see both how heavily he relies on Marx and how and why he takes Marx in new directions.

Social and libidinal machines

Although his historical analysis is patterned on Marx's universal history, Deleuze does not define different social formations in terms of contrasting modes of production. 'We define social formations by *machinic processes* and not by modes of production (these on the contrary depend on the processes)' (Deleuze and Guattari, 1988: 435). This change in terminology is important: like Althusser, Deleuze wants to think about society without relying on a Hegelian division between essence and phenomena, and without presenting the social whole as an organic totality or fixed unity. Deleuze uses the concept of a machine because a machine is made up of fluid connections: it is a process rather than a static combination of elements. But while he praises Althusser for 'the discovery of social production as "machine" or "machinery"', Deleuze then criticizes him for 'the reduction of the machine to structure, the identification of production with a structural and theatrical representation' (Deleuze and Guattari, 1977: 306). For Deleuze, 'machine' is not reducible to structure: the language of structures implies the existence of a fully-formed whole, rather than dynamic and ever-changing connections. Nor is this talk of machines metaphorical. The term is used literally: a machine is that which interrupts flows, and each particular social formation has its own way of selecting, connecting, and combining different elements, of interrupting and arranging flows – flows of people, of wealth, beliefs, desire, and so on. The concept of a social machine enables Deleuze to identify different elements and levels of analysis without depending on a simplistic base-superstructure model whereby one needs to dive beneath the surface to find the hidden, determining instance, the inner essence that drives the whole. As Lecercle says of the related concept of 'assemblage': 'It makes it possible to go beyond the separation between material infrastructure and ideal superstructure, by demonstrating the imbrication of the material and the ideal' (Lecercle, 2006: 200).[7] Assemblages contain both material and ideal elements, without one determining the other or one acting as the surface effect of the other. Like the Nietzschean Marx Foucault posits, for Deleuze there is nothing beneath the surface.[8]

While this suspicion of the depth-surface model turns Foucault away from a 'productionist' model, for Deleuze – always more the Marxist – 'everything is production' (Deleuze and Guattari, 1977: 4). But, following Marx (and following the arguments presented in the previous chapter), it is not simply goods that are produced, but also individuals. As Jason Read argues, Deleuze's concept of the social machine 'breaks down . . . any division between the production of material things and the production of modes of existence and subjectivity' (Read, 2003: 54). This is a key element of Deleuze's contribution: 'This breaking down of the barriers between the subjective – narrow concepts of desire and libido, even of sexuality – and the allegedly objective – the social, the political, and the economic – is one of Deleuze's most important achievements' (Jameson, 1997: 403). Deleuze does this not only through the concepts of machine and assemblage, but also by reformulating the concept of desire itself. The question of desire remained marginal within Marx's own work: he tended to write instead of needs, appetite, and enjoyment, and to do so mainly in early works like the *Economic and Philosophic Manuscripts*, where they are offered as part of a human nature that requires freeing from repression. The rapid development of consumer capitalism since Marx's death has made the issue of desire more pertinent and pressing, however: at least in those nations where capitalism has been established longest and most firmly, the majority of the population is required to relate to capitalism not simply as exploited workers but also as active consumers. This of course is not to deny the relevance of Marx's analysis of exploitation but to claim that consumer capitalism brings into focus the importance of developing a materialist theory of desire that can help explain the operation of capitalism.

Those who today are charged with maintaining and expanding capitalism are well aware of the importance of desire, as evidenced by this claim about Muslims made by an advertising executive in a recent newspaper interview: 'They are not anti-consumerist. There are things they want. . . . But we have not figured out yet how to invent desire [among the Muslim community]' (quoted in Silver, 2007). This candid statement is helpful not only because it indicates the necessity of desire to capitalism today, but also because it usefully highlights some of the features of the Deleuzian concept of desire. Desire is not a spontaneous energy that just needs channeling: desire, as the executive says, needs inventing; it is a process or assemblage, a fabrication, a way of connecting other processes and flows. Nor is desire a capacity that belongs to a pre-existing individual subject: desire is first and foremost a collective investment (there is a Muslim community), and an individual subject (an individual Muslim consumer) is the effect of a certain kind of investment. Finally, desire is not the desire *for* some object which we want but do not presently have. Desire does not operate by forming a fantasy object that is lacking (as the standard Western philosophical tradition up to and including Freud and Lacan has it). To claim that desire is based on lack is either to posit the idealist notion of another world beyond this one and containing objects that are missing here and now, or to rely on the notion of scarcity, beloved of classical political economy but undercut by Marx's analyses of the ways in which scarcity is produced and managed by definite economic systems. For Deleuze's 'materialist psychiatry', desire produces reality: it creates new connections, objects, flows. To use our example: an advertisement may have the ultimate goal of persuading someone to purchase a particular good, but advertisements themselves tend to work not by stimulating desire for that object itself (which often does not even feature in the advert) but by seeking to effect a more primary investment of desire, unrelated to any specific object.

Desire is a form of production, producing desiring-machines that connect and distribute flows of energy. Deleuze congratulates Freud for having recognized desire as production, as an abstract subjective essence without source or object. But he then criticizes Freud for having immediately 'reterritorialized' the discovery, reobjectifying the essence of desire within the confines of the bourgeois family and the Oedipal subject, so that 'this discovery was soon buried beneath a new brand of idealism' (Deleuze and Guattari, 1977: 24). This critique of Freud is modelled on Marx's critique of Adam Smith, whom Marx termed 'the Luther of political economy' (Marx, 1988: 94): rather than locating the source of wealth in gold (mercantilism) or in the land and agricultural labour (physiocracy), Smith correctly identified labour in general as the subjective essence of wealth and private property – just as Luther recognized that the essence of religion lies in man rather than in an external, objective substance (in the church, priest, Bible, etc.). But just as Luther did not then go on to challenge religion itself, so Smith did not then go on to challenge private property itself. Deleuze reworks the comparison: as Smith discovered the essence of wealth in labour in general but realienated it in private property, so Freud discovered the essence of desire in general but realienated it in the private family and the Oedipus complex. In both cases, the problem is that what needs to be explained – private property, the Oedipal subject – is taken as a given presupposition. If Freud is the Luther of psychiatry then we might call Deleuze the Marx of psychiatry: just as Marx sought not to deny the existence of private property or simply wish it away but to explain its genesis, so Deleuze seeks not to deny the existence or impact of Oedipus but to explain its genesis – to explain why capitalism requires the Oedipal subject.

Deleuze cites Marx's critique of Smith not simply to use it as a model for his own critique of Freud. For Deleuze this is in fact much more than a simple comparison or parallel, because political economy and psychoanalysis have discovered the same thing, namely a subjective essence of production in general, an identity of labour and desire. Social production and 'desiring-production' are identical for Deleuze: he refutes the idea that there is on the one hand a social production of real objects and on the other hand a libido which can only access this real world through the mediation of fantasy. Desire immediately invests the social and thus, as Read and Jameson both suggest, Deleuze breaks down the division between that which is supposedly objective, political, and real and that which is supposedly subjective, libidinal, and fantastic or ideological. This division is not merely an epistemic error or illusion, however: capitalism really has effected this division, by constraining social production within the boundaries of private property and sexual reproduction within the bourgeois family unit. Deleuze's combination of Marx and Freud is therefore quite unlike earlier Freudo-Marxisms, which sought to draw parallels between a libidinal economy and a political economy. Deleuze instead attempts to offer a genuinely materialist account of desire, in which labour and desire are only two regimes of the same production. His account of desire is not without its problems, as we shall see later. For now, however, we shall focus on his analysis of capitalism, returning to potential criticisms later.

Coding and deterritorialization

Deleuze posits that in every process of production there is an opposing element of 'anti-production': a non-productive attitude which falls back on production and constitutes 'a surface over which the forces and agents of production are distributed' and recorded, 'whereupon the entire process appears to emanate from this recording surface' (Deleuze and Guattari, 1977: 10). In desiring-production this surface takes the form of the 'body-without-organs', while in social-production it takes the form of the socius. Body-without-organs in particular is a difficult concept – so much so that it is not clear that Deleuze and Guattari themselves were talking about the same thing when they used it: Deleuze has said that he and his co-author 'never did understand [it] in quite the same way' (Deleuze, 2006: 239). Nonetheless, it is important, for it connects Deleuze's Marxian analysis of capitalism to his broader philosophy. In *A Thousand Plateaus* the body-without-organs is presented as a plane of immanence or a plane of consistency: an unformed body permeated by 'free intensities or nomad singularities' (Deleuze and Guattari, 1988: 40), prior to any organization and where relation and identities have not yet been differentiated. So it is something like the field of virtuality, the primary potential of being as difference before actualization or individuation. It is on this body-without-organs that the flows of desire are organized; it is on the socius that social flows are organized: 'The prime function incumbent upon the socius has always been to codify the flows of desire, to inscribe them, to record them, to see to it that no flow exists that is not properly dammed up, channeled, regulated' (Deleuze and Guattari, 1977: 33).

In capitalism the socius is capital itself: capital is the site where social flows are recorded, yet it appears as the source and cause of all production. 'This is the body that Marx is referring to when he says that it is not the product of labor, but rather appears as its natural or divine presupposition' (Deleuze and Guattari, 1977: 10). Deleuze is here drawing from volume three of *Capital*: 'Capital thereby already becomes a very mystical being, since all the productive forces of social labour appear attributable to it, and not to labour as such, as a power springing forth from its own womb' (Marx, 1981: 966). Deleuze claims that capitalism is constantly nearing a point where the socius becomes a body-without-organs – in other words, a point where there is a complete free play of desire, an unconstrained liberation of flows. So capitalism nears the point that Deleuze's own philosophy aims at: the plane of immanence before all organization and actualization, a reinvigoration of the creative potential of life. Thus Deleuze is not straightforwardly anti-capitalist, any more than Marx is. Deleuze like Lyotard follows Marx's analysis of the dynamics of capitalism, seeing capitalism as both an opportunity and a disaster, a social form that is at once revolutionary and reactionary. Where Lyotard writes of capitalism's reproductive drive – annulling, repeating, reserving – and its destructive drive – enriching, creating, maximizing – Deleuze writes of coding and decoding, reterritorialization and deterritorialization. In both cases, in Lyotard and Deleuze, the analyses are meant to capture the rhythm of capitalism, its unique properties in contrast to other social forms, without lapsing into nostalgia for some pre-capitalist naturality that may one day be restored.

We have seen that in order to avoid a base-superstructure model, Deleuze offers the concept of a social machine to cover a mode of living rather than just a mode of production, incorporating the production of goods, people, beliefs, meanings, customs, and so on. In a mixture of ethnological and Marxist historical analysis, in *Anti-Oedipus* Deleuze puts forward three different social machines: the primitive territorial machine of savage society; the imperial despotic machine of barbarian society; and the capitalist immanent machine of civilized society. In *A Thousand Plateaus* this arrangement is subject to an implicit critique: in the later book, Deleuze writes in the preface to its Italian edition, 'universal history assumes a much greater variety. . . . We no longer have to follow, as in *Anti-Oedipus*, the traditional succession of Savages, Barbarians, and Civilized Peoples. Now we come face to face with coexisting formations of every sort' (Deleuze, 2006: 310).[9] Nonetheless, while these social machines are not to be understood in terms of a straightforward linear succession, they can be profitably used as analytical distinctions that bring into better focus capitalism's specificity.

Each society relates its flows (of goods, people, desires, etc.) to certain codes. Savage societies restrict flows in a strict system of belief, meaning, and custom. Here the socius is the earth itself: all production seems to emanate from the earth. Primitive societies may be 'captured' by a despotic state. These barbarian societies – Deleuze's explication of which is heavily indebted to Marx's scattered comments on both feudalism and the Asiatic mode of production – are characterized by overcoding: old systems of meaning, belief, and organization remain but are submitted to a new, transcendent law.

> The objects, the organs, the persons, and the groups retain at least a part of their intrinsic coding, but these coded flows of the former [savage-territorial] régime find themselves overcoded by the transcendent unity [i.e. the despotic state] that appropriates surplus value. (Deleuze and Guattari, 1977: 196)

Here the socius is the despot: everything seems to flow from him, he 'is the sole quasi cause, the source and fountainhead and estuary of the apparent objective movement' (Deleuze and Guattari, 1977: 194).

The movement from savage-territorial machine to imperial-despotic machine marks what Deleuze calls the first great movement of deterritorialization: flows are freed from the body of the earth only to be reterritorialized on the body of the despot.[10] The second great movement of deterritorialization marks the movement from the imperial-despotic machine to the civilized-capitalist machine. In this instance Deleuze talks of deterritorialized workers – the same workers that Marx writes of, who are 'freed' from their land (now given over to deer hunting). But there is no overcoding following this deterritorialization: no despotic state submits everything to its law. The capitalist state has no transcendent status, but rather simply acts as a 'regulator of decoded flows': 'it no longer determines a social system; it is itself determined by the social system into which it is incorporated in the exercise of its functions' (Deleuze and Guattari, 1977: 252, 221). Capitalism is marked by decoding rather than overcoding, as all hitherto existing beliefs and faiths are destroyed. 'All fixed, fast-frozen relations, with their train of ancient and venerable prejudices and opinions are swept away, all new-formed ones become antiquated before they can ossify' (Marx and Engels, 1998: 6). Private property, the growth of wealth, the rise of classes, the production of commodities all signify the '*breakdown of codes*. The appearance, the surging forth of now decoded flows that pour over the socius, crossing it from one end to the other' (Deleuze and Guattari, 1977: 218). It is in this sense that 'capitalism is the universal truth': its decoding operation reveals the coding and overcoding of previous societies (Deleuze and Guattari, 1977: 153).

Immanent limits

Deleuze retranscribes Marx to take account of post-structuralist concerns and interests, but this retranscription simultaneously brings out Marx's strengths – in particular his analysis of the dynamic of capitalism. As we have seen in previous chapters, capitalism is not characterized merely by decoded flows released in a movement of deterritorialization, but by a particular encounter of certain flows: deterritorialized workers, freed from working in one particular place and available for hire, and decoded money, freed from wealth tied up in landed property.

> Flows of property that is sold, flows of money that circulates, flows of production and means of production making ready in the shadows, flows of workers becoming deterritorialized: the encounter of all these flows will be necessary, their conjunction, and their reaction on one another – and the contingent nature of this encounter, this conjunction, and this reaction, which occur one time – in order for capitalism to be born. . . . The only universal history is the history of contingency. (Deleuze and Guattari, 1977: 223–4)

Capitalism forms when the flow of unqualified wealth encounters the flow of unqualified labour and conjugates with it: here Deleuze, like Althusser, has drawn from 'the heart of *Capital*' (Deleuze and Guattari, 1977: 225).

Instead of codes, capitalism has an axiomatic. 'In contrast with the ancient empires that carried out transcendent overcodings, capitalism functions as an immanent axiomatic of decoded flows (of money, labour, products)' (Deleuze and Guattari, 1994: 106). An axiomatic does not enforce any beliefs; it has no meaning and requires no faith. Echoing Marx's views on classical political economy, Deleuze names capitalism the age of cynicism (Deleuze and Guattari, 1977: 225): the capitalist axiomatic functions without belief.[11] In this sense Deleuze's diagnosis is akin to Marx's analysis of commodity fetishism: an axiomatic imposes a way of acting that does not depend on ideas or beliefs, and hence does not rely on illusion or mystification. As we saw in relation to Althusser in Chapter 1, the inversion of fetishism affects our very behaviour, our actions: we do not need to believe that value is a property of things, but we must act *as if* it is (cf. Read, 2003: 71). Whereas a code functions indirectly and extra-economically and determines the qualities of flows, an axiomatic functions directly and economically – it is no longer 'veiled by religious and political illusions' (Marx and Engels, 1998: 5) – and has no need for collective systems of belief or meaning: it is indifferent to the qualities of the flows. Money is the universal standard: all that is important is the generation of surplus value and profit.

The existence of the axiomatic points to a strange tension in capitalism: that double-movement recognized by Lyotard (after Marx). Deleuze claims that capitalism 'axiomatizes with one hand what it decodes with the other.... The flows are decoded *and* axiomatized by capitalism at the same time' (Deleuze, 1977: 246). In addition, capitalism constantly reterritorializes as it deterritorializes: everything under capitalism is given free reign, freed from traditional codes, meanings, qualities, and processes but everything is also and simultaneously reterritorialized on 'neoterritorialities' (the family, the State, the nation, religion). Old codes are revived in an attempt to rechannel flows, to bind them.

> Capitalism therefore liberates the flows of desire, but under the social conditions that define its limit and the possibility of its own dissolution, so that it is constantly opposing with all its exasperated strength the movement that drives it toward this limit. (Deleuze and Guattari, 1977: 139–40)

Hence the theories and practices of the New Right – which saw a massive deterritorialization of wealth and capital and a simultaneous reterritorialization on the nuclear family, the nation-state, traditional moral values, and so on – would not be some distasteful anomaly, or an unpredictable extreme: the fusion of neo-liberalism and neo-conservatism simply follows the rhythm of capitalism in its purest and clearest form. This is 'the age of cynicism, accompanied by a strange piety' (Deleuze and Guattari, 1977: 225).

Capitalism cannot bear its own effects and consequences and does its best to counteract them. It is constantly pushing towards a limit and yet constantly displacing this limit: 'continually drawing near the wall, while at the same time pushing the wall further away' (Deleuze and Guattari, 1977: 176). Deleuze claims that capitalism faces two limits: an absolute, exterior limit that he calls schizophrenia – where fully decoded flows are free to travel across a fully deterritorialized socius, a liberation of the flows of desire on the body-without-organs – and a relative, interior limit that is capitalism itself. The former is constantly pushed back and exorcized, leaving only the latter, which capitalism is continually going beyond, 'but by displacing this limit – that is, by reconstituting it, by rediscovering it as an internal limit to be surpassed again by means of a displacement' (230). In support of this analysis Deleuze frequently quotes a passage from volume three of *Capital*: 'Capitalist production constantly strives to overcome these immanent barriers, but it overcomes them only by means that set up the barriers afresh and on a more powerful scale. . . . The *true barrier* to capitalist production is *capital itself*' (Marx, 1981: 358). This, claims Deleuze, is Marx's greatest innovation: his portrayal of capitalism as the conjugation of 'free', naked labour and pure wealth in an axiomatic system which constantly comes up against its own shifting, immanent limits.

But Deleuze is not interested simply in capturing the rhythm of capitalism, in presenting a picture of it. Like the other post-structuralists, he calls on Marx as a radical, political figure, a thinker who does not simply offer a diagnosis of our society but who does so in order to initiate change. Yet also like the other post-structuralists, Deleuze cannot follow Marx in everything; certain of Marx's paths are blocked: capitalism cannot be resisted in the name of some natural given now alienated, repressed, or lost, yet to be restored – be it human essence, the use-value of labour-power, or the immediacy and unity of non-capitalist society. Deleuze's task is that of the other post-structuralists, but also that of a certain Marx, and of materialist philosophy in general: how to resist or criticize, how to posit some alternative, when one can no longer formulate that critique in the name of an ontological given which must be rescued or defended. For while Deleuze explicitly develops an ontology, it is not the kind of ontology which offers some stable, reassuring ground which can then orient and anchor a critical attack on existing conditions. The absence of a pre-existing ground or outside – a transcendent standard by which to judge that which exists – does not lead Deleuze to abandon critique, however, but to offer an immanent critique of capitalism as a system with only immanent limits, but also with an immanent potential for revolution.

Repression and Revolution

Let us now address Deleuze's response to two questions: what is wrong with capitalism, and how might we change it? As we have already seen, for post-structuralism certain responses are illegitimate. Deleuze cannot answer: it denies human nature, and we wait for the inevitable resolution of its contradictions. But he does have answers: in short, he argues that capitalism is repressive, and the possibility of change lies in revolution. But what can Deleuze mean by repression? After Foucault, it seems as if the notion of repression depends upon some rather suspect ideas: on the one hand, a unified subject with an essential set of attributes that are then repressed; on the other hand, a central power that does the repressing. There is also a further problem for Deleuze: given his analysis of capitalism as a social form that is always deterritorializing, destroying traditional political and cultural authorities, how can capitalism repress anything? What or who is doing the repressing if all authority is being ceaselessly undermined? We need to establish, therefore, both the target and the mechanisms of repression according to Deleuze. To do so, we need to investigate further Deleuze's methodological commitments, especially as they impact on his analysis of capitalism. We shall interpret Deleuze as sympathetically as possible before bringing in some criticisms.

Lines of flight

Deleuze's study of power does not focus on the obvious centres of power (State, family, schools, etc.): in place of these 'molar aggregates' it offers a micropolitics that examines 'molecular' elements. This micropolitics is something like a mix of Foucault and Lyotard, concentrating on the multiple social practices and unconscious libidinal investments which form and sustain larger centres of power. The molar centres are not ignored but they are not the focus of analysis. The distinctiveness of micropolitics does not lie in a difference of scale, however: it is not about looking at the details of little groups in place of large collectivities and organizations, still less about the individual in place of society.[12] A state, a family, an individual: all have both molar and molecular elements and can be analysed with respect to both. Micropolitics is about the analysis of lines: in any society there are lines that segment us into clearly defined, rigid oppositions – between our job and our family, work and leisure, public and private, between sexes, ages, classes, and races. But then there are more supple lines, connections and distributions of greater subtlety and fluidity. At this latter, molecular level there can be found 'microfascisms' that reinforce and sustain the stable, binarized centres of power. Yet there are also lines of flight: something which escapes and provides new connections, a rupture that offers the possibility of change, 'as if something carried us away, across our [molar, rigid] segments, but also across our [molecular, supple] thresholds, towards a destination which is unknown, not foreseeable, not pre-existent' (Deleuze and Parnet, 2002: 125). These lines of flight are what define any society.

In a short but fascinating text on Foucault, Deleuze argues that a key difference between him and Foucault is that whereas the latter begins from power, Deleuze begins from the claim that society takes flight. Thus whereas Foucault's problem – as we saw in the previous chapter – is how to explain how power might be challenged and our existing circumstances transformed, for Deleuze 'the problem for a society is how to stop it from flowing. For me, the powers come later' (Deleuze, 2006: 280). It is assemblages of desire that are primary for Deleuze: power is only one element of an assemblage, which are defined by their lines of flight. This is where repression comes in for Deleuze. Repression does not act on desire as a spontaneous natural given. In a sense repression does not act *on* desire at all: repression is a dimension of assemblages of desire, as the blunting of a line of flight. Repression is therefore something like a reterritorialization: a recapturing of flows set free, a stabilization of identities, freezing the immanent potential of the virtual. Deleuze does not use fixed, transhistorical standards to show that people desire the wrong thing (because they are alienated or suffering from ideological delusion); rather, he wants to loosen up forms of desire that have become fixed. It is not some eternal essence that is repressed but the potential to be different, to be otherwise: 'if we're so oppressed, it's because our movement's being restricted, not because our eternal values are being violated' (Deleuze, 1995*b*: 122). In this sense Deleuze here is not unlike Foucault, despite the latter's rejection of the language of repression and desire.

Thus for Deleuze there is no unified subject with essential attributes who is the target of repression, nor any central repressive power. This may seem very far from Marx – as indeed Deleuze himself implies:

> It is wrongly said (in Marxism in particular) that a society is defined by its contradictions. That is true only on the larger scale of things. From the viewpoint of micropolitics, a society is defined by its lines of flight, which are molecular. (Deleuze and Guattari, 1988: 216)

But here in fact we return to Marx, for lines of flight help define the specificity of capitalism. A line of flight is like a deterritorialization without any corresponding reterritorialization, an escape without recapture – and capitalism is constantly, necessarily, deterritorializing: it is, as Marx claims, a revolutionary social form. It cannot control all the flows it releases: though perpetually reterritorializing, and though it submits its flows to its own axiomatic, there is always something that leaks out. Capitalism

> continually sets and then repels its own limits, but in so doing gives rise to numerous flows in all directions that escape its axiomatic. . . . It does not effect the 'conjugation' of the deterritorialized and decoded flows without those flows forging farther ahead; without their escaping both the axiomatic that conjugates them and the models that reterritorialize them. (Deleuze and Guattari, 1988: 472)

What makes capitalism unique is not that it deterritorializes, that it has these lines of flight; what makes capitalism unique is that 'its lines of escape are not just difficulties that arise, they are the very conditions of its operation' (Deleuze, 2004: 270). An example which Deleuze offers is highly pertinent to the current situation in Europe and elsewhere: the capitalist axiomatic gives rise to a problematic deterritorialized flow of population while simultaneously denying itself the means of resolving this problem (Deleuze and Guattari, 1988: 468). This can explain the problems faced by liberal-capitalist societies and their governments across Europe, wavering between encouragement of this deterritorialized flow – opening borders, dismantling trade barriers, encouraging investment, growth, freedom of movement and employment – and a fear of the consequences that produces a desperate attempt to reterritorialize and block the flows – reimposing border controls, applying quotas, enforcing citizenship tests, encouraging suspicion, hostility, racism. This tension arises because the flow is not just a side effect of global capitalism that can be ignored or eliminated but a condition of its functioning: there is a constant need for cheap, flexible labour that can follow demand across borders. The state must encourage the flow while all the time trying to block it.

This begins to answer the question of how capitalism can be repressive: as well as perpetually deterritorializing, it is perpetually reterritorializing, via the state, the church, traditional values, and so on. Perhaps the most important agent of reterritorialization under capitalism is the family, however. Because older forms of public authority are constantly being undermined, mechanisms of repression need to be privatized: taken on by the bourgeois family rather than left to outside institutions. More than this, it can be said that in capitalism repression is internalized. The Oedipus complex is not a universal structure of human life, yet nor is it simply a myth: it is the primary mechanism of repression in capitalist society, restricting desire within the bourgeois family and producing a subject who does not need an external authority because he polices himself. Here we can also begin to understand what Deleuze means by revolution. If repression is something like reterritorialization, cutting off lines of flight, then '[r]evolution is absolute deterritorialization' (Deleuze and Guattari, 1994: 101). The path of resistance does not lie in smoothing the sharp edges of capitalism through the welfare state or stronger trades unions or restrictions on banking practices – for these are only additional axioms, enlarging capitalism's internal limits. Nor will it do to wait for capitalism's contradictions to explode in a moment of revolutionary resolution. Revolution 'will be a decoded flow, a deterritorialized flow that runs too far and cuts too sharply, thereby escaping from the axiomatic of capitalism' (Deleuze and Guattari, 1977: 378). Rather than trying to contain or block the lines of flight upon which capitalism depends, revolution means pushing the deterritorialization of capitalism even further.

Deleuze's vitalism

Deleuze's arguments here are not unlike those of Lyotard: using a mixture of Marx, Nietzsche, and Freud, he presents a non-dialectical analysis of capitalism that captures the fluid dynamism of a social form defined not by contradictions but by shifting, constantly transgressed limits and boundaries. Rather than calling for social-democratic-style restrictions on capitalism, both Lyotard and Deleuze demand that it be pushed further. Yet in *Libidinal Economy* this demand comes close to a provocative celebration of capitalism: after all, if we have given up critique as religious and metaphysical, then from what position can we judge or condemn capitalism? We must stop commiserating and recognize that even exploitation is a form of *jouissance*. *Anti-Oedipus*, in contrast, articulates the demand in explicitly revolutionary terms, upholding a distinction between revolutionary and repressive investments of desire. The question is whether Deleuze is able to do this without relying on an outdated, religious notion of critique. From the point of view of *Libidinal Economy*, the suspicion must be that rather than offering a philosophy of immanence, *Anti-Oedipus* has reintroduced transcendent critique: against a bad, reactionary investment, there is a good, revolutionary investment that liberates desire as an original purity long repressed. Desire would act here both as a standard with which to judge and condemn capitalism and as a force that is capable of resisting capitalism. The problem with *Libidinal Economy* may be that it seems to abandon a critical standpoint, but the challenge it poses to *Anti-Oedipus* is to explain how it can continue to distinguish between different investments of desire without resorting to something like a nostalgia for lost origins.

Lyotard is not the only writer to offer criticism of Deleuze's concept of desire. Parallel to her critique of Foucault, discussed in the previous chapter, Butler argues that despite his claim to provide a historical understanding, Deleuze in fact presents desire as 'an ahistorical absolute', 'a universal ontological truth, long suppressed, essential to human emancipation' (Butler, 1987: 215, 206). It thus effectively functions in onto-teleological fashion: a libidinal plenitude is the *telos* of desire as 'a revolutionary return to a natural Eros' (Butler, 1987: 217). As with Foucault, it is difficult to dismiss Butler's critique of Deleuze as nothing more than a bad or uncharitable reading, for commentators more sympathetic (and attentive) to Deleuze's work have read him in a similar way. For example, Reidar Due (2007: 115) argues that *Anti-Oedipus* is 'dualistic and Romantic in its idealization of a primary force of alienated desire'. It is Romantic because it is nostalgic for an original and spontaneous desire free from the alienations of modern life; it is dualistic because against the oppressed Oedipal subject of capitalism it opposes a nomadic-schizophrenic subject, but without explaining how there could be a transition between the two or how the schizophrenic subject could have any political potency when it seems to be condemned to the margins of society.

The problem that Deleuze faces is similar to that faced by Foucault. We saw that there was a tension in Foucault's work: he seemed to equivocate between abdication of critique and dependence on ahistorical notions of life or pleasure – what Balibar called Foucault's 'vitalism'. This issue becomes even more noticeable in Deleuze's work because, like Negri, far from trying to deny or disguise Foucault's vitalism, he actively praises it. Earlier we saw Deleuze distinguish his work from that of Foucault: whereas the former argues that it is lines of flight that define a society, because the latter begins from power (so Deleuze argues), he finds it difficult to account for resistance. In his book on Foucault, however, Deleuze puts forward a rather different argument. Eager to draw comparisons between his work and that of Foucault, Deleuze now suggests that Foucault may not have difficulty in counterbalancing power relations, because in fact he starts with resistance: *'resistance comes first'* in Foucault (Deleuze, 1988b: 89). Using what he calls 'the best pages of *The History of Sexuality*' (92) – the same pages that we examined at the end of the previous chapter when considering the critical commentaries of Balibar, Butler, and Vikser – Deleuze argues that resistance is prior to power because resistance is outside the 'diagram' that maps and organizes relations between forces. This outside is Life itself. He writes of Foucault:

> When power becomes bio-power, resistance becomes the power of life, a vital power that cannot be confined within species, environment or the paths of a particular diagram. Is not the force that comes from outside a certain idea of Life, a certain vitalism, in which Foucault's thought culminates? (Deleuze, 1988b: 92–3)

Some have suggested that Deleuze's Foucault book tells us far more about Deleuze than it does about Foucault: whatever the truth of this claim, it is clear that Deleuze is also talking about himself when he speaks of a species of thought that culminates in vitalism. Claire Colebrook (2006, 2008) has argued that we should not think of Deleuze's philosophy as vitalist, because he does not think of life in organicist terms, but expands the category to include inorganic matter such as machines. This is a persuasive case, but it disregards Deleuze's own explicit pronouncements on this matter. Elsewhere, for example, he has claimed: 'Everything I've written is vitalistic' (Deleuze, 1995b: 143). Of course, we cannot simply take these words as proof of Deleuze's vitalism and leave it at that – but it does suggest that the charge of vitalism cannot be easily dismissed. Rather than undertaking a detailed investigation of the place of vitalism in Deleuze's thought, however, I would like to pursue some of these issues in the terms within which we have examined the other post-structuralists. Can Deleuze retain the prospect of social change – and can he do so without the use of ahistorical and suspiciously idealist concepts?

Deleuze phrases himself carefully: like the other post-structuralists, in his discussions of the future he is careful to avoid providing concrete plans or a manifesto to be implemented. 'No political program will be elaborated within the framework of schizoanalysis' (Deleuze and Guattari, 1977: 380). Yet he does not abandon the possibility of social transformation: although every society has its lines of flight, in capitalism these lines 'take on a new character, and a new kind of revolutionary potential. So, you see, there is hope' (Deleuze, 2004: 270). The lines of flight that Deleuze seeks are not solipsistic retreats from reality, but collective movements where the question becomes, 'what can we do so that these escapes may no longer be individual attempts or small communities, but may instead truly constitute a revolutionary machine?' (279). The difficulty is in following a line of flight that does not lead to a dead end – whether by destroying itself, or by hardening into a sedentary rigidity (as in the bureaucratization of a revolution, for example). Deleuze emphasizes that the aim is not to liberate a repressed essence, but to render possible transformations, deterritorializations without reterritorializations: 'it isn't a question of liberty as against submission, but only a question of a line of escape or, rather, of a simple *way out*' (Deleuze and Guattari, 1986: 6).

It could be argued, then, that Deleuze does not need to rely on vitalism, because he views the future not as the unfolding or recovery of a dehistoricized notion of Life, but as an open possibility that develops immanently from the present. Against the suspicion that Deleuze views desire as a natural Eros, we can note that in *Anti-Oedipus* he claims that 'desire is a machine, a synthesis of machines, a machinic arrangement' (Deleuze and Guattari, 1977: 296). As Colebrook notes, this is a machinic, not an organicist concept of desire: desire is assembled rather than given; it is part of a machine rather than a natural force or energy. This is made much clearer in *A Thousand Plateaus*: 'Desire is never an undifferentiated instinctual energy, but itself results from a highly developed, engineered setup rich in interactions' (Deleuze and Guattari, 1988: 215). Depending on how one looks at it, this claim from *A Thousand Plateaus* might be taken as reiteration of the arguments made in the first volume of *Capitalism and Schizophrenia*, or as a subtle change of position in response to criticisms of the first volume: implicit acknowledgement that *Anti-Oedipus* does tend to celebrate a rather naïve notion of libidinal liberation. The latter argument is perhaps most convincing: there is a nostalgic naturalism in the first volume that is much less evident in the second volume.

Deleuze's dualism

Despite the clarifications and changes in Deleuze's philosophy, however, problems remain. Reidar Due suggests that *A Thousand Plateaus* is a marked improvement on *Anti-Oedipus*, having abandoned the residual romanticism of the latter. Yet the charge of dualism that Due directs at *Anti-Oedipus* is in many ways even more applicable to *A Thousand Plateaus*. This is a book that is dominated by dualisms: an almost limitless series of pairings in which one side seems to have priority over the other. Rhizome and tree-root, deterritorialization and reterritorialization, molecular and molar, smooth space and striated space, minor and major, nomadic and sedentary: the impression conveyed is of a series of hierarchical distinctions, or even simply expressions of the same basic hierarchy. John Mullarkey (2006: 19–20) lucidly identifies the problem here: the existence of these hierarchies transgresses Deleuze's own philosophical principle of immanence. The selection and exclusion that it presupposes should be precluded from a philosophy that rejects transcendent order and aspires to a monist ontology that refuses to posit the existence of two worlds. We have already seen that Deleuze's rereading of Marx undermines a whole succession of oppositions: subjective and objective, base and superstructure, labour and desire, material and ideal, social and private, political and libidinal. Yet alongside this destabilization of oppositions, it appears that there is a constant construction of new sets of pairs.

How can the persistence of dualism in Deleuze's work be explained? Mullarkey suggests that Deleuze believes that he needs the central dualism in his work – that between the virtual and the actual –to account for change and the emergence of the new. Yet, he adds, it is an awareness of the need to prevent this dualism from reifying into a strict dichotomy that drives Deleuze perpetually to reinvent his philosophical language (Mullarkey, 2006: 46–8, 17). Thus the conceptual promiscuity of Deleuze's work can at least in part be attributed to a tension between a belief in the need to retain a distinction between the virtual and the actual and a desire to resist the dualisms that have dogged the Western philosophical tradition but which should have no place in a philosophy of immanence: 'constant renaming in the face of dualities continually re-appearing' (Mullarkey, 2006: 188). This philosophical creativity is nowhere more evident in Deleuze's corpus than in *A Thousand Plateaus*, where it reaches an astonishing level as the authors roam over philosophy, linguistics, politics, psychoanalysis, semiotics, geology, literature, and beyond, inventing an extraordinary plethora of new terms. Rather than resisting the entrenchment of dualism, however, this conceptual proliferation merely reinforces it even further, as ever more dualities are introduced. Deleuze repeatedly insists that these pairs should not be considered oppositions: they are always intertwined and neither has priority over the other. But the effect, far from disrupting or displacing these divisions, is merely to expand their number, creating an ever-lengthening list of pairs. The problem is that this throws into doubt Deleuze's attempt to create a materialist philosophy. In the terms outlined in Chapter 1, the postulation of these dualisms would effectively make Deleuze an idealist, dividing between that which is primary, original, and essential and that which is secondary, derived, and accidental. In addition, it casts doubt on Deleuze's Marxist credentials. In his assessment of Deleuze's relation to Marx, Jameson has suggested that dualism is 'the strong form of ideology as such': rather than supplying a critical analysis of a situation that identifies immanent possibilities for change – in other words the kind of analysis that Deleuze himself would like to provide and that can be found in Marx – it reduces everything to a facile question of good versus evil, 'call[ing] for judgement where none is appropriate' (Jameson, 1997: 411–12).

To conclude our examination of Deleuze's reading of Marx, we shall consider how Deleuze might be rescued from these accusations, which threaten to distance him from the Marx that we have been constructing through post-structuralism. Can we have a Deleuze who is neither a dualist nor a vitalist? One possible solution is offered by Badiou (2000), who argues that while dualism may influence Deleuze's philosophical rhetoric, it has little ontological significance in his work. Far from being a thinker of the Two, for Badiou Deleuze is a thinker of the One. There are important pairings in Deleuze's work according to Badiou – like the virtual-actual, for example – but what the existence of these pairs reflects is Deleuze's insistence on the necessity of grasping both the univocity of Being and the equivocity of beings as modalities of Being. The role of thought for Deleuze, says Badiou, is to grasp the movement from Being to beings – but only in order to recognize that ultimately this movement is the movement of Being itself. This has political consequences: because every existing thing is only an expression of the One, Badiou argues, Deleuze cannot account for difference or the emergence of the new. This means that Deleuze cannot adequately account for political events like revolutions. In developing this line of argument, Peter Hallward has done most to pursue the political implications of this reading of Deleuze. If Badiou questions the political consequences of Deleuze's work, Hallward effectively denies that it has any political relevance at all. Following Badiou's claim that Deleuze is a philosopher of the One, Hallward argues that for Deleuze '[a]ll existent individuals are simply so many divergent facets of one and the same creative force, variously termed desire or desiring-production, life, *élan vital*, power' (Hallward, 2006: 16). Hallward thus argues that far from being a materialist thinker, Deleuze is a spiritualist thinker 'preoccupied with the mechanics of *dis*-embodiment and *de*-materialisation', and who therefore 'offers few resources for thinking the consequences of what happens within the actually existing world as such' (3, 162).

This interpretation of Deleuze does tackle the problem of dualism in Deleuze's work, but only at the expense of rejecting Deleuze as a political thinker: Deleuze's monism, it is argued, can tell us little about actual relations and events. Moreover, in effect it only deals with the problem by denying that it exists: the dualisms in Deleuze's work, it is claimed, either have no genuine philosophical significance, or they exist only in order ultimately to testify to the univocity of Being. The dualities in Deleuze's work, however, cannot be dismissed as little more than rhetoric, nor dissolved into a single 'creative force'. They are far too persistent for either strategy to be persuasive. Rather than merely influencing his philosophical language, Deleuze's dualisms have a prominent role in the very structure of his philosophical arguments: they provide an evaluative dimension to his work, ensuring that it is not merely descriptive but also critical. To this extent, it could be argued that the dominant duality in Deleuze's work is not the Bergson-inspired distinction between the virtual and the actual, but the Nietzsche-inspired division between active and reactive forces. However, this reintroduces the suspicion articulated by Jameson that Deleuze is resorting to a (seemingly very non-Nietzschean) split between good and evil, and poses the question of how Deleuze can make such a judgement: from what position is Deleuze judging, and why is the active preferable to the reactive anyway? How can such an evaluation be made within a philosophy of immanence? Why are the categories of active and reactive not submitted to criticism?

One way to respond to these questions is to think of Deleuze's dualisms not in terms of Nietzsche but of Marx. In his Marx-inspired analysis of capitalism, the active-reactive pairing becomes the distinction between deterritorialization and reterritorialization. Rather than a transcendent evaluation of capitalism, this distinction identifies different tendencies within capitalism – for example, the subversion of all traditional values by the profit imperative and the simultaneous reinscription of traditional values in an attempt to guard against revolt. This is not an evaluative distinction between good and evil but, following Marx, recognition of the dual nature of capitalism itself, as a social form that is both loaded with possibility and potentially catastrophic. These tendencies can then provide the basis for an immanent critique of capitalism: not by judging it from the outside, but by exposing its workings and pushing it to its own limits and beyond. It is not a question of uncritically endorsing or encouraging deterritorialization wherever it happens, but of attending to specific instances of deterritorialization. Philosophy will not be given the final word on what should happen and how we should proceed because – as we saw Deleuze claim at the end of the previous chapter – philosophy is only one practice among many, itself subject to judgement rather than offering definitive criteria of judgement.

If the dualisms in Deleuze's work are not just rhetoric, then nor do they exist only so one side can be dissolved into the other. Deleuze is a philosopher of process: his aim is not to dissolve that which exists into a vital, originary force. His argument is that simply looking at what exists does not tell us much; specifically, it tells us little about how that which exists came to be. As before, Marx provides a useful orientation point here for a sympathetic reading of Deleuze. In *Anti-Oedipus*, Deleuze states: 'Let us remember once again one of Marx's caveats: we cannot tell from the mere taste of wheat who grew it; the product gives us no hint as to the system and the relations of production.'[13] Rather than taking products as given, we need to analyse the exact mechanisms by which they were produced: 'the moment that one describes . . . the material process of production, the specificity of the product tends to evaporate, while at the same time the possibility of another outcome, another end result of the process appears' (Deleuze and Guattari, 1977: 24). Thus if the specificity of the product evaporates, it is not into an abstract, generalized, primordial creative force, but into the specific processes that generated the product. Far from being unable to account for actually existing relations, Deleuze refers us precisely to those relations – and he does so not to lead us 'out of this world' (as the title of Hallward's book on Deleuze has it) but to show us that the development of this world was not inevitable, and that another world is possible.

Such might be a generous reading of Deleuze – one that confirmed his claims to be both a materialist and a Marxist. We might also, however, use Marx to criticize Deleuze here. Marx sets out to explain the genesis not only of products but of ideas too – in particular, he aims (as we saw in Chapter 3) to study the genesis of abstraction. For Deleuze, in contrast, it often seems that abstraction is an end in itself. The paradox of *A Thousand Plateaus*, for instance, is that the more varied its range becomes – the more fields of enquiry that it explores – the more formal and abstract it becomes, so that each area that it interrogates seems only to reinforce Deleuze's own ontological commitments. This is a wider problem in Deleuze's work, including his analysis of capitalism. The risk here is similar to that faced by Lyotard: just as *The Differend* tended to reduce capitalist exploitation to only another example of a differend (and, to a lesser extent, just as in *Libidinal Economy* questions of historical development tended to get lost in the relation between representation and desire), so the danger with Deleuze is that his analysis of capitalism, rather than attending to the historical specificity of this unique social form, is moulded to fit his existing philosophical concepts. Deterritorialization and reterritorialization can be very useful concepts for analysing present-day capitalism – but if this basic duality can in some form also be applied to any phenomena whatsoever, then what can they tell us about the specificity of capitalism? The dualities of Deleuze's philosophy become just as abstract as the categories of the dialectic: they become concepts which will fit anything but which show us nothing. That is not to say that Deleuze's analysis of capitalism is without worth – on the contrary, it is extremely valuable and productive – but it means, I would suggest, that if we want to get the best out of it then we should do our best to read Deleuze as a Marxist. As Deleuze himself says, we need to follow Marx's rules exactly.

Conclusion

Consonant with post-structuralist aims, Deleuze offers what might be called a practical reading of Marx: not an academic commentary, but an energetic use of Marx. Like the other post-structuralists, Deleuze rejects Marx's idealist side, though Deleuze's critique is implicit rather than explicit. When it comes to Marx's positive legacy, on the other hand, Deleuze is the most vocal of the post-structuralists, and his use of Marx is perhaps the most inventive, with several important post-structuralist themes congregating in his work: he aligns Marx with Nietzsche rather than Hegel in order to offer a universal history of contingency and a non-dialectical analysis of capitalism which examines the micro-processes by which subjects are produced. Yet if in Deleuze the strengths of post-structuralist readings of Marx are most clearly dramatized, then so are their failures: despite its historical perspective, its demand to begin from concrete situations, and its search for revolutionary opportunities in specific moments, Deleuze's philosophy risks falling back on ontological abstractions, with concrete and specific differences dissipating. The problems that Deleuze faces are those of post-structuralism more generally, and in the next chapter I want to go back to Marx for an alternative escape from idealism, and in doing so to articulate more clearly the form of Marx's materialism.

Chapter 6

Marx Through Post-Structuralism

Communism is for us not a state of affairs *which is to be established, an* ideal *to which reality [will] have to adjust itself. We call communism the* real *movement which abolishes the present state of things.*

(Marx and Engels, 1976: 49)

What can be made of Marx after post-structuralism? What is Marx without ideology, with no dialectic, where the economic is not determinant, where class is not centre stage? In this chapter we shall revisit Marx, having read him through post-structuralism. If we return to Marx, however, it is not to the original purity of a Marx unadulterated by interpretation, but to a Marx renewed by his encounter with post-structuralism, as we examine what post-structuralist uses and criticisms of Marx can tell us about his work. We shall go on to outline a characterization of materialism, using the readings of Marx we have analysed. We begin, however, by revisiting post-structuralism itself. There is no one, single post-structuralist Marx, but the commonalities in their readings of his work allow us now to provide a sharper picture of post-structuralism than that provided in Chapter 1. To develop this picture, we shall also return to Althusser. I shall argue that the originality of the post-structuralist approach is further demonstrated by the fact that there is evidence that Althusser himself later adapted his work in the light of post-structuralist insights.

Post-Structuralism and Althusser Revisited

We need to be careful when using a term like 'post-structuralism': as I have tried to show, there are many differences between the thinkers who are brought under this heading. Nonetheless, the term is more than a mere label of convenience: there exist common uses and points of interest, shared enemies and allies, that justify bringing certain writers together. I have argued that Marx has been a key influence on post-structuralism, and as such looking at post-structuralist engagements with Marx can reveal something about post-structuralism in general, about what it is that makes it distinctive. As we review the four readings of Marx we have examined, it will be useful to return to Althusser, comparing and contrasting his work with that of the post-structuralists. The readings of Marx given by the latter are recognizably post-Althusserian – but just as post-structuralism has an ambivalent relation to structuralism, so 'post-Althusserian' indicates an ambivalent relation to Althusser. Althusser's reading of Marx is singled out for praise by the post-structuralists, and with good reason: the post-structuralists build on the work Althusser did, making use of his insights. But they also take things in a different direction, producing new insights which make Althusser's seem naïve or clumsy by comparison, and offering a distinctively post-structuralist engagement with Marx.

Distinguishing post-structuralism

The most important similarity between the post-structuralists that emerges from their readings of Marx is a common defence of Marx's contemporary relevance: post-structuralism is not a rejection of Marx, nor an attempt to surpass him and render him irrelevant. It is true that this defence does not have a uniform intensity: it varies from Lyotard's somewhat nostalgic tributes to Deleuze's sustained and passionate praise. But each post-structuralist welcomes Marx, even embraces him. At its lowest level, this embrace is simply reconfirmation that all of us are, in Derrida's words, heirs of Marx, whether we know it or not: one cannot talk of capitalism, or begin to criticize society, or even begin to write history, without constantly reaffirming Marx's insights. More than this universal relevance, however, post-structuralism praises Marx as a central and specific influence on post-structuralism itself: post-structuralism would not have been possible in 'a pre-Marxist space', to borrow a phrase from Derrida (1994: 92). This goes beyond mere recognition of Marx's impact: there is a united post-structuralist defence of Marx's contemporary *political* importance. Both Derrida and Foucault warn against 'academicizing' Marx: neutralizing him by neglecting or smothering his radical significance and treating him as just another step in the history of philosophy. Likewise, Deleuze never tires of emphasizing the importance of Marx's critical analysis of capitalism, while even Lyotard stresses the need to retain Marx as something more than simply an influence: as a voice for the voiceless. It is important to stress this point because there is a temptation to overlook or even directly deny the influence of Marx upon post-structuralism – a temptation strongly bound up with the reception of these thinkers in the Anglo-American academy. In Lyotard's case this is perhaps understandable: the most committed Marxist to begin with, his reorientation could (albeit incorrectly) be interpreted as a repudiation of Marx, in line with the *nouveaux philosophes*. Similarly, we have seen that Foucault's playful comments on Marx and his hostility to orthodox Marxism led many to conclude that this hostility extended to Marx himself. Long before *Specters of Marx*, reception of Derrida was dominated by the 'Yale Derrida' – not a Derrida friendly with Marx. Even once the Marx book was published, long-formed perceptions were difficult to challenge. It might be said that with Deleuze the reverse applies, yet the effect has been similar: with Derrida, long-standing silence on Marx bred suspicions that were difficult to shift; the early reception of Deleuze, on the other hand, was strongly associated with *Anti-Oedipus*, a book so saturated with Marx that many current commentators have tried to distance Deleuze from Marx simply in order to show that another Deleuze exists.[1] The recent explosion of interest in Deleuze has thus coincided with a conscious effort to move Deleuze away from or beyond Marx.

Overall, the effacement of Marx from post-structuralism can perhaps best be understood in terms of the political context: post-structuralism seemed to offer an alternative to a Marxism that appeared not only exhausted but irredeemably corrupted. But this attempt to oppose Marx to the post-structuralists ignores a crucial distinction that the latter make: while the degradation of Marxism led many commentators to conflate Marx and Marxism in an effort to contrast them both unfavourably with post-structuralism, it led the post-structuralists themselves to resist this conflation so as to be able to continue to call upon Marx. This does not mean that they do not make use of certain Marxist philosophers, nor that they repudiate the history of Marxism or retreat from political activism. But it is really from Marx himself they draw inspiration, and not Marxism as a wider political movement, nor as a kind of organizational precedent, with its parties and revolutions. This tells us a number of things about post-structuralism. In part it is to do with a common post-structuralist attitude to political action: the micropolitical scale of their analyses and the desire to keep the future open leads the post-structuralists to a distrust of parties and manifestoes. This is not a rejection of collective action but wariness of such action ossifying into bureaucratic stasis, or something worse. The context within which the post-structuralists wrote can help explain these suspicions. Comparison with Althusser is pertinent here. Althusser, slightly older than the post-structuralists and imprisoned by the Nazis in the war, fixed his allegiance to the party that had played a vital role in the Resistance: he sought to free Marx by challenging existing orthodoxy from within the French Communist Party (PCF). Rather than simply detaching Marx from theoretical dogma, leaving him 'free and floating' (to adapt Lyotard's phrase), Althusser sought to change the direction of the Party itself: to posit an alternative Marx in opposition to the Party but also for the sake of the Party. The post-structuralists came to Marx in a different context and with different aims. Loyal attachment to Marxism had become a sign more of delusional folly than of ideological probity. Suspicions were raised not just by the Soviet Union but by the Communist Party in France itself. The two official positions adopted by the postwar PCF – first a doctrinaire Stalinism, and then the subjective, humanist Marxism propounded by Garaudy – were unpalatable to the post-structuralists. Outside the Party as well, Marxism had become a stultifying deadweight: in the universities Marx was filtered through Hegel and joined to phenomenology, his radical potential blunted by official recognition and assimilation into idealist currents of thought. All this meant that none of the post-structuralists were inside the Communist Party in the way that Althusser was – indeed, none were really 'inside' Marxism in the way that Althusser was. Lyotard's most interesting work came after breaking with Marxism, and in their two different ways both Derrida and Foucault maintained a distance from Marxism. Even Deleuze, happy to proclaim himself a Marxist, was not a Marxist like Althusser: Deleuze's proclamation signified a specific allegiance to Marx rather than to any party or organization. This does not align the post-structuralists with the conventional anti-Marxist hysteria that began to grip mainstream opinion in France in the 1970s: to the contrary, one aim of distinguishing Marx from Marxism was to combat and undermine the crude and clumsy attacks made by the *nouveaux philosophes*, for whom Stalin is the genuine heir of Marx.[2] While they do not straightforwardly dismiss the connection between Marx and Stalin, the post-structuralists do not accept that the gulag is enough to discredit Marx: any connections must be studied in their specificity and with care.[3] Marx offers many routes – for there are many Marxes.

This postulation of many Marxes reflects epistemological and hermeneutic concerns as well as the immediate socio-political context. Misgivings about the forms of institutional Marxism in France combined with suspicion of the conceptual formalism and theoretical system-building of a more structuralist approach to help generate a relation to Marx that is more supple and flexible than Althusser's own relation to Marx. For all his emphasis on avoiding mere repetition of Marx, it is often the case that Althusser seems to be trying to return to the true Marx, searching for the correct reading (hence Lyotard's jibe at 'the little Althusserians'). This is not the goal of the post-structuralists. The post-structuralists do not distinguish Marx from Marxism so that they may return to a truer Marx, as if to scrape away all historical accretions in order that the real Marx may shine through, his philosophical system once again clear for all to see. Marx is approached as an open resource. In part this treatment of Marx is a necessary consequence of the diversity of his work (which we shall discuss later), but it also stems from a distinctively post-structuralist attitude: Marx is read in this way because this is the way that post-structuralism reads all texts, in the spirit of what Derrida calls an 'active interpretation', filtering and using a text rather than simply repeating it or trying to reconstruct its internal coherence. Any reader of Marx will need to be selective – but the post-structuralists differ in that they affirm this selectivity, rather than pretending there is a single Marx.

This treatment of Marx as a non-systematic, heterogeneous resource is part of the attempt to liberate Marx from the constraints of a wider institutional Marxism (whether that institution be the party or the university): for it is frequently Marxism itself which has tried to subdue Marx by forcing him into a system. 'I will always wonder', says Derrida, 'if the idea of Marxism – the self-identity of a Marxist discourse or system or even a science or philosophy – is not in principle incompatible with the event-Marx' (Derrida, 2002*b*: 188). It is this 'event-Marx' which post-structuralism tries to liberate. The point is neither to attempt to absolve Marx of blame for actions carried out in his name and return to a Marx of purely philosophical interest, nor to treat Marx as an infinitely fluid mixture of which any interpretation or use is legitimate, but rather to reaffirm Marx's importance and recapture his novelty, to draw on what Marx and no one else provides. This does not mean that the post-structuralists simply approach Marx in a fashion of careless, haphazard eclecticism that leads to readings of Marx lacking in rigour. On the contrary, if anything they give closer and more revealing readings than those of Althusser: while Althusser was all too ready to suppress that which did not fit into his version of Marx, the post-structuralists are far more willing to acknowledge and highlight the tensions and paradoxes in Marx's work. Freed from the duty to present the correct Marx, the post-structuralists are more attentive to the irresolvable problems in his work. Although Althusser does not only divide between a Young and an Old Marx, he does place great emphasis on the 1845 break – but he then struggles to account for the re-emergence and persistence of certain themes and concepts in Marx's work, dividing Marx into more and more periods. For the post-structuralists, in contrast, the heterogeneity of Marx's texts is captured not by periodizing Marx, but by acknowledging the simultaneous coexistence of contrasting elements throughout his work, and selectively drawing from across his oeuvre.

The targets of Althusser's critiques – essentially idealism, particularly in its Hegelian forms – remain those of post-structuralism as well, but the post-structuralists deal with them in a different way. Althusser seemed to struggle with Hegel, at once wanting to claim that Marx broke definitively with him, even that he was never a Hegelian, and to acknowledge Marx's debt to Hegel's dialectic and his continuing reliance on Hegelian terminology. The post-structuralists do not have this problem. In part this is because they do not try to divide Marx into Hegelian and non-Hegelian periods, aiming (as Althusser sometimes seems to be) to pinpoint the moment when Marx relieves himself of his Hegelian inheritance. But it is also because the post-structuralists pursue their suspicions of Hegel with greater rigour than Althusser, repudiating dialectical thinking. Hegel's logic suppresses the differend for Lyotard; his *Aufhebung* is destroyed by *différance* for Derrida; his dialectics cannot possibly account for the relations of social conflict for Foucault; he is the primary antagonist for Deleuze, for whom contradiction is always 'a perpetual misinterpretation of difference itself' (Deleuze, 1983: 157). Read in the light of post-structuralism, Althusser's position seems rather strange, and perhaps untenable as it stands: both wanting to purge Marx of Hegel and to retain that most Hegelian mechanism, the dialectic; to establish Marx's specificity while forever placing him in Hegel's debt, with the gift of the dialectic at the heart of his work. The post-structuralists, in contrast, construct not merely a non-Hegelian Marx, but a non-dialectical Marx: a Marx who points to movements and forces that cannot be contained within the framework of contradiction and negation. Althusser's attitude towards the dialectic is reflective of a broader tension in his work: he wants to rid Marx of idealism, yet there is a 'residual idealism' in Althusser's own work, encapsulated by what Derrida calls the 'metaphysical anchoring' of the concept of overdetermination: it is as if Althusser fails fully to escape idealism, retaining something like that structuralist nostalgia for origins and presence of which Derrida writes. The post-structuralists have different problems: rather than remaining entangled in idealism, they have to face the problems that accompany the attempt to abandon idealism altogether – primarily, the difficulty of maintaining a critical orientation. Althusser himself comes to face these problems in his later work – and this, I want now to argue, is because that later work is in its turn influenced by post-structuralism.

Influencing Althusser

It is difficult to say for certain whether Althusser consciously borrowed from the post-structuralists when working on his later writings. It seems likely that he read Lyotard, though he does not discuss him. Derrida's work on Marx appeared only after Althusser's death, but Althusser certainly read his earlier work (which laid the basis for Derrida's later critique of Marx's onto-teleology). Both Derrida and Deleuze are named by Althusser as part of the suppressed current of materialism in Western philosophy (Althusser, 2006: 167, 189). He read the work of his ex-student Foucault very carefully: as early as 1962 Althusser was giving seminars on Foucault, and he is praised in *Reading Capital*; thereafter the two were involved in what Montag calls a 'strange "dialogue", whose participants did not directly address or even name each other' (Montag, 1995: 71).[4] Whether or not Althusser consciously adjusted his work in the light of these four, he clearly saw something interesting in post-structuralism. Moreover, as he developed his ideas, his position came more and more to resemble a post-structuralist position on Marx, so that it began to seem as if Althusser was following in the wake of post-structuralism rather than vice versa. He does not repudiate his earlier work, but he does develop it, and the changes reflect the work the post-structuralists had done in the meantime. This is not to claim that Althusser simply modified his position in response to or as a result of post-structuralist work on Marx. There are numerous continuities between the early and later Althussers, as we have seen, suggesting that it would be simplistic to posit too strong a break. Moreover, any changes that did take place were the result of a number of factors: Althusser reworked his ideas not only in acknowledgement of the internal theoretical weaknesses of his programme, but also in response to the wider socio-political situation that he faced. Nonetheless, it is not unreasonable to suggest that Althusser drew on themes and insights developed by the post-structuralists – and at the very least consideration of this possibility can help us refine our portrait of post-structuralism.

The most obvious way in which Althusser's later work echoes post-structuralism is in its reformulation of the critique of idealism as a critique of philosophies of Origins and Ends. As I argued in Chapter 1, this reformulation confirms Althusser's earlier readings of Marx. But the terms in which the critique is redrawn reflect the work done by the post-structuralists: Lyotard's attack on eschatological philosophies nostalgic for a lost origin; Derrida's suspicion of onto-teleology (not yet applied to Marx by the time Althusser is writing, but already well-developed in relation to other thinkers); Foucault's discussion of humanist portrayals of Man as a truth reduced and promised; Deleuze's attempt to forge a materialism that does not replicate the problems of idealism. Hence, although I used Althusser in Chapter 1 to set the scene, this does not imply strict chronological priority: on the contrary, his critique of idealism can be used to set the scene for post-structuralist critiques because it comes after these post-structuralist critiques, synthesizing and summarizing them (albeit implicitly). It is not only in his newly sharpened definition of idealism that one can see the reflection of post-structuralism in Althusser: it is also apparent in new analyses of the place of idealism in Marx's work. Whereas the earlier Althusser often seemed to be trying to establish the exact point at which Marx broke with idealism, the later Althusser, like the post-structuralists, seems more willing to acknowledge tensions in Marx's work, finding even in *Capital* that idealist theses sit alongside materialist innovations. No longer content to illuminate the heterogeneity of Marx's texts through periodization, Althusser's later writings exhibit a more post-structuralist recognition of the complexity of Marx's work, acknowledging the contiguity of opposing elements in Marx's work.

Althusser's reassessment of Marx is accompanied by a reassessment of his own work: a reinvigorated materialism sees him alter his terms. There is far less emphasis on ideology and the dialectic, both of which had been attacked and abandoned by post-structuralism. Overdetermination gives way to aleatory materialism; the metaphysical anchoring of determination in the last instance gives way to a greater sensitivity to the contingent singularity of events. Here, in fact, Althusser explicitly indicates that he has been influenced by a post-structuralist approach to Marx, citing Deleuze's analysis of capitalism in *Anti-Oedipus*: when Althusser writes of the contingent encounter between workers and money, he is drawing on a Marx filtered through Deleuze (Althusser, 2006: 197). This new proximity to post-structuralism leads Althusser to the kinds of difficulties that the post-structuralists face. Rather than finding himself still tethered to a metaphysical idealism, the danger Althusser now faces is that he cannot find any critical footing at all, able only to register a chaotic indeterminacy that mirrors the very determinism he wishes to oppose.

The relations between Althusser and post-structuralism are complicated; neither side forms a homogeneous block that can be compared simply to the other: the post-structuralists offer different Marxes and Althusser subtly changes position over time. But in changing position Althusser comes closer to a post-structuralist approach. At the risk of oversimplifying, one name can usefully illuminate the differences and connections between Althusser and post-structuralism: Nietzsche appears with more frequency in Althusser's later writings, and it is the influence of Nietzsche that stands as a key difference between post-structuralism and Althusser's earlier work. Named by Althusser as an aleatory materialist, Nietzsche's presence makes Althusser look more post-structuralist. Nietzsche's shadow falls over post-structuralist readings of Marx in various places. He is there in the way they approach Marx, in their refusal to systematize; but he is also found in the kind of Marx they construct. It is Deleuze, of course, who most explicitly opposes Nietzsche to dialectical thinking, but his influence can be felt in other post-structuralist attempts to extract a non-dialectical Marx attentive to more subtle and fluid forces and movements. More generally, Nietzsche facilitates the post-structuralist critique of Marx's onto-teleology. Nietzsche stands as an ally against those narratives of *ressentiment* – including those of a certain Marx – whose subject is the victim of a wrong seeking redress: where the recovery of some loss is promised as an ultimate end (communism as an end to the suffering of the proletariat). Marx is read by the post-structuralists in this Nietzchean style, challenging traditional ontologies with the rejection of notions of deeper, underlying realities or fixed essences, and undermining teleology as philosophies of history are rejected in favour of histories of contingency. This is not to say that the post-structuralists take these themes – this hostility to systematization, dialectics, onto-teleology – and simply apply them to Marx. Nietzsche's shadow certainly falls on post-structuralism, and he can act as a useful shorthand for some of the differences between (early) Althusser and post-structuralism; but things cannot be reduced to easy formulas (Althusser + Nietzsche = post-structuralism!). What can be said, however, is that the post-structuralists offer readings of Marx that are quite different from Althusser's readings. Yet we should not be led to disparage Althusser's contribution: in his attempt to bring Marxist theory 'back to life' Althusser remains in many ways a trailblazer for post-structuralism.

Distinctions within post-structuralism

Though they share much in common, it is important not simply to conflate the work of the four post-structuralists we have examined. Thinking about how they differ can tell us as much about their work as can analysis of common features. Clearly, there is an almost endless number of ways in which we might distinguish between these thinkers, especially if we were simply to try to isolate each one from the rest in turn. It might be more productive to try to identify different groupings within post-structuralism. Giorgio Agamben's essay 'Absolute Immanence' (1999: 220–39) provides a potentially useful division. Agamben differentiates between a line of immanence and a line of transcendence: the latter runs from Spinoza and Nietzsche to Deleuze and Foucault, while the former runs from Kant and Husserl to Levinas and Derrida; both lines converge in the middle on Heidegger. If we follow this distinction, then it could be said that the Lyotard of *Libidinal Economy* would be aligned with the line of immanence, while the Lyotard of *The Differend* would belong to the line of transcendence. Agamben illustrates this distinction with a diagram, but does not elaborate on it much further (the essay as a whole is a reading of Deleuze's 'Immanence: A Life . . .'). Daniel Smith (2003*a*) has taken Agamben's essay as the starting point for a valuable comparative study of the philosophies of Deleuze and Derrida in terms of subjectivity, ontology, and epistemology. Rather than extending Smith's study and offering a comprehensive analysis of all four thinkers in terms of immanence and transcendence, I would like to present some brief, preliminary remarks about how such a distinction might relate to the materialist philosophy that we have been outlining.

I have suggested that a key challenge faced by materialist philosophy is how to remain critical. How can a critical position be maintained if one abandons the themes of a lost origin or of a quasi-exterior ground from which critique can be secured? More specifically, how can the possibility of an alternative future be held open without the postulation of some solid, unshifting ontological given or the promise of a redemptive *telos*? One answer to this question is to say that we should abandon critique – a position which both Lyotard and Foucault sometimes seem to accept. At other times, however, both pursue different strategies. From the late 1970s, Lyotard alters his position, in recognition that questions of judgement and justice cannot be neglected. The question that Lyotard now asks is how to retain a notion of justice that cannot be reduced to the application of pre-given criteria and can always remain open to a future that cannot be determined in advance. In this way, he affirms the simultaneous necessity and impossibility of judgement: we must judge, but there can be no final judgement. These, *mutatis mutandis*, are also the questions posed by Derrida: how can we preserve a concept of justice irreducible to the law that can welcome the unforeseeable without lapsing into relativism? In both cases, this need for sensitivity to the unexpected is phrased in terms of the event. It is in the nature of the event that it cannot be anticipated: once it has been recognized as an event and recuperated into existing epistemic, ethical, or ontological frameworks, then it ceases to be an event. Lyotard and Derrida can here both be said to be following a logic of transcendence. There is a formal or structural transcendence of the event as that which is absolutely unattainable: it cannot be fully grasped in its 'eventness'. Or more accurately, this is a logic of quasi-transcendence, for there can be no pure transcendence: it is always contaminated by the limited, determined realm of empirical reality. An event must at some point be recuperated in order to have occurred at all, and at some point a decision or judgement must be made.

If this is the logic that Lyotard pursues in *The Differend*, then in *Libidinal Economy* he puts forward an analysis much closer to that of Foucault and Deleuze. Rather than turning to the event as the motif of an open future, Foucault and Deleuze suggest that alternatives to the present emerge out of the present itself. The possibility of change is guaranteed not by the postulation of an unattainable event-to-come, but within a historically determined space of struggle between different forces. Deleuze's lines of flight develop out of existing circumstances, from moments of deterritorialization within definite socio-historical conditions: 'it is in concrete social fields, at specific moments, that the comparative moments of deterritorialization, the continuums of intensity and the combinations of flux they form must be studied' (Deleuze and Parent, 2002: 135). Similarly, Foucault indicates alternatives by analysing existing power relations: relations which are defined by their positivity and singularity and are immanent to the subjects and events that they shape. For both Foucault and Deleuze, these conditions of change are thus not (quasi-) transcendent but immanent to the present: there is no inaccessible 'other' (even if always contaminated by the here and now) because there is only this one world and one life, with nothing beyond or beneath. This immanent potential should not be confused with inevitability: it does not mean that the seeds of the future will grow inexorably from the present. It is not the predetermination of the future but the connection of the future with the present.

From the point of view of the strategy of immanence pursued by Foucault and Deleuze, the logic of transcendence has several weaknesses. Perhaps above all, it is suspiciously ahistorical, ignoring the multiplicity and specificity of existing practices and forces and committing us to an impossible obligation (to welcome that which can never arrive) rather than encouraging us to analyse present conditions in an attempt to find new ways forward. There is a sense in which a philosophy of the event is as empty as the teleology that it is supposed to oppose: neither have much to say about concrete circumstances. We also saw, however, that the work of Foucault and Deleuze is not without its problems. At its limit, their strategy leads to a vitalism that, rather than determining existing power relations, conceives of the immanent potential of the present in terms of a notion of Life as an 'outside' which resists all relations of power. In this way, rather than simply rejecting the theme of the event, their philosophies of immanence lead to a concept of the event different from that found in Derrida or *The Differend*, but equally flawed: the event not as an unexpected break in the chain of history, but as the realization of the power of Life. As Badiou puts it, in Deleuze's work '[t]he event is the ontological realisation of the eternal truth of the One, the infinite power of Life' (Badiou, 2007: 38). This 'Life' is ultimately no less ahistorical than the 'event' of Derrida and Lyotard.

Thus in a sense we come full circle: a central charge against Marx made by post-structuralism is that his teleology – his presupposition of a *telos* that would be the return of a lost origin – cancels historicity and negates the future. Teleology, which is supposed to tell us how history will develop, is effectively ahistorical. But the two strategies of transcendence and immanence, in part both offered as alternatives to the perceived weaknesses of Marx's thought, tend to fall prey to the same fault. They are, at their limit, also ahistorical. In order to think about whether there may be alternative resources in Marx, we need now to examine his work more carefully: not to return to a pure, original Marx, however, but to revisit him through the lens of post-structuralism.

Back to Marx

The idea in returning to Marx through post-structuralism is not to look for what it is in Marx that has withstood post-structuralism, like a survey of damage after a storm or a search for survivors as the floodwaters recede. Such an approach would suggest that post-structuralism confronts Marx as an unrelated system of thought, when I have argued that the latter is a key influence upon the former. Hence in what follows, we shall take our lead from those areas of Marx that interest the post-structuralists: what is it in Marx – what texts, arguments, phrases, concepts – that the post-structuralists keep coming back to, and so what now catches the eye when rereading Marx? It was noted in the previous section that all four post-structuralists defend Marx's significance – but what does this defence involve? What exactly are they defending? In addressing these questions, we shall turn more specifically to the uses the post-structuralists have made of Marx, having already looked more broadly at how we can understand post-structuralism. Yet I also want to go beyond post-structuralist readings of Marx: to use those readings, and the debates they raise, as a springboard; to elaborate on them in order to reconstruct a certain Marx. In revisiting the grounds in Marx that have proved most fertile for post-structuralism, it will be important not only to draw on post-structuralist *uses* of Marx, but also on their errors and misjudgements: to develop a Marx that arises from an analysis of post-structuralist readings which is at once sympathetic and critical. Hence, not straightforwardly to ask: what have the post-structuralists done with Marx? But rather: given post-structuralist readings, what can now be done with Marx?

Philosophy and history

The first thing to note is that post-structuralism helps reveal the plurality of possibilities contained within Marx. We saw that post-structuralism draws on

Marx as an open resource, making use of parts of his legacy and ignoring or rejecting others, and that this active interpretation is a feature of post-structuralism's approach to all texts. But it can be said that it is also inspired by the specific nature of Marx's works themselves. There is no grand, monolithic system here; his ideas must be mined from a massive range of sources: published books, rough drafts, marginal commentaries, prefaces, afterwords, short summaries, manifestoes, newspaper articles, letters, revisions, critiques, plans which come to nothing or are perpetually deferred. As Lyotard has suggested, we can think of Marx's oeuvre as a body of work whose completion is continually postponed and which can never form a whole – in part for existential, psychological, and theoretical reasons, no doubt, but also because he is always changing his ideas in response to changing socio-economic conditions and political setbacks and advances. Anyone coming to this work is necessarily obliged to undertake a task of interpretation and reconstruction that will produce a new Marx rather than simply mirror an existing one or replicate a supposed original. The choices involved in this task will always be political, and hence any use of Marx is always a political one. This is true even – perhaps especially – of those readings that deny their own political status, offering themselves as purely philosophical readings that present Marx as just another philosopher whose unfortunate political pronouncements we can quietly ignore. These attempted depoliticizations are in fact deeply political: attempts to eradicate Marx's potential political impact, anaesthetizing him in the name of protecting the status quo.

Although any reading of Marx will be partial and politicized, it is possible to pretend otherwise: post-structuralism, on the other hand, explicitly affirms that its usage of Marx is political, just as it explicitly acknowledges that it offers a reconstruction rather than a duplication of Marx. This political use of Marx is not a violent imposition, but is in the spirit of his work, in which political radicalism and philosophical innovation are inseparable. It is Marx who politicizes philosophy, introducing a new notion of critical philosophy that post-structuralism will follow, situating philosophy in the political field and deflating its pretensions to autonomy and eternity by demonstrating its historical-political function, its role in social struggle. Critical philosophy after Marx is no longer inspired by a love of knowledge, attempting to distinguish Truth from Error and separate correct ideas from false ideas; it now aims to relate the genesis, development, and entrenchment of ideas to the movement and interplay of different forces and to material social conditions. In *The German Ideology* and other early pieces, Marx tends merely to oppose these two different elements: the material against the ideal, the reality of concrete actuality against the illusions of philosophical speculation. But as his work develops, the rigidity of this opposition dissolves. Far from remaining caught in the metaphysical dualisms of the Western philosophical tradition, oppositions break down and blur throughout Marx's work: between the material and the ideal, politics and philosophy, the political and the economic, nature and man, nature and history. What is left is something like a philosophy of the mixed or impure (even a philosophy of the spectral). This feature of Marx's work emerges through examination of the ways in which the post-structuralists both use and criticize Marx. On the one hand, they take up and radicalize Marx's own proto-deconstruction of the binaries of metaphysics; on the other hand, through their criticisms they bring to light the manner in which Marx is still beholden to a certain binary way of thinking, thereby allowing us to distinguish more carefully between Marx's own contribution and his continued entanglement in Western metaphysics.

Marx's reinvention of critical philosophy is intimately linked to his historiographical innovations. Part of Marx's innovation is to introduce history into philosophy, historicizing both critique and its object: neither society nor our knowledge of it are eternal. It might be argued that before Marx, Hegel had introduced history into philosophy. But Hegel conceptualizes history in a very different way. In Hegel, history has a static quality: as Althusser argues, in Hegel every historical period expresses every other. Rather than disrupting what appears eternal and essential, as happens in Marx, Hegel's history reaffirms the eternal and essential. With neither origin nor end in doubt, Hegel effectively neutralizes history. Rather than applying Hegel to political economy, Marx fundamentally alters the concept of history. Once again, this is revealed by both post-structuralist uses and criticisms of Marx, and in a different way by each post-structuralist: in Lyotard there is a vigorous attack on Marx's teleology; in Derrida there is the claim that a thinking of time and historicity distinct from any philosophy of history can be found in Marx; in Foucault, the development of a non-teleological historical methodology inspired in large part by Marx; in Deleuze, explicit use of Marx's universal history. Read in succession, these four post-structuralist analyses of Marx offer a kind of cumulative critique that gradually builds a distinctive picture of his contribution. This Marx provides a universal history as a genealogy: not the history of necessity and continuity but a history of contingencies and ruptures, in which present bourgeois society is seen to contain the key to earlier societies not because it is eternal and natural or the logical endpoint of a predictable progression, but because it is historical and impermanent, built out of the ruins of 'vanished social formations' (Marx, 1973: 105) and open to change. Sensitive to concrete events, it does not posit a predetermined End or offer a narrative of smooth and expected progress, but records the specific and heterogeneous development of social forms.

With Hegel, in contrast, all is reduced to a core essence, with singular historical events merely the phenomenal expressions of this essence. It may be thought that we find something similar in Marx, with the Economy replacing Mind as the sovereign essence governing the Whole. This, indeed, is a common charge levelled at Marx: he effaces the political by reducing it to the economic.

But we have seen that rather than maintaining hierarchical oppositions, Marx deconstructs them. In this instance, there is in Marx what Balibar calls a 'short circuit' between the political and the economic: 'the labour relation (as a relation of exploitation) is *immediately* economic *and* political' (Balibar, 1994: 138).[5] This short-circuiting is nowhere clearer than in Marx's historical account of the transition to capitalism, in particular in *Capital*'s section on primitive accumulation. In order both to establish and maintain the conditions of capitalism and to ensure its functioning, Marx notes, whole populations were 'forcibly expropriated from the soil, driven from their homes, turned into vagabonds, and then whipped, branded and tortured by grotesquely terroristic laws' introduced by successive governments (Marx, 1976a: 899). Marx's record of this governmental intervention demonstrates not that he thinks that capitalism was established as part of a grand plan, but that no clear and final distinction can be made between the political and the economic. Political change is not merely a consequence of the dissolution of old economic forms: governments themselves 'appear as conditions of the historic dissolution process and as makers of the conditions for the existence of capital' (Marx, 1973: 507).

Yet how can this be reconciled with Marx's insistence that under capitalism property 'receives its purely economic form by the stripping away of all its former political and social embellishments and admixtures' (Marx, 1981: 755)? We saw in Chapter 2 that Marx demonstrates that the dissolution of communal bonds is a necessary precondition for a capitalist system 'in which all political etc. relations are obliterated' (Marx, 1973: 503). This is why Deleuze claims that capitalism functions axiomatically, that is, directly and economically, without the need for codes, political or otherwise. But it should not be thought that there is a contradiction here: between, on the one hand, Marx's demonstration that the establishment and maintenance of capitalism is at once economic *and political*, and, on the other hand, his claim that political relations are obliterated under capitalism. In each case, it is the same process at work: the direct 'economic' functioning of capitalism, and the consequent marginalization of 'political' codes and relations, is based upon the fact that the 'economic' becomes simultaneously 'political' under capitalism – and hence that political relations of force that were once distinct from, and even dominant over, economic relations have now become absorbed into the economic, creating a situation in which the old political forms have become irrelevant and the economic and the political are entwined. This entwinement of the political and the economic occurs not only during the establishment of capitalism, but continues long after feudalism has been dissolved: the continuing extraction of surplus value under capitalism presupposes a set of conditions that require perpetual renewal and maintenance, and these conditions are, as Balibar argues, 'eminently "political"' (Balibar, 1994: 139).[6] What Balibar is here referring to is the process by which capitalism creates the workers it needs: a process that is part of a conflictual relationship made up of battles like those of the struggle over the working day. This leads to another aspect of Marx that emerges from his post-structuralist encounter: the production of subjectivity.[7]

Subjectivity and capitalism

Marx, before Nietzsche, is the inaugurator of that decentring of man to which post-structuralism owes so much. In a response to Stirner in *The German Ideology*, Marx at one point remarks sardonically that '"communism" is not at all of the opinion that "man" "needs" anything apart from a brief critical elucidation' (Marx and Engels, 1976: 208). In fact this 'brief' critical elucidation stretches not only throughout the massive bulk of *The German Ideology* but throughout Marx's work as a whole, from the sixth thesis on Feuerbach that frames 'the essence of man' as 'the ensemble of the social relations' (Marx, 1976b: 4) to the late notes on Wagner that emphasize the practical relations of social man against the theoretical relations of 'man' in general. One may, of course, find humanist elements in Marx, as one may find other idealist elements. But the post-structuralists help us to distinguish between that in Marx which he uncritically inherits and that which is genuinely new: a matter of identifying the novelty of Marx's contribution, which puts forward an approach that deals with individuals 'only in so far as they are the personifications of economic categories, the bearers of particular class-relations and interests' (Marx, 1976a: 92).

With Althusser and other structuralist-influenced approaches, this decentring of the subject often amounted to a displacement into relational terms. But the post-structuralists show that in Marx it involves more than this (just as it involves more than a polemical battle against those who depend on notions of human nature). The subject is not the empty, shifting centre of a network of social relations: the subject is not simply dissolved, it is *produced*. This is one way in which post-structuralism differs from structuralism: in its attitude to the subject, developing a focus on the various pre-individual drives and forces from which subjectivity is derived and formed. In this sense post-structuralism brings something new to Marx; this can be seen in Lyotard and Deleuze's analysis of capitalism in terms of desire, for example. But this shift beyond structuralism also takes something more directly from Marx, and that is an examination of the processes whereby subjects are created. Marx's anti-humanism is not simply a negative movement in which Man is erased, nor simply a critique of other theoretical positions: it recounts the actual material processes through which individuals are constituted. The 'individual' is not merely an abstraction, the invention of liberal ideology, or the product or precondition of the exchange process. The individual is created through a series of minute but concrete operations: forming, training, and disciplining workers until they fit into the production process as cogs into a machine.[8]

This construction of the individuals that capitalism requires depends upon the dissolution of distinctions between the economic and the political that we have already observed. This is made clear by Foucault, who of all the post-structuralists most obviously draws on Marx's detailed recreation of the processes of individualization. Echoing Balibar, Read argues that Foucault's notion of bio-power 'is constituted at the point at which political power becomes inseparable from economic power. Biopolitics, like Marx's critique of political economy, short-circuits the division between the economic and the political' (Read, 2003: 141).

These different elements of Marx's work – his politicization of philosophy and reconceptualization of history and subjectivity – are of course united by his analysis of capitalism. At least from 1844 onwards, a critique of capitalism is the centre and focus of Marx's work: the target of his politicized philosophy is capitalism, his histories recount the emergence and development of capitalism as a specific social form, and he details the production of subject positions within the capitalist production process. We should not assume that the post-structuralists seek to play down this Marx – the critic of capitalism – as if he were a dated and slightly embarrassing relic who can be pushed aside in order to get at what is still useful and relevant. On the contrary, all four call upon this Marx. This may seem obvious – for what else is Marx but a critic of capitalism? But there are other things to be taken from Marx: it is possible to smother or ignore Marx's contribution here. Everyone, as Derrida has highlighted, is in some way an heir to Marx – but not everyone is a critic of capitalism. It was not inevitable or necessary that the post-structuralists draw on this aspect of Marx, and it is significant that they do.

After his break from Marxism, Lyotard clearly tries to distance himself somewhat from Marx, yet he continues to borrow Marx's insights into capitalism (though not always with acknowledgement). *Libidinal Economy* adapts these insights, reworking them in non-dialectical and anti-idealist terms, while continuing to rely on Marx's account of the rhythm and energy of capitalism. While this Marx-inspired analysis becomes fainter in Lyotard's later work, it is still as a critic of capitalism that Lyotard calls on Marx: in *The Differend* it is as a voice against the capitalist social order and its attempts to stifle differends that Marx is held to be valuable. Derrida offers no analysis of capitalism comparable to that found in *Libidinal Economy* – or even *The Differend* – yet he too calls on this Marx: for help in analysing contemporary relations between states, markets, law, and capital; in combating the 'ten plagues' of the new world order; and in countering the 'euphoria of liberal-democrat capitalism' (Derrida, 1994: 80). While Derrida does not produce his own analyses of contemporary capitalist relations (and thereby use Marx in this way), it is clear that he values Marx's contribution here: indeed, in *Specters of Marx* it is only really in his praise of Marx as a critic of capitalism that Derrida breaks away from his usual (and somewhat predictable) terrain and seems to be enlivened by Marx, doing something else with him other than passing him through the familiar machinery of deconstruction. Foucault's somewhat mischievous attitude towards Marx means that he does not often say what it is that he admires in Marx's work. He does however explicitly cite Marx's contribution as an innovative historian: yet what draws Foucault to Marx is not only the latter's historical methodology, but also the object of that methodology – namely, the genesis, development, and functioning of capitalism. In detailing the links between the organization of men and the accumulation of capital, between the development of disciplinary power and the rise of a capitalist economy, Foucault's work (especially *Discipline and Punish*) can at times seem like an addendum to *Capital*. Finally, this particular use of Marx is most conspicuous in Deleuze, who states explicitly and repeatedly that he takes from Marx his specific conceptualization of capitalism as the meeting of free money and free labour in an axiomatic system. Hence the Marx that emerges from post-structuralism is not some sort of 'postmodern' Marx, relieved of his obsessive interest in capitalism and so now fit to join in the conversations at Richard Rorty's liberal dinner parties. On the contrary, the post-structuralists strongly oppose this kind of dilution of Marx – and they oppose it not only by explicitly rejecting the academic or liberal anaesthetization of Marx, but also by actively drawing on his work on capitalism.

Materialist philosophy

I have argued that one thing that unites Marx and all four post-structuralists is a desire to pursue a materialist philosophy. Having examined the kind of Marx who emerges from post-structuralism, and developed a firmer definition of post-structuralism itself, we are now in a better position to put forward a definition of materialism. In Chapter 1, we sought to distinguish materialism from idealism, which was defined in terms of onto-teleology: the Origin of history is simultaneously posited as its End; the goal and meaning of history is therefore to recover this lost origin. It was claimed that materialism cannot simply be the opposite of idealism, for such a materialism would in effect remain idealist. One can replace Mind with Matter, but in doing so one has not escaped the framework of idealism. 'There is no very great difference between false materialism and typical forms of idealism' (Deleuze and Guattari, 1977: 22). Such an idealist materialism certainly exists in Marx's work, with the role of the lost origin taking on various forms: the essence of human nature, pure use-value, unalienated labour, the simplicity and transparency of non-capitalist social relations, the unity and harmony of man and nature, the immediacy of concrete material actuality. But at the same time, Marx recognizes that a productive materialism must be more than the opposite of idealism: there is a need for a new materialism that escapes the idealist-materialist dichotomy that has persisted throughout Western philosophy. By outlining a post-structuralist Marx, we have simultaneously been sketching the contours of this new materialism. What are its features?

Defining materialism

We have identified at least three features. First, it revolutionizes philosophy: no longer simply a reflection on truth, philosophy now directly intervenes into political struggles, and does not depend on a central unifying term or on abstract oppositions. Materialism is not a philosophical reflection on matter, but a political intervention aware of its own material conditions and potential consequences. Second, it recognizes the contingency, complexity, and importance of history – not as a smooth development but in terms of ruptures and breaks and without offering an endpoint to which we are heading. Third, it decentres the subject and dethrones the sovereignty of consciousness, instead detailing the production of different forms of subjectivity. If we are to take seriously the first of these claims – namely that materialist philosophy must be a form of political intervention – then these three aspects cannot merely be suggestions that alter the way we can study philosophy, history, or subjectivity. Instead, they must be closer to something like practical imperatives. They can thus be reformulated in the following way. First, materialist philosophy must be critical: it cannot simply offer a picture of a situation and leave it at that, but must be able to challenge the status quo and offer the possibility of social change. Second, it must be historical: it must examine the genesis, development, and specificity of a situation in contrast to other historical periods. Finally, it must focus on existing social relations, and not on the 'essential' properties of pregiven entities or on 'ideal' relations (either through nostalgia for a lost past or in expectation of a certain future).

Using this outline of materialist philosophy – as critical, historical, and focused on existing social relations – it is possible to re-evaluate the work of the four post-structuralists. First, some post-structuralist work seems to abandon a critical standpoint. This is especially true of Lyotard's *Libidinal Economy* and much of Foucault's work: their refusal of teleology in places begins to look like indifference towards the future or resignation in the face of the immutability of our present situation. Second, some post-structuralist work also lacks historical perspective. The analyses of capitalism provided by Lyotard and Deleuze are provocative and insightful, yet there is little of the kind of concrete historical detail provided by Marx (or, for that matter, by Foucault), and there is a tendency to slip into a philosophical abstraction productive of ahistorical concepts. This lack of historical perspective can also apply to the ways in which Marx is read: when Derrida reads Marx's work, for example, he does little to place that work in its historical context, instead simply assimilating it to the tradition of Western metaphysics that Derrida deconstructs. Finally, some post-structuralist work fails to focus on existing social relations. Of all the post-structuralists, it would seem to be Foucault who most obviously fulfils this requirement. Yet Foucault's focus is almost always historical: his genealogies help us understand how we reached the present, but rarely examine present configurations in any detail. Moreover, as we saw in Chapter 4, there is a risk in Foucault's work that he slides away from analysis of social relations to postulation of notions like 'bodies' and 'life'. In Deleuze this risk is even more pronounced, for Deleuze explicitly embraces the vitalism that Foucault approaches. Equally, the concept of the event used by Lyotard and Derrida becomes abstracted from existing social relations. In its attempts to develop a materialist philosophy, post-structuralism risks repeating the ahistoricism and abstraction of idealism.

In making these criticisms, we are not singling out post-structuralism for criticism while we leave Marx untouched – for we have already seen Marx subjected to a series of wide-ranging criticisms. Far from being immune to the charge of relapsing into idealism, this accusation forms the basis of the post-structuralist critique of Marx. Nor are we using Marx as a yardstick with which to judge post-structuralism – for the materialist philosophy that we are referring to has been developed through analysis of the work of the post-structuralists themselves. We are seeing if they live up to their own standards, not those of Marx. Nor are we repeating the pseudo-Marxist criticisms of Habermas and his like. The problem is not that the post-structuralists cannot ground their critical perspectives. In fact we might even say that they face problems precisely *because* they continue to try to ground their critical perspectives: it is this continued effort that leads them to rely on notions like the event and Life. The challenge of materialist philosophy – particularly well illuminated by looking at post-structuralist readings of Marx – is how to pursue critique without ontology or teleology: how critique continues if it is not made in the name of something lost or something to come (or both). The Habermasians in effect deal with this challenge by pretending that it does not exist, and thus continuing to make the same old demands. But as Paul Veyne argues – in a discussion of Foucault – the desire for foundations does not prove that such foundations exist. To the objection that 'Foucault cannot found norms', Veyne replies simply: 'nor could anyone else'. He continues:

> For Foucault the worry about finding foundations was specific to the 'anthropological age': it was from Kant to Husserl that attempts were made to found, to get back to the unquestionable *arche*; to get beyond the anthropological age is to abandon the project of foundation in favour of something else. (Veyne, 1992: 342–3)

To move beyond the idealism of 'the anthropological age' is to abandon the attempt to found norms and face with maturity and care the challenge of doing without absolute normative foundations. Yet if the challenge of materialism cannot be evaded by pretending that it does not exist, then nor can it be evaded by playing down its significance. Veyne is quite correct to argue that our age is no longer anthropological, but he is perhaps a little too relaxed about the consequences of this change. As we have seen, if we are not careful then abandoning foundations can lead to an abandonment of critical thought, or the reappearance of idealism by other means. To avoid this happening, I suggest we take our lead from Marx.

Class struggle

We turn to Marx again not in search of a solid unshakeable ground on which critique can rest: we need not call for a re-ontologized Marx. If we look in Marx for a reformulated materialism then it is a Marx re-read through post-structuralism. At the same time, however, we can find in Marx conceptual resources that exceed those of post-structuralism. Marx's way of securing critique is to root philosophy in active social struggles. This is how we can understand the epigraph to this chapter. There are numerous ways to interpret this famous but somewhat enigmatic remark. Taken from *The German Ideology*, the surrounding paragraphs are still infused with idealism. But by identifying communism as a real movement rather than an ideal aim, Marx points the way to a genuinely materialist position, where philosophy is about practical intervention rather than theoretical application, negotiating a path between the immanent potential of the present and the unpredictability of the future. It does not offer a list of principles or criteria by which to measure and judge the present state of things, but actively engages with and emerges out of existing struggles.

For Marx, of course, these are *class* struggles. Marx's emphasis on class is not something that needs to be elided when he is read through post-structuralism. This does not mean that it can straightforwardly be taken from Marx – but, then, as Derrida has argued, no inheritance is ever straightforward. The post-structuralists themselves are by no means implacably opposed to the use of class. On the contrary, it is a concept that they robustly defend. Nevertheless, they are at the same time clearly a little suspicious of it. A remark by Foucault hints at the complex ambiguities of the post-structuralist position. Asked about social class in an interview, he responded: 'Ah, here we are at the centre of the problem, and no doubt also of the obscurities of my own discourse' (Foucault, 1980: 203). This comment itself is a little obscure, but it is clear that Foucault has no desire to do away with class: he frequently makes use of the concept in *Discipline and Punish* and elsewhere. In places he is even more explicit: 'I label political everything that has to do with class struggle, and social everything that derives from and is a consequence of the class struggle' (Foucault, 1996: 104). The simplicity of this statement (taken from an interview) should not obscure the complexities of Foucault's attitude, but it does show that Foucault was not scared of using 'class' and 'class struggle'. Similarly, Derrida is vociferous in berating a critic who accuses him of 'a refusal of class politics'; the accusation inspires a response of rare clarity and force: 'If I had wanted to say that I believed there were no more social classes and that all struggle over this subject was passé, I would have' (Derrida, 1999b: 236).[9] He goes on to claim: 'I took and take very seriously the existence of some "thing" like that which one calls, since Marx, social classes' – even if '[w]hat seemed especially problematic to me . . . was the insufficiently "differentiated" nature of the concept of social class as it had been "inherited"' (237). Likewise, Deleuze does not do away with class, but tries to reformulate and reposition the concept: in *Anti-Oedipus* using it as a figure for the decoding of capitalism – 'All history can . . . be read under the sign of classes' (Deleuze and Guattari, 1977: 153) – and in *A Thousand Plateaus* distinguishing between classes as molar segments and masses as molecular flows – 'The bourgeoisie considered as a mass *and* as a class . . .' (Deleuze and Guattari, 1988: 221). Even Lyotard does not abandon class. While he rejects the idea of the working class as the universal subject, it is nevertheless where Marx speaks of class that Lyotard claims that Marxism has not come to an end: as testament to the conflict between labourer and capitalist.

What the post-structuralists object to is not the concept of class as such, but Hegelian-inspired, idealist uses of it. Such uses can certainly be found in Marx, who often presents the proletariat as the universal class, whose triumph will return humankind to a lost Eden: class as both an ontological category, referring to a kind of fixed essence, and a teleological category, with the proletariat identified by its destiny, its role in demanding and securing the goal of communism. Hence in *The Holy Family* Marx argues that it is not important what the proletariat 'at the moment *regards* as its aim. It is a question of *what the proletariat is*, and what, in accordance with this *being*, it will historically be compelled to do' (Marx and Engels, 1975: 37). But there is another possibility in Marx, another way of looking at class which can address post-structuralist criticisms – yet perhaps also disclose Marx's advantages over post-structuralism. For although the post-structuralists do not reject the concept of class, it remains – to borrow Foucault's phrase – an obscure point in their work.

Class need not be an ontological given or a teleological destiny; in a sense, it is not even a fixed object of study at all. It instead points to a set of relations, a series of variable determinations: 'a system of relations structured by struggle', as Bensaïd (2002: 99) puts it. Bensaïd argues that Marx 'does not "define" *a* class; he apprehends relations of conflict between classes. He does not photograph a social fact labelled "class"; he has his sights set on the class relation in its conflictual dynamic' (Bensaïd, 2002: 111). It is in this way that Marx's claim that history is the history of class struggles should be understood: in 'class struggle' it is *struggle* and not class which is primary (Read, 2003: 154). There do not exist a priori, fixed entities called classes which then enter into a struggle with each other; there is a conflictual relation within which different class positions are determined. 'Marx', argues Balibar, 'paradoxically thought that the existence and the very identity of classes is the tendential effect of their struggle' (Balibar, 1994: 138). It is in this sense that Balibar writes of 'class struggle without class': class struggle here is 'a *process of transformation without pre-established end*, in other words an endless transformation of the identity of social classes' (Balibar, 1991: 168). To show that Marx does not hold a simplistic view of class, commentators are fond of pointing to *The Eighteenth Brumaire*, with its plurality of different classes and their various interactions. But the complexity of Marx's conceptualization of class lies not merely in an accretionary proliferation in the number of classes, creating an ever-enlarged taxonomy of social categories. Rather, it lies in treating classes as relations rather than things: this is a de-ontologized and non-teleological conception of class. This approach is not limited to Marx's 'political' texts like *The Eighteenth Brumaire*, but is central to *Capital* and Marx's critique of political economy. Thinking of class in this way is not at all a form of economic reductionism. On the contrary, it undoes economic reductionism: as I have argued, these struggles – to which Marx devotes the bulk of *Capital* – are both economic *and* political (and neither purely economic nor purely political). This concept of class – which I think all four post-structuralists would accept – fits well with the outline of materialism that we have developed. Beginning from class struggles allows one to take a critical position without reference to ideal norms. In addition, class is a historical concept: classes change over time and can only be understood with reference to their historical formation and development. Finally, classes allow us to trace the production of subjectivity within a network of social relations.

Conclusion

These brief remarks that I have ended with are not meant to offer a definitive account of the issue of class. I have discussed it here to show how Marx can be read through post-structuralism: with post-structuralist criticisms and insights helping to highlight a certain Marx – for whom class is not an onto-teleological concept – and with Marx counterbalancing the shortcomings of post-structuralism – developing the rigorous analysis of class that the post-structuralists recognize is vital but which they do not provide themselves. All this is achieved not through simple comparison of Marx and post-structuralism, but by looking at how the latter have read the former. Nor is the outline of materialist philosophy that I have traced supposed to be exhaustive. The very nature of materialist philosophy as conceptualized here means that it is impossible to do much more than sketch its outline: any definition will always be insufficient. Unlike idealism, which applies a pre-established schema to the world, materialism must deal with concrete situations – and it is in pursuing concrete analysis that it defines itself. It cannot determine its content in advance. There are no ready-made formulas; there is always work to be done.

Notes

Introduction

1. It is a version of the latter approach that I examine in the final section of Chapter 1. The former approach is most frequently articulated with respect to one particular thinker: for example, Barry Smart's (1983) claim that Foucault's work can be seen as a remedy for the deleterious faults of a Marxism in crisis. Where appropriate I have listed relevant texts that deal with the relation between Marx and post-structuralism.
2. Stuart Sim (2000), for example, discusses all four thinkers in relation to post-Marxism. Extracts from Lyotard's *Libidinal Economy* and Derrida's *Specters of Marx* are provided in Sim's (1998) post-Marxist reader.
3. The connections between post-structuralism and the work of Laclau and Mouffe – or, more specifically, 'the *possibilities* that post-structuralism opens up to think and deepen the project of a radical democracy' – are discussed in more detail in Laclau (1990: 191–4).
4. In a 1988 interview, Laclau admits that in *Hegemony and Socialist Strategy* 'we have dealt with Marx's work only marginally'. Strangely, he goes on to imply that because they dealt with the history of Marxism, starting with the Second International, there was little need to investigate Marx further: 'it would doubtless be wrong to assume that Plekhanov or Kautsky, who devoted a considerable part of their lives to the study of Marx's work – and who were certainly not hacks – have simply misread Marx' (Laclau, 1990: 181–2).
5. Kellner's critique of Baudrillard may in part have been provoked by Arthur Kroker, who had earlier claimed that Baudrillard 'has managed to radicalise *Capital*, and to make Marx dangerous once more' (Kroker, 1985: 77). In contrast, Kellner argues that 'while Baudrillard provides a strong polemic against reductionist, naturalistic and economistic readings of Marx, his broadside attack and dismissal of Marxism *tout court* is unfair and unwarranted', and he 'sets up something of a straw-man Marx' (Kellner, 1989: 53, 35). Kellner concludes that '[i]n political terms . . . Baudrillard's project comes down to . . . capitulation to the hegemony of the Right and a secret complicity with aristocratic conservatism' (Kellner, 1989: 215). This verdict is typical of judgements on Baudrillard, especially from Marxists. (As I shall show in the last section of Chapter 1, it is not untypical of Marxist judgements on Lyotard, Derrida, Foucault, and Deleuze.) It has since been challenged, however. Mike Gane (1991) has explicitly rejected Kellner's reading of Baudrillard, instead situating Baudrillard's work in both the Marxist and Durkheimian traditions. (The influence of Durkheim, widely

acknowledged since Gane, further distances Baudrillard from the other four post-structuralists, for Durkheim is not a major reference point for them.) Gane does not provide a full account of the relation between Marx and Baudrillard, however; such an account is still to be written. It would be a difficult task: Kellner is certainly correct when he states that 'Baudrillard's relation to Marx is extremely complex and volatile' (Kellner, 1989: 33).

6 An analysis of post-structuralist readings of Hegel would certainly be a fascinating, if formidable, project to pursue. The last two chapters of Bruce Baugh's (2003) book on French receptions of Hegel offer some guide as to what such a project might look like – though like me, Baugh declares that he is not 'concerned with the truth or accuracy of French interpretations of Hegel' (Baugh, 2003: 6).

Chapter 1

1 A more comprehensive survey of this period than I can offer here is given by Poster (1975). Tiersky (1974) looks at the political background, including the role of the French Communist Party.
2 Glucksmann (1980) and Levy (1977) are representative texts of this new fashion. A useful exploration of the *nouveaux philosophes* and their place in the French intellectual scene is found in Christofferson (2004).
3 As usual, things are more complicated than simple classifications allow. Lévi-Strauss had dedicated *The Savage Mind* to the memory of Merleau-Ponty: clearly he was not unremittingly hostile to his work. Foucault has suggested that 'Merleau-Ponty's encounter with language' marks a 'critical point' in the 'movement from phenomenology toward structuralism', and tells of Merleau-Ponty discussing Saussure before he was well known in France (Foucault, 1998: 436). Nonetheless, despite the subtleties of their respective positions, there are clear differences between Sartre and Merleau-Ponty on the one hand and those who can be termed structuralists and post-structuralists on the other. As Foucault notes elsewhere, Merleau-Ponty can be grouped with Sartre as a philosopher of the subject (Foucault, 1998: 466). Lévi-Strauss's dedication represents homage to a past master rather than solidarity with a contemporary ally.
4 Of all the post-structuralists, in fact, it was Deleuze who offered the most systematic commentary on structuralism. In 'How Do We Recognize Structuralism?', an essay written in 1967 but not published until 1972, Deleuze discusses a number of 'structuralist' thinkers, each of whom 'discovers problems, methods, solutions that are analogically related, as if sharing in a free atmosphere or spirit of the time, but one that distributes itself into singular creations and discoveries' in different domains of thought (Deleuze, 2004: 170). The thinkers discussed include Lévi-Strauss, Jakobson, Barthes, Althusser, and Foucault. In an extremely dense and subtle analysis, Deleuze emphasizes the importance of structuralism's focus on differential relations, its anti-essentialist thinking of structures, and its dissipation of the subject.
5 Alan Schrift (1995: 3) suggests that 'if one wishes to distinguish what – in the English-speaking world – is called "poststructuralism" from its structural and

existential predecessors, perhaps the most obvious way to do so is precisely in terms of the appearance of Nietzsche as an important reference for virtually all those writers who would be characterized as "poststructuralist"'. While acknowledging other influences, Schrift argues that it was through Nietzsche that post-structuralism reintroduced discussion of subjectivity and history, themes neglected by structuralism. Although I agree that the influence of Nietzsche is crucial, I want to show that it is also through Marx that these themes are reintroduced.

6 Like Derrida, Foucault recognizes the difficulty of this escape: 'to make a real escape from Hegel presupposes an exact appreciation of what it costs to detach ourselves from him. It presupposes a knowledge of how close Hegel has come to us, perhaps insidiously. It presupposes a knowledge of what is still Hegelian in that which allows us to think against Hegel' (Foucault, 1981: 74).

7 This definition of philosophy is only explicitly formulated by Althusser after *For Marx* and *Reading Capital*. See in particular the interview titled 'Philosophy as a Revolutionary Weapon' in Althusser (1971).

8 It should be noted that not all the claims made in this autobiography should be taken at a purely literal level: many of them are demonstrably false. Elliott is not the only reader to suggest that *The Future Lasts a Long Time* itself requires a symptomatic reading (Elliott, 2006: 324; cf. Montag, 2003).

9 Althusser's early writings on Hegel are collected in Althusser (1997). Even as late as 1984 he was writing of a Hegel 'who remains, after all, the fundamental reference for everyone, since he is himself such a "continent" that it takes practically a whole lifetime to come to know him well' (Althusser, 2006: 229).

10 In a critique of idealism that has many similarities with that of Althusser, Laclau and Mouffe point out that 'the most determinist tendencies within Marxism are also the most idealist, since they have to base their analyses and predictions on inexorable laws which are not immediately legible in the surface of historical life; they must base themselves on the internal logic of a closed conceptual model and transform that model into the (conceptual) essence of the real' (Laclau and Mouffe, 1987: 88). For Laclau and Mouffe, '[t]here is in [Marx's] work the beginning, but only the beginning, of a movement in the direction of materialism' (Laclau and Mouffe, 1987: 90). Writing in 1987, Laclau and Mouffe would not have been influenced by Althusser's late works, but Laclau has claimed that 'a good deal of my later works can be seen as a radicalization of many themes already hinted at in *For Marx*' (Laclau, 1990: 178). They are not uncritical of Althusser, however. In a critique which anticipates Derrida's comments on the same subject, in *Hegemony and Socialist Strategy* the authors claim that the radical potential of Althusser's concept of overdetermination is compromised by the concomitant concept of 'determination in the last instance by the economy' (Laclau and Mouffe, 2001: 97–9).

11 Marx writes that in the fetishism of commodities, '[t]o the producers . . . the social relations between their private labours appear *as what they are*, i.e. they do not appear as direct social relations between persons in their work, but rather as material relations between persons and social relations between things' (Marx, 1976a: 165–6; my emphasis). We are not dealing with illusions, nor even simply necessary appearances, but with necessary behaviour.

[12] For all its faults, Anderson (1998) offers a good history of the term 'postmodern', as does Bertens (1995).

[13] Jencks (1977) and Venturi et al. (1972) offer perhaps the most significant discussions of this form of architecture.

[14] Rorty uses the phrase 'postmodernist bourgeois liberalism' in a number of places; it is the title of an essay in Rorty (1991b). While sometimes sympathetic to Marx, he has more often spoken of 'dumping Marx' (cf. Rorty, 1982: 207). Even when sympathetic, Marx is presented as little more than a 'fellow citizen', like Mill or Dewey 'engaged in a shared, social effort – the effort to make our institutions and practices more just and less cruel' (Rorty, 1989: xiv). Rorty has said elsewhere of the relationship between Marx and twentieth-century Continental philosophy: 'I think that to get caught up on Adorno and Marcuse one has to take Marx more seriously than he has been taken in America. Derrida, Foucault, and Heidegger don't ask you to take Marx all that seriously' (Rorty, 2006: 39). I aim to show that, with respect to Derrida and Foucault at least, Rorty is wrong.

[15] For examples of individual readings, see Jameson's review of Derrida's *Specters of Marx* (Jameson, 1999), or his essay on Deleuze (Jameson, 1997); he also provides the foreword to Lyotard (1984b).

[16] Even Habermas, seeking to explain why Foucault took up Nietzsche's theory of power, claims that Foucault 'experienced *sudden* disappointment with a political engagement' and 'joined the choir of disappointed Maoists of 1968' (Habermas, 1987: 257).

[17] The 'debates' between Habermas and both Derrida and Foucault have inspired a lot of commentary, even though they are somewhat one-sided. Derrida offered no extended response to Habermas's accusations, though three years after the publication of Habermas's book he commented: 'Those who accuse me of reducing philosophy to literature or logic to rhetoric (see, for example, the latest book by Habermas, *The Philosophical Discourse of Modernity*) have visibly and carefully avoided reading me' (Derrida, 1995c: 218). Towards the end of Derrida's life the relationship became more amicable and productive (even collaborative): it is explored in Thomassen (2006), which contains articles by both men and by other commentators. The equivalent volume with respect to Foucault is Kelly (1994); see also Ashenden and Owen (1999). Foucault died before the publication of *The Philosophical Discourse of Modernity*, but some comments from a 1984 interview suggest an interesting and potentially fruitful debate could have taken place. Foucault says: 'I am quite interested in [Habermas's] work, although I know he completely disagrees with my views. While I, for my part, tend to be a little more in agreement with what he says, I have always had a problem insofar as he gives communicative relations this place which is so important and, above all, a function that I would call "utopian"' (Foucault, 1997: 298).

[18] Lyotard is mentioned at the very start of *The Philosophical Discourse of Modernity* (Habermas, 1987: xix), but Habermas does not provide any detailed treatment of his work. Lyotard has been more willing to comment on Habermas but, certain sarcastic jibes aside, his criticisms of Habermas are often implicit (Jameson calls *The Postmodern Condition* 'a thinly veiled polemic' against Habermas [Jameson, 1984: vii]). For a discussion of the debate, see Steuerman (1992); also

Rorty's essay on the two in Rorty (1991a). Habermas has in passing linked Deleuze to the kind of *Lebensphilosophie* and general metaphysical obscurantism of which he accuses Foucault (Habermas, 1992: 212). Deleuze has said little on Habermas, and there is (as yet) almost no secondary literature on the relation between the two.

[19] By this Foucault is referring to the idea that 'one has to be "for" or "against" the Enlightenment'. For Foucault, 'one must refuse everything that might present itself in the form of a simplistic and authoritarian alternative: you either accept the Enlightenment and remain within the tradition of its rationalism (this is considered a positive term by some and used by others, on the contrary, as a reproach), or else you criticize the Enlightenment and then try to escape from its principles of rationality (which may be seen once again as good or bad). And we do not break free of this blackmail by introducing "dialectical" nuances while seeking to determine what good and bad elements there may have been in the Enlightenment' (Foucault, 1997: 313).

[20] The 'non-bullshit' Marxism of G. A. Cohen, with its defence of 'those standards of clarity and rigour which distinguish twentieth-century analytical philosophy' (Cohen, 2000: *xxv*, *ix*) gives forceful (if crude and unconvincing) expression to this tendency, though these sentiments are not limited to so-called analytical Marxists: one does not have to be an analytical philosopher to join Cohen in lamenting that 'logical positivism . . . never caught on in Paris' (Cohen, 2000: *x*).

[21] Though each of the post-structuralists is criticized, there is a noticeable, though informal, hierarchical ranking of the four thinkers: Derrida and Foucault are occasionally afforded praise (in particular, Norris greatly admires Derrida), but such praise is very rarely given to Deleuze (who is rarely mentioned at all) and almost never to Lyotard (usually dismissed alongside Baudrillard as what Callinicos calls 'the *epigone* of poststructuralism' [Callinicos, 1989: 5]).

Chapter 2

[1] While there are some useful commentaries on Lyotard – see, for example, Bennington (1988) and Readings (1991) – there is no good study of the relation between Lyotard and Marx: both Lyotard's defenders and detractors accept his repudiation of Marxism at face value, and thus tend to ignore his comments on Marx. In contrast, one of my claims in this chapter is that Marx remained vital to Lyotard's thought: the latter only developed a distinctive philosophical stance in an intense and ambivalent struggle with Marx, who was never fully discarded.

[2] See, for example, his essay 'The Name of Algeria' in Lyotard (1993c).

[3] These themes are especially prominent in the essay 'The State and Politics in the France of 1960', available in Lyotard (1993c).

[4] This rejection of critique is anticipated in Lyotard's 1972 essay on *Anti-Oedipus*: 'Just as atheism is religion extended into its negative form . . . so does the critique make itself the object of its object and settle down into the field of the other, accepting the latter's dimensions, directions and space at the very moment that

it contests them' (Lyotard, 1977: 11). In this essay, Lyotard links this stance to Marx's objections to the still religious critique of religion offered by Feuerbach.

5   Lyotard is thinking not only of *Anti-Oedipus* here, but also of Baudrillard, who in *The Mirror of Production* (published a year before *Libidinal Economy*) had rejected the Marxist faith in a revolutionary working class in favour of a celebration of 'the radicality of desire' (Baudrillard, 1975: 155) and the subversive potential of marginal groups. For Lyotard (1993b: 108, 135), Baudrillard's '*subversive reference*, that of the good savage and the good hippy' risks replicating Marx's metaphysics: 'the constitution of a theatricality through exteriorization (of the peasant, of Robinson, of the socialist worker, of the marginal), critique made possible by the position of an uncritiqued'. The danger is that desire becomes assimilated to a notion of 'a *good rebel nature*, of a nature good insofar as it is rebellious, insofar therefore as it is left outside, *forgotten*, foreclosed' (Lyotard, 1993b: 107). Lyotard does not simply reject Baudrillard's work, however: 'We are', he says, 'very close and very far . . . from what Baudrillard is doing' (104). This statement of partial affiliation is unsurprising, given that Baudrillard's views on Marx are in places very similar to those of Lyotard, and of post-structuralism more generally. Baudrillard argues that Marx's 'denaturalization' of the categories of classical political economy left in place certain unquestioned naturalist assumptions, his critique ultimately reliant on a 'seething metaphysic of needs and use-values' (Baudrillard, 1981: 135). For Baudrillard, '[i]t is here that Marxian idealism goes to work' (130–1). Like Lyotard, Baudrillard rejects the ontological prioritization of use-value, arguing that '[u]se value and needs are only an effect of exchange value' (137). Marxism for Baudrillard remains tied to a humanist schema, trapped between Hegelian eschatology and the anthropologism of political economy, perpetuating 'the *idea* of man *producing* himself in his infinite determination, and continually surpassing himself toward his own end' (Baudrillard, 1975: 33).

6   The full claim made by Lyotard is, in fact: 'The "disappearance" of the organic body is the accusation, in sum, made by Marx and Baudrillard (but this goes further, in both senses), by which the *dispositif* of capital stands condemned' (Lyotard, 1993b: 139). But I am concerned here with Marx, not Baudrillard.

7   To this extent, Habermasian accusations of post-structuralism's 'cryptonormativity' are legitimate. However, unlike the Habermasians, I do not want to insist that the post-structuralists make their normative positions clearer. Rather, I shall argue later that a materialist philosophy – such as both Marx and the post-structuralists wish to achieve – is better pursued by abandoning the search for normative foundations and instead beginning from existing struggles.

8   Adorno remains important to *The Differend*, though for Lyotard it is not simply Auschwitz that signals the end of speculative dialectics: there are many 'names' other than Auschwitz – though this particular name holds a unique place and Lyotard dedicates an extended discussion to it in *The Differend* – and these names signal the bankruptcy of metanarratives in general.

9   Hence one cannot expect that the famous unfinished chapter at the end of the third volume of *Capital*, with its unanswered question 'What makes a class?' (Marx, 1981: 1025), would have furnished such a definition, as if the lack of this definition stands as an enigmatic or frustrating lacuna in Marx's work.

10 In *Libidinal Economy* Lyotard had cited this passage from Marx as an example of 'his thoroughly religious love for a lost consubstantiality of men amongst themselves and nature', 'weaving the absolutely Christian scenario of the martyr of the proletariat as the sacrificial episode necessary to the final salvation' (Lyotard, 1993*b*: 107–8).
11 Lyotard recognizes that he may be committing this particular performative contradiction (as Habermas would call it), asking: 'Are "we" not telling, whether bitterly or gladly, the great narrative of the end of great narratives?' (Lyotard, 1988*a*: 135). He does not answer this question directly: in part, this is because rather than trying to overcome such paradoxes, Lyotard enjoys playing with them (compare his 'laughter' when faced with the possibility of issuing a universal prescription forbidding universal prescriptions in Lyotard and Thébaud [1985: 100]). But it is also because in *The Differend* (in contrast to *The Postmodern Condition*) the bankruptcy of grand narratives and the heterogeneity of genres is not established by some overarching metadiscourse, but is validated by signs which evoke a feeling of sorrow 'that can reach the level of the sublime and attest to the heterogeneity between Ideas and realities' (Lyotard, 1988*a*: 180).
12 These themes are developed in particular in Lyotard (1991*a*: especially the Introduction) and Lyotard (1997: especially chapters 5 and 6). Lyotard distinguishes 'development' from progress: 'It seems to proceed of its own accord, with a force, an autonomous motoricity that is independent of ourselves' (Lyotard, 1992: 92). It is not directed by human beings, driven to pursue the true or the good; rather, '[t]he human race is, so to speak, "pulled forward" by this process without possessing the slightest capacity for mastering it' (Lyotard, 1991*a*: 64). Humanity is a subsystem of the system, driven by it, its vehicle and not its author. This is Lyotard's anti-humanism pushed to its extremes.

Chapter 3

1 The book was followed in 1999 by an essay called 'Marx & Sons', in which Derrida further clarifies his ideas by responding directly to some of his critics. Here he also alludes to the 'longstanding demand' to write about Marx (Derrida, 1999*b*: 213). It is the final essay in Sprinker (1999), which contains a number of responses to *Specters of Marx*. Of these responses, perspicacious comments are offered in the essays by Negri, Macherey, Jameson, Montag, and Hamacher (though in rather oblique fashion from the last). Unfortunately, the essays by Marxist critics – Eagleton, Ahmad, and Lewis – are much weaker, and often seem to be little more than crude attempts to score points against postmodernism/post-structuralism rather than considered attempts to deal with any of the issues raised by the book. More measured and perceptive assessments are offered elsewhere by Laclau (1995) and Callinicos (1996), the latter from a Marxist perspective. Because he had said so little on the subject prior to *Specters of Marx*, the literature on Derrida and Marx focuses on this book. An exception is the early study by Ryan (1982). Even after the publication of *Specters of Marx*, commentators explicitly addressing Derrida's contribution to political

philosophy apparently felt little need to mention Marx other than in passing (cf. Beardsworth, 1996).
2. These themes overlap and recur throughout Derrida's later work, including and especially in *Specters of Marx*. They are dealt with at greater length in the following places: hospitality in Derrida (1997b, 1999a, 2000, 2001) and the essay 'Hospitality' in Derrida (2002a: 358–420); responsibility in Derrida (1995a); duty in the essay 'Passions: An Oblique Offering' in Derrida (1995b) and in Derrida (1992b, 1993); the gift in Derrida (1992a); and the promise in Derrida (1986) (especially the third lecture).
3. One reviewer has proposed that Derrida's interview 'is seriously marred by the embarrassing ease with which historical hindsight masquerades as political prescience, and eventually becomes yet another apologia for deconstructionism' (Macey, 1994: 47).
4. Throughout the discussion that follows, 'spectre' and ghost' can be taken as synonymous – though, as I shall show, they need to be distinguished from 'spirit'.
5. Notwithstanding Derrida's argument, it is clear that it is *also* a habit of writing for Marx. In 1837 Marx finished a letter to his father in this way: 'Forgive, dear father, the illegible handwriting and bad style; it is almost four o'clock. The candle is burnt right down and my eyes are sore; a real anxiety has come over me and I will not be able to quieten the ghosts I have roused until I am near you again' (Marx, 1971b: 10). It seems that even as a young student Marx was troubled by spectres.
6. Moreover, even the concept of exchange itself breaks down – cannot be maintained in a pure state – for it is also 'affected by the same overflowing contamination', in this case 'inscribed and exceeded by a promise of gift beyond exchange' (Derrida, 1994: 163, 160). Derrida is here extrapolating from his work on the gift in Derrida (1992a). Comparisons can be made with the effort of Baudrillard – under the influence of Mauss and Bataille – to elucidate the symbolic order of the gift distinct from commodity exchange.
7. This theme – messianicity – is anticipated, very briefly, in 'Force of Law' (Derrida, 2002a: 254), but it is most fully developed in Derrida's book and essay on Marx. It also recurs in later work, including in a late interview in which he points to the 'alter-globalization movements' as one incarnation of this kind of messianicity (Derrida and Cauter, 2006: 268). In his final interview, Derrida links anti-globalization movements back to *Specters to Marx*: 'Beyond "cosmopolitanism," beyond the "global citizen" as a new global nation-state, this book [*Specters of Marx*] anticipates all the anti-globalization imperatives that I believe in and that are coming more clearly into view now' (Derrida, 2004). This final comment, one might uncharitably suggest, is further evidence of Derrida's unfortunate tendency retrospectively to overplay the significance of his own work.
8. On the question of Benjamin's Judaism and its link to his politics, especially as expressed in the 1940 fragment from which I have quoted, see the essay by Tiedmann (1989) and the discussions in Buse et al. (2005).
9. Derrida himself implies that the theme has, like so much of his work, been developed through readings of Husserl and Heidegger (cf. Derrida, 1999b: 250).

[10] He claims, among other things: 'My ambition (which is perhaps excessive) is to call for a new reading of Marx – a greater ambition than many Marxists' (Derrida, 2002b: 185).

[11] Cf. John Protevi (2001: 44, 9), one of Derrida's most perceptive and sympathetic commentators, who notes 'Derrida's inability to engage with matter outside metaphysical conceptuality', but goes on to add: 'This is not to say that Derridean political intervention is useless – far from it. . . . Nonetheless, it is important to demonstrate where Derrida can help us and where he cannot.'

[12] Following the initial reception of Derrida's writings, which in the Anglophone world took place mainly in literature departments, over the last ten or fifteen years there has been growing interest in the potential political dimensions of deconstruction. This interest has been fed both by Derrida's own work (which in the final two decades of his life seemed increasingly to offer more obviously political interventions in specific situations – on issues like immigration, for instance) and by numerous secondary commentaries. Of the latter, Simon Critchley's (1992) *The Ethics of Deconstruction* was extremely influential, claiming that 'Derrida's work results in a certain *impasse* of the political' (while of course emphasizing its 'ethical demand') (Critchley, 1992: 189). Recent defences of the radical political potential of deconstruction can be found in Thomson (2005) and Thomassen (2007). See also the essays in McQuillan (2007b).

Chapter 4

[1] Most of the literature on the relation between Marx and Foucault has focused on – or at least begins from – Foucault's supposed hostility towards Marxism. In turn, this literature can be roughly divided into two: that which criticizes Foucault from a Marxist position and that which criticizes Marx from a Foucauldian position. Nicos Poulantzas (1978: 44) provides a classic Marxist critique of Foucault, arguing that he caricatures Marxism, cannot account for resistance, and (along with Deleuze) 'seriously underestimate[s] the importance of classes and the class struggle'. Smart (1983), Wapner (1989), and Olssen (2004) tend to favour Foucault, though with varying degrees of hostility towards Marx, and varying degrees of recognition that the work of Foucault and Marx may be compatible. Even those authors who have been much more willing to forge an alliance between Marx and Foucault have tended to assume that a large gap separates the thinkers: Poster (1984), for example, presents Foucault as a supplement to Marxism, while Hunt (2004) assumes that Foucault would have rejected any such alliance. Richard Marsden (1999) has sought to challenge the assumption that Marx and Foucault are incompatible, though Marsden's approach – analysing postmodernity from the perspective of organization studies filtered through critical realism – produces some strange and not always edifying results. Even though he does not explicitly address Foucault's attitude towards Marx, Jason Read (2003) is perhaps the best guide to the relation between the two thinkers, subtly revealing numerous points of convergence.

2. In 1969 Foucault himself offered a straightforward riposte to Sartre's criticisms of his book: 'he hasn't read it' (Foucault, 1996: 54).
3. In addition, *The Order of Things* anticipates Baudrillard's argument that Marx remained tied to the conceptual logic of production: 'Marx made a radical critique of political economy, but still in the form of political economy' (Baudrillard, 1975: 50).
4. Foucault sometimes characterized his work as a 'critical ontology of ourselves' or a 'historical ontology of ourselves' (cf. Foucault, 1997: 319, 262). However, it is clear that this critical ontology is not the same as the idealist ontology that I outlined in Chapter 1: Foucault does not search for the underlying essence of things; on the contrary, he tries to show that there is no essence underlying things. In this sense, then, it can be said that Foucault as much as Lyotard and Derrida seeks to undermine (idealist) ontology.
5. Foucault gives a relevant and significant example: 'it can be said that political economy has a role in capitalist society, that it serves the interests of the bourgeois class, that it was made by and for that class, and that it bears the mark of its origins even in its concepts and logical architecture' (Foucault, 1977a: 185) – but for Foucault it must still be analysed at the archaeological level, examining its system of formation: the manner in which it makes possible the formation and articulation of objects of knowledge, concepts, and strategies.
6. An interview from 1978, for example, sees Foucault stating: 'Out of the visions of Marx, the visions of socialists, from their thoughts and their analyses, which were among the most objective, rational, and seemingly accurate thoughts and analyses, emerged in actuality political systems, social organizations, and economic mechanisms that today are condemned and ought to be discarded' (Foucault, 2005a: 185). See also Foucault's (1994: 277–81) review of Glucksmann's *The Master Thinkers*. Christofferson (2004: especially 198–201) offers a useful discussion of the relationship between Foucault and the *nouveaux philosophes*; see also Dews (1979).
7. The notion of a theory as a toolbox is raised by Deleuze (2004: 208) in a discussion with Foucault. Elsewhere Foucault clarifies: 'The notion of theory as a toolkit means: (i) The theory to be constructed is not a system but an instrument, a *logic* of the specificity of power relations and the struggles around them; (ii) That this investigation can only be carried out step by step on the basis of reflection (which will necessarily be historical in some of its aspects) on given situations' (Foucault, 1980: 145).
8. Strangely, Marsden (1999: 20–1) takes this statement as one of the 'clear signs of Foucault's hostility to Marx' – though it is clear that Foucault here is not rejecting Marx *tout court*. Rather, he is warning against the kind of 'academization' of Marx that would mean 'misconceiving the kind of break [Marx] effected' (Foucault, 1980: 76).
9. The direct references to Marx in *Discipline and Punish* are few but significant, citing *Capital*'s insights into the optimization of productive forces through cooperation (Foucault, 1977b: 163–4), the disciplinary function of surveillance (175), and the role of technological and disciplinary innovations in the accumulation of capital (221).

10. This point is well made by Poulantzas (1978: 63–7), who recognizes the value of Foucault's contribution here. While critical of Foucault, to his credit Poulantzas claims that Foucault's analyses not only often concur with Marxism but may even enrich it; indeed, '[s]everal of his analyses are not only compatible with Marxism: they can be understood only if it is taken as their starting-point' (67–8). Smart (1983: 105, 102) argues that Poulantzas' modest attempt to reconcile Foucault with Marx 'has diluted the radical and critical potential of Foucault's work', ultimately revealing 'a significant degree of incompatibility between Foucault's genealogical analyses and Marxist analysis'.
11. In the introductory volume of *The History of Sexuality* Foucault declares: 'One needs to be nominalistic, no doubt' (Foucault, 1979: 93).
12. Foucault defines bio-power as simultaneously 'an *anatamo-politics of the human body*', shaping the individual subject, forming docile, efficient bodies, and '*a bio-politics of the population*', operating at the level of the human species as a whole, monitoring birth and death rates, regulating public health (all those techniques and procedures that Foucault has grouped under the name of 'governmentality'). He claims that 'bio-power was without question an indispensable element in the development of capitalism; the latter would not have been possible without the controlled insertion of bodies into the machinery of production and the adjustment of the the phenomena of population to economic processes' (1979: 139–41).

Chapter 5

1. Despite (or perhaps because of) its brevity and limited focus (on the philosophy of language), Lecercle's (2005) article is in many ways the best analysis of Deleuze's relation to Marx, clearly elucidating points of influence and connection. The essay is adapted from a chapter in Lecercle (2006: 118–38), and some of its themes and arguments reflect discussions in Lecercle (2002). There are few detailed studies of the relation between Marx and Deleuze. Nicholas Thoburn's book *Deleuze, Marx and Politics* (2003) makes some interesting arguments, but rather than looking at the way Deleuze has read Marx, it examines 'zone[s] of engagement' between the two (Thoburn, 2003: 12). Moreover, despite its criticisms of Negri's work, the Marx who emerges often seems much closer to Negri and the Italian tradition than to Deleuze. As with Foucault, Read (2003) rarely comments directly on Deleuze's reading of Marx, but he nonetheless produces a subtle and intelligent analysis that reveals much about the relation between the two thinkers. Holland (2009) offers a helpful introduction to Deleuze and Guattari's use of Marx.
2. If in this chapter I refer only to Deleuze, even when speaking about *Anti-Oedipus* and the three other Deleuze-Guattari books, it is out of convenience, and because this chapter is about Deleuze; I do not underestimate the influence of Guattari. Genosko (2009) offers a useful introduction to Guattari's work.
3. In a very early piece – a 1954 review of Hyppolite's *Logic and Existence* – Deleuze notes approvingly that 'Hyppolite starts from a precise idea to make a precise

point: *Philosophy must be ontology, it cannot be anything else; but there is no ontology of essence, there is only an ontology of sense*' (Deleuze, 2004: 15). Towards the end of the review, Deleuze wonders 'whether an ontology of difference couldn't be created that would not go all the way to contradiction, since contradiction would be less and not more than difference' (18). This proposed project is what would occupy Deleuze for the rest of his career; it is undertaken most systematically in *Difference and Repetition*.

4. Again like the other post-structuralists, Deleuze has an ambivalent attitude towards Althusser. Lecercle (2002: 200) perhaps overstates the case a little when he claims that 'Althusser is the frequent object of implicit, and sometimes entirely explicit criticism', but there are certainly points of disagreement – especially, as Lecercle (183–4) argues, and as I shall briefly discuss in the next section, over the concept of the machine.

5. Deleuze borrows the 'baggy clothes' analogy from Bergson, though rather than using this analogy to refer to dialectics, Bergson uses it to criticize a 'philosophical empiricism' (opposed to a 'true', metaphysical empiricism) in which 'unity and multiplicity are representations one need not cut according to the object, that one finds already made and that one has only to choose from the pile, – ready-made garments which will suit Peter as well as Paul because they do not show off the figure of either of them' (Bergson, 1946: 206–7).

6. More accurately, and as we shall see in Chapter 6, Althusser reads Marx in Deleuzian style.

7. Deleuze himself claims: 'There is no base or superstructure in an assemblage' (Deleuze and Parnet, 2002: 71). The relation between 'machine' and 'assemblage' is complex, as are their respective definitions. Deleuze writes of 'machinic assemblages', but the two terms are distinct: concrete assemblages effectuate or actualize abstract machines and '[a]bstract machines operate within concrete assemblages' (Deleuze and Guattari, 1988: 510). Machines set assemblages in motion, connecting them to other assemblages. The important point here, however, is that both concepts testify to that mixing of the material and the ideal of which Lecercle speaks, and which, as I argued in Chapter 3, is a key feature of Marx's work.

8. Deleuze claims this is 'Foucault's greatest historical principle: behind the curtain there is nothing to see, but it was all the more important each time to describe the curtain, or the base, since there was nothing either behind or beneath it' (Deleuze, 1988*b*: 54). An intriguing anticipation of this statement – and of Foucault's own remarks in 'Nietzsche, Genealogy, History' – is found in Deleuze's 1954 review of Hyppolite: 'Absolute knowledge is what is closest, so to speak, what is most simple: it *is here*. "Behind the curtain there is nothing to see," or as Hyppolite says: "the secret is that there is no secret"' (Deleuze, 2004: 17). Given Hyppolite's interests, this suggests that – though it lies beyond the scope of my present enquiry – an interesting study could be made of the precise role of (readings of) Hegel in Deleuze's philosophical development.

9. Holland (1991) offers a cogent analysis of some of the differences and connections between *Anti-Oedipus* and *A Thousand Plateaus*, centred on the concept of deterritorialization.

10. The term 'deterritorialization' is adapted from Lacan: see Holland (1999: 19–20) for a brief but useful elucidation; also Holland (1991).
11. See, for example, Marx (1988: 95) on the 'growth in the *cynicism* of political economy from Smith through Say to Ricardo, Mill, etc.'
12. Thus Deleuze's micropolitics is very different from the analytical Marxists' search for 'the *micro-foundations* of macro-structural theory' (Wright, 1994: 190). That search was based on the belief that 'a satisfactory explanation of collective action must provide micro-foundations for the behaviour, that is explain it in terms of the desires and beliefs that enter into the motivation of the individuals participating in it' (Elster, 1985: 15–6). This rational choice-inspired approach is almost diametrically opposed to the anti-humanist micropolitical analyses of post-structuralism – and, in fact, to the analyses of Marx.
13. The reference is to *A Contribution to the Critique of Political Economy*: 'From the taste of wheat it is not possible to tell who provided it, a Russian serf, a French peasant, or an English capitalist' (Marx, 1971a: 28).

Chapter 6

1. I think that this is one way to understand recent attempts to integrate Deleuze with liberal-democratic thought, albeit via a critical interrogation rather than simple assimilation: see Patton (2005, 2007, 2008), Tampio (2009), Smith (2003*b*). For a more direct attempt to decouple Deleuze from Marx, see DeLanda (2006, 2008).
2. Foucault's occasional sympathy for the *nouveaux philosophes* should not obscure the fact that he never fully accepts their facile denigration of Marx.
3. Foucault gives clearest expression to this feeling. He argues that it is necessary to avoid '[r]efusing to question the Gulag on the basis of the texts of Marx or Lenin or to ask oneself how, through what error, deviation, misunderstanding or distortion of speculation of practice, their theory could have been betrayed to such a degree. On the contrary, it [i.e. posing the Gulag question] means questioning all these theoretical texts, however old, from the standpoint of the reality of the Gulag. Rather than searching in those texts for a condemnation in advance of the Gulag, it is a matter of asking what in those texts could have made the Gulag possible' (Foucault, 1980: 135). Yet he argues further that 'we must insist on the specificity of the Gulag question against all theoretical reductions (which make the Gulag an error already to be read in the texts)' (Foucault, 1980: 137). It is this qualification that is crucial, and distances Foucault from the *nouveaux philosophes*.
4. Among other remarks, in *Reading Capital* Althusser places Foucault alongside Canguilhem and Bachelard as one of 'our masters in reading learned works' (Althusser and Balibar, 1970: 16n1). In a letter from Althusser to the English translator of *Reading Capital*, this praise is balanced by the claim that ' "something" from my writings has passed into his [i.e. Foucault's]' (Althusser and Balibar, 1970: 323).

5. To this extent, at least, Laclau and Mouffe's move to a post-Marxist terrain is unnecessary, for the recognition that 'the economy is itself structured as a political space' (Laclau and Mouffe, 2001: 76–7) is already present in Marx.
6. Moreover, the entwinement of the economic and the political manifests itself today not only in the maintenance and reinforcement of capitalism, but in the establishment of capitalism in other parts of the world. For all Marx's insistence that he offered no master key of explanation, *Capital*'s pages on expropriation and the role of the state shed an interesting light on present-day China, where an authoritarian state has proved extremely useful in the transition to a free-market economy. As one current observer comments, 'what China proves (though this is left unsaid) is that an authoritarian system helps rather than hinders economic growth on the neo-liberal model, by ensuring that labour laws, trade unions, the legislature, the judiciary and the fear of environmental destruction do not impede the privatisation of state assets, the appropriation of agricultural land, the provision of subsides and tax cuts to businessmen, or the concentration of wealth in fewer hands' (Mishra, 2006: 5). '*Tantae molis erat* to unleash the "eternal natural laws" of the capitalist mode of production' (Marx, 1976a: 925)!
7. It is not my argument here that it is only through post-structuralism – through examination of its insights and errors – that Marx's blurring of the political and the economic is revealed; only that it is one way of approaching and understanding this important issue. It is a feature of Marx's work that has been discussed by other commentators. In addition to Balibar, for example, Jacques Bidet (2007: 318) states that *Capital* 'constitutes a "*political* economy", but in the singular sense that the programme of historical materialism defines, this sense being first of all that of conceiving the inseparable conjunction of these two terms'.
8. In *Capital*, Marx repeats the words of a manager of a glass works, who testifies that his child workers 'cannot well neglect their work; when they once begin, they must go on; they are just the same as parts of a machine' (Marx, 1976a: 469n22).
9. The accusation comes from Tom Lewis, who uses his review of *Specters of Marx* to dispel 'some post-structuralist myths about the working class today' (Lewis, 1999: 149).

Bibliography

Agamben, Giorgio (1999) *Potentialities: Collected Essays in Philosophy.* Stanford, California: Stanford University Press.
Althusser, Louis (1969) *For Marx,* trans. Ben Brewster. London: NLB.
— (1971) *Lenin and Philosophy and Other Essays,* trans. Ben Brewster. London: NLB.
— (1972) *Politics and History: Montesquieu, Rousseau, Hegel and Marx,* trans. Ben Brewster. London: NLB.
—(1976) *Essays in Self-Criticism,* trans. Grahame Lock. London: NLB.
—(1978) 'What Must Change in the Party', trans. Patrick Camiller, *New Left Review* 109: 19–45.
—(1990) *Philosophy and the Spontaneous Philosophy of the Scientists and Other Essays,* ed. Gregory Elliott, trans. Ben Brewster *et al.* London: Verso.
—(1993) *The Future Lasts a Long Time and The Facts,* ed. Olivier Corpet and Yann Moulier Boutang, trans. Richard Veasey. London: Chatto and Windus.
—(1996) *Writings on Psychoanalysis: Freud and Lacan,* ed. Olivier Corpet and François Matheron, trans. Jeffrey Mehlman. New York: Columbia University Press.
—(1997) *The Spectre of Hegel: Early Writings,* ed. François Matheron, trans. G. M. Goshgarian. London: Verso.
—(2003) *The Humanist Controversy and Other Writings (1966–67),* ed. François Matheron, trans. G. M. Goshgarian. London: Verso.
—(2006) *Philosophy of the Encounter: Later Writings, 1978–87,* ed. Olivier Corpet and François Matheron, trans. G. M. Goshgarian. London: Verso.
Althusser, Louis and Étienne Balibar (1970) *Reading Capital,* trans. Ben Brewster. London: NLB.
Anderson, Perry (1976) *Considerations on Western Marxism.* London: NLB.
—(1984) *In the Tracks of Historical Materialism.* London: Verso.
—(1998) *The Origins of Postmodernity.* London: Verso.
Aron, Raymond (1990) *Memoirs: Fifty Years of Political Reflection,* trans. George Holoch. New York: Holmes & Meier.
Ashenden, Samantha and David Owen, eds. (1999) *Foucault contra Habermas: Recasting the Dialogue Between Genealogy and Critical Theory.* London: Sage Publications.
Badiou, Alain (2000) *Deleuze: The Clamour of Being,* trans. Louise Burchill. Minneapolis: University of Minnesota Press.
—(2005) 'The Adventures of French Philosophy', *New Left Review* 35: 67–77.
—(2007) 'The Event in Deleuze', trans. Jon Roffe, *Parrhesia* 2: 37–44. www.parrhesiajournal.org/parrhesia02/parrhesia02_badiou2.pdf. Last accessed 26 July 2007.

Balibar, Étienne (1991) 'From Class Struggle to Classless Struggle', trans. Chris Turner, in Étienne Balibar and Immanuel Wallerstein, *Race, Nation, Class: Ambiguous Identities*. London: Verso.
—(1992) 'Foucault and Marx: The Question of Nominalism', in Timothy J. Armstrong, ed., *Michel Foucault Philosopher*. New York: Routledge.
—(1994) *Masses, Classes, Ideas: Studies on Politics and Philosophy Before and After Marx*, trans. James Swenson. New York: Routledge.
—(1995) *The Philosophy of Marx*, trans. Chris Turner. London: Verso.
Baudrillard, Jean (1975) *The Mirror of Production*, trans. Mark Poster. St Louis: Telos Press.
—(1981) *For a Critique of the Political Economy of the Sign*, trans. Charles Levin. St Louis: Telos Press.
Baugh, Bruce (2003) *French Hegel: From Surrealism to Postmodernism*. New York: Routledge.
Beardsworth, Richard (1996) *Derrida and the Political*. London: Routledge.
Benjamin Walter (2003) *Selected Writings Volume 4: 1938–1940*, trans. Edmund Jephcott et al., ed. Howard Eiland and Michael W. Jennings. Cambridge, MA: The Belknapp Press of Harvard University Press.
Bennington, Geoffrey (1988) *Lyotard: Writing the Event*. Manchester: Manchester University Press.
—(2000) *Interrupting Derrida*. London: Routledge.
Bensaïd, Daniel (2002) *Marx for Our Times: Adventures and Misadventures of a Critique*, trans. Gregory Elliott. London: Verso.
Bergson, Henri (1946) *The Creative Mind*, trans. Mabelle L. Andison. New York: Philosophical Library.
Bertens, Hans (1995) *The Idea of the Postmodern: A History*. London and New York: Routledge.
Bidet, Jacques (2007) *Exploring Marx's* Capital*: Philosophical, Economic and Political Dimensions*, trans. David Fernbach. Leiden, The Netherlands: Brill.
Buse, Peter, Ken Hirschkop, Scott McCracken, and Bertrand Taithe (2005) *Benjamin's* Arcades*: An Unguided Tour*. Manchester: Manchester University Press.
Butler, Judith (1987) *Subjects of Desire: Hegelian Reflections in Twentieth Century France*. New York: Columbia University Press.
—(1990) *Gender Trouble: Feminism and the Subversion of Identity*. New York: Routledge.
Callinicos, Alex (1989) *Against Postmodernism: A Marxist Critique*. Cambridge: Polity Press.
—(1996) 'Messianic Ruminations: Derrida, Stirner and Marx', *Radical Philosophy* 75: 37–41.
Castoriadis, Cornelius (1988) *Political and Social Writings. Volume Two, 1955–1960: From the Workers' Struggle Against Bureaucracy to Revolution in the Age of Modern Capitalism*, trans. and ed. David Ames Curtis. Minneapolis: University of Minnesota Press.
—(1993) *Political and Social Writings. Volume Three, 1961–1979: Recommencing the Revolution: From Socialism to the Autonomous Society*, trans. and ed. David Ames Curtis. Minneapolis: University of Minnesota Press.

Christofferson, Michael Scott (2004) *French Intellectuals Against the Left: The Antitotalitarian Moment of the 1970s*. New York: Berghahn Books.
Cohen, G. A. (2000) *Karl Marx's Theory of History: A Defence*. Oxford: Clarendon Press.
Colebrook, Claire (2006) *Deleuze: A Guide for the Perplexed*. London: Continuum.
—(2008) 'On Not Becoming Man: The Materialist Politics of Unactualized Potential', in Stacy Alaimo and Susan Hekman, eds., *Material Feminisms*. Bloomington, IN: Indiana University Press.
Critchley, Simon (1992) *The Ethics of Deconstruction: Derrida and Levinas*. Oxford: Blackwell.
DeLanda, Manuel (2006) *A New Philosophy of Society: Assemblage Theory and Social Complexity*. London: Continuum.
—(2008) 'Deleuze, Materialism and Politics', in Ian Buchanan and Nicholas Thoburn, eds., *Deleuze and Politics*. Edinburgh: Edinburgh University Press.
Deleuze, Gilles (1983) *Nietzsche and Philosophy*, trans. Hugh Tomlinson. London: The Athlone Press.
—(1988a) *Bergsonism*, trans. Hugh Tomlinson and Barbara Habberjam. New York: Zone Books.
—(1988b) *Foucault*, trans. Seán Hand. London: The Athlone Press.
—(1989) *Cinema 2: The Time-Image*, trans. Hugh Tomlinson and Robert Galeta. London: The Athlone Press.
—(1994) *Difference and Repetition*, trans. Paul Patton. London: The Athlone Press.
—(1995a) 'Le "Je me souviens" de Gilles Deleuze', *Le Nouvel Observateur* 1619: 50–1.
—(1995b) *Negotiations 1972–1990*, trans. Martin Joughin. New York: Columbia University Press.
—(2001) *Pure Immanence: Essays on A Life*, trans. Anne Boyman. New York: Zone Books.
—(2004) *Desert Islands and Other Texts 1953–1974*, ed. David Lapoujade, trans. Michael Taormina. Los Angeles: Semiotext(e).
—(2006) *Two Regimes of Madness: Texts and Interviews 1975–1995*, ed. David Lapoujade, trans. Ames Hodges and Michael Taormina. Los Angeles: Semiotext(e).
Deleuze, Gilles and Félix Guattari (1977) *Anti-Oedipus: Capitalism and Schizophrenia*, trans. Robert Hurley, Mark Seem and Helen R. Lane. New York: The Viking Press.
—(1986) *Kafka: Toward a Minor Literature*, trans. Dana Polan. Minneapolis: University of Minnesota Press.
—(1988) *A Thousand Plateaus: Capitalism and Schizophrenia*, trans. Brian Massumi. London: The Athlone Press.
—(1994) *What is Philosophy?*, trans. Hugh Tomlinson and Graham Burchill. London: Verso.
Deleuze, Gilles and Claire Parnet (2002) *Dialogues II*, trans. Hugh Tomlinson and Barbara Habberjam. London: Continuum.
Derrida, Jacques (1976) *Of Grammatology*, trans. Gayatri Chakravorty Spivak. Baltimore: The Johns Hopkins University Press.
—(1978) *Writing and Difference*, trans. Alan Bass. London: Routledge & Kegan Paul.

—(1981) *Positions*, trans. Alan Bass. London: Continuum.
—(1982) *Margins of Philosophy*, trans. Alan Bass. New York: Harvester Wheatsheaf.
—(1983) 'The Time of a Thesis: Punctuations', in Alan Montefiore, ed., *Philosophy in France today*. Cambridge: Cambridge University Press.
—(1984) 'Deconstruction and the other' (interview with Richard Kearney), in Richard Kearney, *Dialogues with Contemporary Continental Thinkers: the Phenomenological Heritage*. Manchester: Manchester University Press.
—(1986) *Memoires for Paul de Man*, trans. Cecile Lindsay, Jonathan Culler, and Eduardo Cadava. New York: Columbia University Press.
—(1989) 'In Discussion with Christopher Norris', in Andreas Papadakis, Catherine Cooke and Andrew Benjamin, eds., *Deconstruction: Omnibus Volume*. London: Academy Editions.
—(1991) *A Derrida Reader: Between the Blinds*, ed. Peggy Kamuf. New York: Columbia University Press.
—(1992a) *Given Time: I. Counterfeit Money*, trans. Peggy Kamuf. Chicago: The University of Chicago Press.
—(1992b) *The Other Heading: Reflections on Today's Europe*, trans. Pascale-Anne Brault and Michael Naas. Bloomington: Indiana University Press.
—(1993) *Aporias*, trans. Thomas Dutoit. Stanford, California: Stanford University Press.
—(1994) *Specters of Marx: The State of the Debt, the Work of Mourning and the New International*, trans. Peggy Kamuf. New York: Routledge.
—(1995a) *The Gift of Death*, trans. David Wills. Chicago: The University of Chicago Press.
—(1995b) *On the Name*, ed. Thomas Dutoit. Stanford, California: Stanford University Press.
—(1995c) *Points... Interviews, 1974–1991*, ed. Elisabeth Weber. Stanford, California: Stanford University Press.
—(1997a) '"Perhaps or Maybe", Jacques Derrida in conversation with Alexander Garcia Düttmann', *PLI: Warwick Journal of Philosophy* 6: 1–18.
—(1997b) *Politics of Friendship*, trans. George Collins. London: Verso.
—(1999a) *Adieu to Emmanuel Levinas*, trans. Pascale-Anne Brault and Michael Naas. Stanford, CA: Stanford University Press.
—(1999b) 'Marx & Sons', trans. G. M. Goshgarian, in Michael Sprinker, ed., *Ghostly Demarcations: A Symposium on Jacques Derrida's Specters of Marx*. London: Verso.
—(2000) *Of Hospitality: Anne Dufourmantelle Invites Jacques Derrida to Respond*, trans. Rachel Bowlby. Stanford, CA: Stanford University Press.
—(2001) *On Cosmopolitanism and Forgiveness*, trans. Mark Dooley and Michael Hughes. London: Routledge.
—(2002a) *Acts of Religion*, ed. Gil Anidjar. New York: Routledge.
—(2002b) *Negotiations: Interventions and Interviews, 1971–2001*, ed. and trans. Elizabeth Rottenberg. Stanford, CA: Stanford University Press.
—(2002c) 'The Three Ages of Jacques Derrida: An Interview with the Father of Deconstructionism by Kristine McKenna', *LA Weekly*. www.laweekly.com/general/features/the-three-ages-of-jacques-derrida/3438/#Continuation. Last accessed 27 July 2006.

—(2004) 'The Last Interview', *Studio Visit*. www.studiovisit.net/SV.Derrida.pdf. Last accessed 16 July 2007.
Derrida, Jacques and Lieven de Cauter (2006) 'For a Justice to Come: An Interview with Jacques Derrida', in Lasse Thomassen, ed., *The Derrida-Habermas Reader*. Edinburgh: Edinburgh University Press.
Derrida, Jacques and Maurizio Ferraris (2001) *A Taste for the Secret*, trans. Giacomo Donis, ed. Giacomo Donis and David Webb. Cambridge: Cambridge University Press.
Descombes, Vincent (1980) *Modern French Philosophy*, trans. L. Scott-Fox and J. M. Harding. Cambridge: Cambridge University Press.
Dews, Peter (1979) 'The *Nouvelle Philosophie* and Foucault', *Economy and Society* 8(2): 127–71.
—(1987) *Logics of Disintegration: Post-Structuralist Thought and the Claims of Critical Theory*. London: Verso.
Donzelot, Jacques (1977) 'An Anti-Sociology', trans. Mark Seem, *Semiotext(e)* 2(3): 27–44.
Dreyfus, Hubert L. and Paul Rabinow (1982) *Michel Foucault: Beyond Structuralism and Hermeneutics*. Brighton, Sussex: The Harvester Press.
Due, Reidar (2007) *Deleuze*. Cambridge: Polity.
Eagleton, Terry (1988) *Against the Grain: Essays 1975–1985*. London: Verso.
—(1992) *The Ideology of the Aesthetic*. Oxford: Blackwell.
—(1997) *The Illusions of Postmodernism*. Oxford: Basil Blackwell.
Elliott, Gregory (2006) *Althusser: The Detour of Theory*. Leiden, the Netherlands: Brill.
Elster, Jon (1985) *Making Sense of Marx*. Cambridge: Cambridge University Press.
Eribon, Didier (1991) *Michel Foucault*, trans. Betsy Wing. Cambridge, MA: Harvard University Press.
Foucault, Michel (1970) *The Order of Things: An Archaeology of the Human Sciences*. London: Tavistock Publications.
—(1977a) *The Archaeology of Knowledge*, trans. A. M. Sheridan Smith. London: Tavistock Publications.
—(1977b) *Discipline and Punish: The Birth of the Prison*, trans. Alan Sheridan. London: Allen Lane.
—(1977c) *Language, Counter-Memory, Practice: Selected Essays and Interviews*, ed. Donald F. Bouchard, trans. Donald F. Bouchard and Sherry Simon. Ithaca, NY: Cornell University Press.
—(1979) *The History of Sexuality Volume One: An Introduction*, trans. Robert Hurley. London: Allen Lane.
—(1980) *Power/Knowledge: Selected Interviews and Other Writings 1972–1977*, ed. Colin Gordon, trans. Colin Gordon et al. New York: Pantheon Books.
—(1981) 'The Order of Discourse', trans. Ian McLeod, in Robert Young, ed., *Untying the Text: A Post-Structuralist Reader*. Boston, MA: Routledge and Kegan Paul.
—(1986) *Death and the Labyrinth: The World of Raymond Roussel*, trans. Charles Ruas. Garden City, NY: Doubleday and Company, Inc.
—(1988) *Politics, Philosophy, Culture: Interviews and Other Writings 1977–1984*, ed. Lawrence D. Kritzman, trans. Alan Sheridan et al. New York: Routledge.

—(1992) *The History of Sexuality Volume Two: The Use of Pleasure*, trans. Robert Hurley. Harmondsworth, Middlesex: Penguin Books.
—(1994) *Dits et écrits 1954–1988 III: 1976–1979*, ed. Daniel Defert and François Ewald. Paris: Gallimard.
—(1996) *Foucault Live: Collected Interviews, 1961–1984*, ed. Sylvère Lotringer, trans. Lysa Hochroth and John Johnston. New York: Semiotext(e).
—(1997) *Essential Works of Foucault 1954–1984 Volume One. Ethics: Subjectivity and Truth*, ed. Paul Rabinow, trans. Robert Hurley et al. Harmondsworth, Middlesex: Allen Lane The Penguin Press.
—(1998) *Essential Works of Foucault 1954–1984 Volume Two. Aesthetics, Method, and Epistemology*, ed. James Faubion, trans. Robert Hurley et al. Harmondsworth, Middlesex: Allen Lane The Penguin Press.
—(2001) *Essential Works of Foucault 1954–1984 Volume Three. Power*, ed. James D. Faubion, trans. Robert Hurley et al. Harmondsworth, Middlesex: Allen Lane The Penguin Press.
—(2003) *"Society Must Be Defended": Lectures at the Collège de France, 1975–76*, ed. Mauro Bertani and Alessandro Fontana, trans. David Macey. London: Allen Lane.
—(2005a) 'Dialogue between Michel Foucault and Baqir Parham', trans. Janet Afary, in Janet Afary and Kevin B. Anderson, eds., *Foucault and the Iranian Revolution: Gender and the Seductions of Islamism*. Chicago: The University of Chicago Press.
—(2005b) 'Foucault Recalled: Interview with Michel Foucault' (by Frank Mort and Roy Peters), *New Formations* 55: 9–22.
—(2006) *History of Madness*, ed. Jean Khalfa, trans. Jonathan Murphy and Jean Khalfa. London: Routledge.
Fukuyama, Francis (1992) *The End of History and the Last Man*. London: Hamish Hamilton.
Gane, Mike (1991) *Baudrillard: Critical and Fatal Theory*. London: Routledge.
Genosko, Gary (2009) *Félix Guattari: A Critical Introduction*. London: Pluto Press.
Glucksmann, André (1980) *The Master Thinkers*, trans. Brian Pearce. Brighton, Sussex: The Harvester Press.
Guattari, Félix (2006) *The Anti-Œdipus Papers*, ed. Stéphane Naduad, trans. Kélina Gotman. Los Angeles: Semiotext(e).
Habermas, Jürgen (1981) 'Modernity versus Postmodernity', trans. Seyla Ben-Habib, *New German Critique* 81(22): 3–14.
—(1987) *The Philosophical Discourse of Modernity: Twelve Lectures*, trans. Frederick Lawrence. Cambridge: Polity Press.
—(1992) *Autonomy and Solidarity: Interviews with Jürgen Habermas*, ed. Peter Dews. London: Verso.
—(2001) 'From Kant's "Ideas" of Pure Reason to the "Idealizing" Presuppositions of Communicative Action: Reflections on the Detranscendentalized "Use of Reason"', in William Rehg and James Bohman, eds., *Pluralism and the Pragmatic Turn: Essays in Honour of Thomas McCarthy*. Cambridge, MA: The MIT Press.
Hallward, Peter (2006) *Out of this World: Deleuze and the Philosophy of Creation*. London: Verso.

Hardt, Michael (1993) *Gilles Deleuze: An Apprenticeship in Philosophy*. London: UCL Press.
Hardt, Michael and Antonio Negri (2000) *Empire*. Cambridge, MA: Harvard University Press.
—(2004) *Multitude: War and Democracy in the Age of Empire*. New York: The Penguin Press.
Harvey, David (1989) *The Condition of Postmodernity: An Enquiry into the Origins of Cultural Change*. Oxford: Basil Blackwell.
Holland, Eugene W. (1991) 'Deterritorializing "Deterritorialization": From the *Anti Oedipus* to *A Thousand Plateaus*', *Substance* 20(3): 55–65.
—(1999) *Deleuze and Guattari's* Anti-Oedipus: *Introduction to Schizoanalysis*. London: Routledge.
—(2009) 'Karl Marx', in Graham Jones and Jon Roffe, eds., *Deleuze's Philosophical Linageage*. Edinburgh: Edinburgh University Press.
Hunt, Alan (2004) 'Getting Marx and Foucault into Bed Together!', *Journal of Law and Society* 31(4): 592–609.
Jacoby, Russell (1981) *Dialectic of Defeat: Contours of Western Marxism*. Cambridge: Cambridge University Press.
Jameson, Fredric (1984) 'Foreword' to Jean-François Lyotard, *The Postmodern Condition: A Report on Knowledge*, trans. Geoff Bennington and Brian Massumi. Manchester: Manchester University Press.
—(1993) *Postmodernism, or, The Cultural Logic of Late Capitalism*. London: Verso.
—(1997) 'Marxism and Dualism in Deleuze', *The South Atlantic Quarterly*, 96(3): 393–416.
—(1999) 'Marx's Purloined Letter', in Michael Sprinker, ed., *Ghostly Demarcations: A Symposium on Jacques Derrida's* Specters of Marx. London: Verso.
Jencks, Charles A. (1977) *The Language of Post-Modern Architecture*. London: Academy Editions.
Kant, Immanuel (1964) *Critique of Pure Reason*, trans. Norman Kemp Smith. London: Macmillan.
Kellner, Douglas (1989) *Jean Baudrillard: From Marxism to Postmodernism and Beyond*. Cambridge: Polity Press.
Kelly, Michael, ed. (1994) *Critique and Power: Recasting the Foucault/Habermas Debate*. Cambridge, MA: The MIT Press.
Kroker, Arthur (1985) 'Baudrillard's Marx', *Theory, Culture and Society* 2(3): 69–83.
Laclau, Ernesto (1990) *New Reflections on the Revolution of Our Time*. London: Verso.
—(1995) ' "The Time is Out of Joint" ', *Diacritics* 25(2): 86–96.
Laclau, Ernesto and Chantal Mouffe (1987) 'Post-Marxism without Apologies', *New Left Review* 166: 79–106.
—(2001) *Hegemony and Socialist Strategy: Towards a Radical Democratic Politics*. London: Verso.
Lecercle, Jean-Jacques (2002) *Deleuze and Language*. Basingstoke, Hampshire: Palgrave Macmillan.
—(2005) 'Deleuze, Guattari and Marxism', *Historical Materialism* 13(3): 35–55.
—(2006) *A Marxist Philosophy of Language*, trans. Gregory Elliott. Leiden, The Netherlands: Brill.

Lenin, V. I. (1966) '*Kommunismus*', in *Collected Works Volume 31*. Moscow: Progress Publishers.
Lévi-Strauss, Claude (1963) *Structural Anthropology*, trans. Claire Jacobson and Brooke Grundfest Schoepf. New York: Basic Books.
—(1966) *The Savage Mind*, trans. anon. London: Weidenfeld and Nicolson.
Levy, Bernard-Henri (1977) *La Barbarie à visage humain*. Paris: Grasset.
Lewis, Tom (1999) 'The Politics of "Hauntololgy" in Derrida's *Specters of Marx*', in Michael Sprinker, ed., *Ghostly Demarcations: A Symposium on Jacques Derrida's Specters of Marx*. London: Verso.
Lyotard, Jean-François (1971) *Discours, figure*. Paris: Klincksieck.
—(1974) 'Adorno as the Devil', trans. Robert Hurley, *Telos* 19: 126–37.
—(1977) 'Energumen Capitalism', trans. James Leigh, *Semiotext(e)* 2(3): 11–26.
—(1984*a*) 'Interview' (with Georges Van Den Abbeele), *Diacritics* 14: 16–21.
—(1984*b*) *The Postmodern Condition: A Report on Knowledge*, trans. Geoff Bennington and Brian Massumi. Manchester: Manchester University Press.
—(1988*a*) *The Differend: Phrases in Dispute*, trans. Georges Van Den Abbeele. Minneapolis: University of Minnesota Press.
—(1988*b*) 'An Interview' (with Willem van Reijen and Dick Veerman), trans. Roy Boyne, *Theory, Culture and Society* 5: 277–309.
—(1988*c*) *Peregrinations: Law, Form, Event*. New York: Columbia University Press.
—(1989) *The Lyotard Reader*, ed. Andrew Benjamin. Oxford: Basil Blackwell.
—(1991*a*) *The Inhuman: Reflections on Time*, trans. Geoffrey Bennington and Rachel Bowlby. Cambridge: Polity Press.
—(1991*b*) *Phenomenology*, trans. Brian Beakley. Albany, NY: State University of New York Press.
—(1992) *The Postmodern Explained to Children: Correspondence 1982–1985*, ed. Julian Pefanis and Morgan Thomas. Sydney: Power Publications.
—(1993*a*) 'Complexity and the Sublime', in Lisa Appignanesi, ed., *Postmodernism: ICA Documents*. London: Free Association Books.
—(1993*b*) *Libidinal Economy*, trans. Iain Hamilton Grant. London: The Athlone Press.
—(1993*c*) *Political Writings*, trans. Bill Readings and Kevin Paul Geiman. London: UCL Press.
—(1994) 'Nietzsche and the Inhuman (interview with Richard Beardsworth)', *Journal of Nietzsche Studies* 7: 67–130.
—(1997) *Postmodern Fables*, trans. Georges Van Den Abbeele. Minneapolis: University of Minnesota Press.
—(2006) *The Lyotard Reader and Guide*, ed. Keith Crome and James Williams. Edinburgh: Edinburgh University Press.
Lyotard, Jean-François and Gilbert Larochelle (1992) 'That Which Resists, After All', *Philosophy Today* 36(4): 402–17.
Lyotard, Jean-François and Jean-Loup Thébaud (1985) *Just Gaming*, trans. Wlad Godzich. Manchester: Manchester University Press.
Macey, David (1994) 'The Lonely Hour of the Final Analysis', *Radical Philosophy* 67: 45–7.

Macherey, Pierre (1999) 'Marx Dematerialized, or the Spirit of Derrida', in Michael Sprinker, ed., *Ghostly Demarcations: A Symposium on Jacques Derrida's Specters of Marx*. London: Verso.

McQuillan, Martin, (2007a) 'Introduction: The Day after Tomorrow . . . or, the Deconstruction of the Future' in Martin McQuillan, ed., *The Politics of Deconstruction: Jacques Derrida and the Other of Philosophy*. London: Pluto Press.

McQuillan, Martin, ed. (2007b) *The Politics of Deconstruction: Jacques Derrida and the Other of Philosophy*. London: Pluto Press.

Marsden, Richard (1999) *The Nature of Capital: Marx after Foucault*. London: Routledge.

Marx, Karl (1970) *Critique of Hegel's 'Philosophy of Right'*, trans. Annette Jolin and Joseph O'Malley, ed. Joseph O'Malley. Cambridge: Cambridge University Press.

—(1971a) *A Contribution to the Critique of Political Economy*, trans. S. W. Ryazanskaya, ed. Maurice Dobb. London: Lawrence and Wishart.

—(1971b) 'Letter to his Father', in Karl Marx, *Early Texts*, trans. and ed. David McLellan. Oxford: Basil Blackwell.

—(1973) *Grundrisse: Foundations of the Critique of Political Economy (Rough Draft)*, trans. Martin Nicolaus. Harmondsworth, Middlesex: Penguin Books.

—(1976a) *Capital: A Critique of Political Economy. Volume One*, trans. Ben Fowkes. Harmondsworth, Middlesex: Penguin Books.

—(1976b) 'Theses on Feuerbach', in Karl Marx and Friedrich Engels, *Collected Works Volume 5*. London: Lawrence and Wishart.

—(1981) *Capital: A Critique of Political Economy. Volume Three*, trans. David Fernbach. Harmondsworth, Middlesex: Penguin Books.

—(1988) *Economic and Philosophic Manuscripts of 1844*, trans. Martin Milligan. Amherst, NY: Prometheus Books.

—(1995) *The Poverty of Philosophy*, trans. H. Quelch. Amherst, NY: Prometheus Books.

—(1996a) *The Eighteenth Brumaire of Louis Bonaparte*, in Karl Marx, *Later Political Writings*, ed. and trans. Terrell Carver. Cambridge: Cambridge University Press.

—(1996b) '"Notes" on Adolph Wagner', in Karl Marx, *Later Political Writings*, ed. and trans. Terrell Carver. Cambridge: Cambridge University Press.

Marx, Karl and Friedrich Engels (1956) *Selected Correspondence*. Moscow: Foreign Languages Publishing House.

—(1975) *The Holy Family, or Critique of Critical Criticism: Against Bruno Bauer and Company*, in Karl Marx and Friedrich Engels, *Collected Works Volume 4*. London: Lawrence and Wishart.

—(1976) *The German Ideology*, in Karl Marx and Friedrich Engels, *Collected Works Volume 5*. London: Lawrence and Wishart.

—(1998) *The Communist Manifesto*, ed. David McLellan. Oxford: Oxford University Press.

Merleau-Ponty, Maurice (1969) *Humanism and Terror: An Essay on the Communist Problem*, trans. John O'Neill. Boston: Beacon Press.

Mishra, Pankaj (2006) 'Getting Rich', *London Review of Books* 28(23): 3–7.

Montag, Warren (1995) '"The Soul is the Prison of the Body": Althusser and Foucault, 1970–1975', *Yale French Studies* 88: 53–77.
—(1998) 'Althusser's Nominalism: Structure and Singularity (1962–6)', *Rethinking Marxism* 10(3): 64–73.
—(2003) *Louis Althusser.* Basingstoke, Hampshire: Palgrave Macmillan.
Mullarkey, John (2006) *Post-Continental Philosophy: An Outline.* London: Continuum.
Negri, Antonio (1984) *Marx Beyond Marx: Lessons on the* Grundrisse, trans. Harry Cleaver, Michael Ryan and Maurizio Viano, ed. Jim Fleming. South Hadley, MA: Bergin and Garvey Publishers.
—(1996) 'Notes on the Evolution of the Thought of the Later Althusser', trans. Olga Vasile, in Antonio Callari and David Ruccio, eds., *Postmodern Materialism and the Future of Marxist Theory: Essays in the Althusserian Tradition.* Hanover, New Hampshire: Wesleyan University Press.
—(1999) *Insurgencies: Constituent Power and the Modern State*, trans. Maurizia Boscagli. Minneapolis: University of Minnesota Press.
Nietzsche, Friedrich (1968) *Twilight of the Idols and the Anti-Christ*, trans. R. J. Hollingdale. Harmondsworth, Middlesex: Penguin Books.
—(1998) *On the Genealogy of Morality: A Polemic*, trans. Douglas Smith. Oxford: Oxford University Press.
Norris, Christopher (1990) *What's Wrong with Postmodernism: Critical Theory and the Ends of Philosophy.* Hemel Hempstead: Harvester Wheatsheaf.
—(1992) *Uncritical Theory: Postmodernism, Intellectuals and the Gulf War.* London: Lawrence and Wishart.
—(1993) *The Truth About Postmodernism.* Oxford: Blackwell.
—(1996) *Reclaiming Truth: Contribution to a Critique of Cultural Relativism.* London: Lawrence and Wishart.
Olssen, Mark (2004) 'Foucault and Marxism: Rewriting the Theory of Historical Materialism', *Policy Futures in Education* 2(3–4): 454–82.
Owen, David (1994) *Maturity and Modernity: Nietzsche, Weber, Foucault and the Ambivalence of Reason.* London: Routledge.
Patton, Paul (2005) 'Deleuze and Democracy', *Contemporary Political Theory* 4(4): 400–13.
—(2007) 'Utopian Political Philosophy: Deleuze and Rawls', *Deleuze Studies* 1(1): 41–59.
—(2008) 'Becoming-Democratic', in Ian Buchanan and Nicholas Thoburn, eds., *Deleuze and Politics.* Edinburgh: Edinburgh University Press.
Poster, Mark (1975) *Existential Marxism in Postwar France: From Sartre to Althusser.* Princeton, NJ: Princeton University Press.
—(1984) *Foucault, Marxism and History: Mode of Production versus Mode of Information.* Cambridge: Polity Press.
Poulantzas, Nicos (1978) *State, Power, Socialism*, trans. Patrick Camiller. London: NLB.
Protevi, John (2001) *Political Physics: Deleuze, Derrida and the Body Politic.* London: Continuum.
—(2003) 'Love', in Paul Patton and John Protevi, eds., *Between Deleuze and Derrida.* London: Continuum.

Readings, Bill (1991) *Introducing Lyotard: Art and Politics*. London: Routledge.
Read, Jason (2003) *The Micro-Politics of Capital: Marx and the Prehistory of the Present*. Albany, NY: State University of New York Press.
Rorty, Richard (1982) *Consequences of Pragmatism (Essays: 1972–1980)*. Brighton, Sussex: The Harvester Press.
—(1989) *Contingency, Irony, and Solidarity*. Cambridge: Cambridge University Press.
—(1991*a*) *Essays on Heidegger and Others: Philosophical Papers Volume 2*. Cambridge: Cambridge University Press.
—(1991*b*) *Objectivity, Relativism, and Truth: Philosophical Papers Volume I*. Cambridge: Cambridge University Press.
—(1996) 'Response to Ernesto Laclau', in Chantal Mouffe, ed., *Deconstruction and Pragmatism*. London: Routledge.
—(1999) *Philosophy and Social Hope*. Harmondsworth, Middlesex: Penguin Books.
—(2006) *Take Care of Freedom and Truth Will Take Care of Itself: Interviews with Richard Rorty*, ed. Eduardo Mendieta. Stanford, CA: Stanford University Press.
Ryan, Michael (1982) *Marxism and Deconstruction: A Critical Articulation*. Baltimore: The John Hopkins University Press.
Sartre, Jean-Paul (1963) *The Problem of Method*, trans. Hazel E. Barnes. London: Methuen & Co. Ltd.
—(1971) 'Replies to Structuralism: An Interview', trans. Robert D'Amico, *Telos* 9: 110–16.
Saussure, Ferdinand de (1960) *Course in General Linguistics*, ed. Charles Bally and Albert Sechehaye, trans. Wade Baskin. London: Peter Owen.
Schrift, Alan D. (1995) *Nietzsche's French Legacy: A Genealogy of Poststructuralism*. New York: Routledge.
Silver, James (2007) 'I don't think papers are about to go away' (interview with Marian Salzman), *The Guardian*. http://media.guardian.co.uk/mediaguardian/story/0,,1984686,00.html. Last accessed 26 January 2007.
Sim, Stuart (1998) *Post-Marxism: A Reader*. Edinburgh: Edinburgh University Press.
—(2000) *Post-Marxism: An Intellectual History*. London: Routledge.
Smart, Barry (1983) *Foucault, Marxism and Critique*. London: Routledge and Kegan Paul.
Smith, Daniel W. (2003*a*) 'Deleuze and Derrida, Immanence and Transcendence: Two Directions in Recent French Thought', in Paul Patton and John Protevi, eds., *Between Deleuze and Derrida*. London: Continuum.
—(2003*b*) 'Deleuze and the Liberal Tradition: Normativity, Freedom and Judgement', *Economy and Society* 32(2): 299–324.
Sprinker, Michael, ed. (1999) *Ghostly Demarcations: A Symposium on Jacques Derrida's Specters of Marx*. London: Verso.
Steuerman, Emilia (1992) 'Habermas vs Lyotard: Modernity vs Postmodernity?', in Andrew Benjamin, ed., *Judging Lyotard*. London: Routledge.
Stirner, Max (1995) *The Ego and Its Own*, ed. David Leopold. Cambridge: Cambridge University Press.
Tampio, Nicholas (2009) 'Assemblages and the Multitude: Deleuze, Hardt, Negri, and the Postmodern Left', *European Journal of Political Theory* 8(3): 383–400.

Thoburn, Nicholas (2003) *Deleuze, Marx and Politics*. London: Routledge.
Thomassen, Lasse, ed. (2006) *The Derrida-Habermas Reader*. Edinburgh: Edinburgh University Press.
Thomassen, Lasse (2007) *Deconstructing Habermas*. London: Routledge.
Thompson, E. P. (1978) *The Poverty of Theory and Other Essays*. London: Merlin Press.
Thomson, Alex (2005) *Deconstruction and Democracy: Derrida's Politics of Friendship*. London: Continuum.
Tiedmann, Rolf (1989) 'Historical Materialism or Political Messianism? An Interpretation of the Theses "On the Concept of History"', trans. Barton Byg, Jeremy Gaines, and Doris L. Jones, in Gary Smith, ed., *Benjamin: Philosophy, History, Aesthetics*. Chicago: The University of Chicago Press.
Tiersky, Ronald (1974) *French Communism, 1920–1972*. New York: Columbia University Press.
Venturi, Robert, Denise Scott Brown and Steven Izenour (1972) *Learning from Las Vegas*. Cambridge, MA: The MIT Press.
Veyne, Paul (1992) 'Foucault and going beyond (or the fulfilment of) nihilism', in Timothy J. Armstrong, ed., *Michel Foucault Philosopher*. New York: Routledge.
Visker, Rudi (2003) 'From Foucault to Heidegger: A One-Way Ticket?', in Alan Milchman and Alan Rosenberg, eds., *Foucault and Heidegger: Critical Encounters*. Minneapolis: University of Minnesota Press.
Wapner, Paul (1989) 'What's Left: Marx, Foucault and Contemporary Problems of Social Change', *Praxis International* 9(1–2): 88–111.
Williams, James (1998) *Lyotard: Towards a Postmodern Philosophy*. Cambridge: Polity Press.
—(2000) *Lyotard and the Political*. London: Routledge.
Wright, Erik Olin (1994) *Interrogating Inequality: Essays on Class Analysis, Socialism and Marxism*. London: Verso.
Žižek, Slavoj (2004) *Organs Without Bodies: Deleuze and Consequences*. New York: Routledge.

Index

Agamben, Giorgio 163
Althusser, Louis 3, 4, 8, 10, 12, 13, 17–29, 34, 35, 36, 52, 63, 79, 87, 109, 110, 112, 142, 155–62, 167, 169, 178, 179
  and Deleuze 131, 133, 135–6, 141, 188
  and Derrida 72–3, 90
  and Foucault 98, 100, 102, 105–6, 189–90
  on idealism 2, 3, 8, 24–7, 71, 83
  and Lyotard 41, 45, 64–5, 83
Anderson, Perry 31–5, 180
anti-humanism 12, 14, 16, 17, 18, 36, 55, 169, 183, 189
Aron, Raymond 10

Badiou, Alain 9, 130, 151, 164–5
Balibar, Étienne 72, 80, 103, 110, 121, 147, 148, 168, 170, 175–6, 190
Baudrillard, Jean 6, 177, 181, 182, 184, 186
Baugh, Bruce 178
Benjamin, Walter 87–9, 112, 184
Bennington, Geoffrey 39, 44, 92, 181
Bensaïd, Daniel 62, 85, 87–8, 113, 175
Bergson, Henri 14, 125, 129, 151, 188
Bidet, Jacques 190
biopolitics 170, 187
bio-power 122, 148, 170, 187
Butler, Judith 121, 123, 147–8

Callinicos, Alex 30, 32, 35, 79, 181
capitalism 3, 26, 156, 190
  Deleuze on 126, 127–8, 133–46 *passim*, 148, 152, 153, 168, 169, 171, 172, 175
  Derrida on 74, 170

Foucault on 116, 118–19, 120, 171, 187
Lyotard on 40, 43–4, 47–55 *passim*, 56, 57–8, 61, 63–4, 139, 147, 153, 169, 170, 172
Marx on 51–3, 57–8, 82–4, 109–10, 111, 112, 119, 139, 143, 152, 168–70
  and postmodernism 31–2
Castoriadis, Cornelius 40, 41–2, 45
class 39–41, 62, 79, 100, 109, 115, 117, 118–19, 120, 141, 144, 155, 169, 182, 185, 186, 190
  class struggle 20, 24, 41, 94, 104, 120, 174–6, 185
  working class 42, 59, 62, 87, 119, 141, 175, 182
Cohen, G. A. 181
Colebrook, Claire 148, 149
commodity fetishism 26, 27, 52, 77, 80–3, 102, 141–2, 179
communism 10, 11, 26, 32, 47–8, 52–3, 59–60, 62, 66, 77, 155, 162, 169, 174, 175

deconstruction 6, 14, chapter 3 *passim*, 167, 171, 184, 185
  provisional definition of 67–71
Deleuze, Gilles 4, 8, 9, 33, chapter 5 *passim*, 168, 171, 175, 177
  and Althusser 18, 19, 131, 133, 135–6, 141, 160, 161, 162, 180, 181
  and Derrida 125–6, 127, 128, 130, 135
  and Foucault 4, 120, 124, 125–6, 128, 130, 132, 133–4, 135, 136, 143, 144–5, 147–8, 164, 173, 185, 186, 187–9

Deleuze, Gilles (*Cont'd*)
    and Lyotard 39, 44, 52, 54, 125, 126, 128, 130, 132, 134, 135, 139, 142, 144, 146–7, 153, 164, 169, 172
    and post-structuralism 1, 2, 5, 13–16, 35–6, 156–60, 163–5, 167, 169, 178
    Anti-Oedipus 13, 44, 49, 50, 54, chapter 5 *passim*, 157, 161, 171, 175, 181, 182, 187, 189
    Difference and Repetition 129, 130, 132, 188
    Foucault 120, 148, 188
    Nietzsche and Philosophy 14, 19, 131–3, 159–60
    A Thousand Plateaus 33, 129, 133, 134, 135, 139, 140, 145, 149, 150, 153, 175, 188, 189
    What is Philosophy? 129–30, 141, 146
    see also deterritorialization *and* reterritorialization
Derrida, Jacques 4, 9, 35, chapter 3 *passim*, 167, 170, 174–5, 177, 179, 180, 181, 183–5
    and Althusser 18, 19, 27, 72–3, 87, 90, 160, 161
    and Deleuze 125–6, 127, 128, 130, 135
    and Foucault 15, 92, 94–5, 96, 98, 101, 103, 104, 108, 110, 112, 113, 114, 124, 186
    and Lyotard 4, 39, 65, 66, 67, 70, 71, 74, 75, 76, 79, 80, 81, 85, 86–7, 89–90, 92–3, 132
    and post-structuralism 1, 2, 5, 6, 8, 13–16, 33, 36, 156–60, 163–5, 170–1, 172–3
    'Force of Law' 69–70, 89, 184
    Specters of Marx 35, chapter 3 *passim*, 94, 157, 170, 177, 180, 183–5, 190
    see also deconstruction
Descombes, Vincent 9, 11
desire 3, 16, 34, 43, 44, 47, 48–9, 50, 53–4, 63, 65, 135–43, 144–5, 146, 147, 149–50, 151, 153, 169, 182, 189

deterritorialization 52, 127, 138–41, 142, 145–6, 149, 152, 153, 164, 189
Dews, Peter 34, 186
dialectics 15, 23, 27, 33, 36, 55, 65, 71, 72, 86, 110, 121, 126, 132–3, 135, 146, 153, 159–60, 161–2, 170, 181, 182, 188
differend 39, 43, 55–9, 61, 63, 65, 114, 153, 159, 170
Donzelot, Jacques 125
Due, Reidar 147, 149

Eagleton, Terry 32, 33–4, 183
Elliott, Gregory 19, 21, 22, 179
event 4, 15, 27, 38, 46, 56–65 *passim*, 66, 67, 70–1, 85–9 *passim*, 93, 95, 104, 113, 124, 129–30, 151, 161, 163–5, 173
exchange-value *see* value

Foucault, Michel 4, 30, 33–4, 35, chapter 4 *passim*, 167, 170, 171, 174, 175, 177, 178, 179, 180, 181, 185–7, 189
    and Althusser 18, 19, 98, 100, 102, 105–6, 160, 161, 189–90
    and Deleuze 120, 124, 125–6, 128, 130, 132, 133–4, 135, 136, 143, 144–5, 147–8, 164, 173, 188
    and Derrida 15, 92, 94–5, 96, 98, 101, 103, 104, 108, 110, 112, 113, 114, 124, 186
    and Lyotard 4, 39, 94–5, 96, 98, 101, 102, 104, 108, 113, 114, 116, 122, 172, 186
    and post-structuralism 1, 2, 5, 8, 13–16, 30, 36, 156–60, 163–5, 173
    The Archaeology of Knowledge 98–9, 100, 102–3, 104–5, 106, 186
    Discipline and Punish 106, 107, 118–19, 120, 171, 174, 186
    History of Madness 15, 19, 92, 116–17
    The History of Sexuality Volume One 100, 114, 115–16, 121, 122, 148, 187
    'Nietzsche, Freud, Marx' 108–9

'Nietzsche, Genealogy,
    History' 106–7, 111, 188
The Order of Things 95–8, 99, 102,
    103, 105, 186
French Communist Party (PCF) 10, 11,
    19, 22, 41, 94, 102, 157, 158
Freud, Sigmund 9, 14, 17, 43, 46, 54, 102,
    108, 128, 137–8, 146
Fukuyama, Francis 74

Gane, Mike 177–8
Garaudy, Roger 11, 22, 158
genealogy 15, 54, 99, 104, 106–7, 111,
    113, 122, 123, 133, 167, 173
Glucksmann, André 100, 178, 186
Goldmann, Lucien 10
Guattari, Félix 13, 33, 44, 54, 125, 126–8,
    139, 187

Habermas, Jürgen 31, 33–4, 63, 107, 123,
    173, 180–1, 182, 183
Hallward, Peter 151, 152
Hardt, Michael 6, 123, 128, 131
Harvey, David 31, 35
Hegel, G. W. F. 7, 9, 11, 39, 79, 158, 167
    and Althusser 18, 19, 20, 22–5, 27,
        28, 159, 179
    and Deleuze 131–3, 135, 153, 188
    and Derrida 67, 72, 77, 87
    and Lyotard 43, 44, 57, 59, 65
    and post-structuralism 15–16, 28,
        36, 159–60, 178, 179
history 3, 12, 15, 156, 162, 165, 171,
    172, 179
    Althusser on 22–3, 24–5, 26, 28, 36,
        72
    Deleuze on 126, 130, 131, 133–5,
        140, 141, 153, 175
    Derrida on 72, 87–9, 92, 93
    Foucault on 94, 95, 96, 97, 103,
        104–14 *passim*, 116, 124
    Lyotard on 58–62
    Marx on 22–3, 62–3, 107–14, 119,
        133–5, 167–8, 175
humanism 8, 10–11, 13, 16, 18, 20, 22–3,
    27, 28, 36, 39, 41, 48, 63, 95–8, 100,
    103, 105, 114, 124, 158, 161, 169, 182

idealism
    Althusser's critique 24–8, 159–60,
        161–2, 179
    defined 2–3, 24–7, 36–7, 171
    Marx's 2–3, 4, 7, 51–3, 121, 174, 182
    post-structuralism's 3, 121–3, 147–50,
        164–5, 173–4
    post-structuralist critique 14, 16,
        71–2, 130–1, 159–60, 161–2
immanence 89, 131, 132–3, 139, 141–3, 145,
    147, 149–50, 152, 163–5, 174

Jacoby, Russell 18
Jakobson, Roman 12, 178
Jameson, Fredric 31–4, 81–2, 136, 138,
    150, 151, 180, 183

Kant, Immanuel 9, 33, 34, 54, 59, 70,
    86, 97, 132, 163, 173
Kellner, Douglas 6, 177–8
Kroker, Arthur 177

Laclau, Ernesto 5–6, 177, 179, 190
Lecercle, Jean-Jacques 125, 135, 136, 187,
    188
Lefebvre, Henri 10
Lenin, V. I. 25, 189
Lévi-Strauss, Claude 11, 12-13, 14, 15, 18,
    25, 27, 72, 178
Lewis, Tom 190
Lyotard, Jean-François 4, 32, 35, 37,
    chapter 2 *passim*, 78, 83, 166,
    167, 170, 175, 177, 180, 181–3
    and Althusser 18, 19, 41, 44, 45–6,
        52, 64, 64, 160, 161
    and Deleuze 39, 44, 52, 54, 125, 126,
        128, 130, 132, 134, 135, 139, 142,
        144, 146–7, 153, 164, 169, 172
    and Derrida 4, 39, 66, 67, 70, 71,
        74, 75, 76, 79, 80, 81, 85, 86–7,
        89–90, 92–3
    and Foucault 4, 39, 94–5, 96, 98,
        101, 102, 104, 108, 113, 114, 116,
        122, 172, 186
    and post-structuralism 1, 2, 5, 8,
        13–16, 30, 36, 156–60, 163–5,
        172–3

Lyotard, Jean-François (*Cont'd*)
  The Differend 16, 55–63, 64, 65, 89, 153, 163–4, 170, 182, 183
  Discours, figure 13, 16, 19, 46
  Just Gaming (*Au Juste*) 55
  Libidinal Economy 14, 15, 41, 44–5, 56, 57, 61, 63, 64, 66, 122, 128, 146–7, 153, 163–4, 170, 172, 177, 182, 183
  The Postmodern Condition 41, 55, 180, 183
  Phenomenology 39–40
  see also differend, *Socialisme ou barbarie*

Macherey, Pierre 80, 183
McQuillan, Martin 92, 185
Marsden, Richard 185, 186
Marx, Karl *passim*
  Capital Volume One 52–3, 57–8, 77, 80–5, 109–10, 113, 119, 168, 169, 176, 179, 190
  Capital Volume Three 58, 139, 143, 168, 182
  The Communist Manifesto 52, 53, 61, 77, 100, 117, 141, 142
  Critique of Hegel's 'Philosophy of Right' 62
  Economic and Philosophic Manuscripts 118, 119, 137–8, 189
  The Eighteenth Brumaire 77, 117, 176
  The German Ideology 20, 53, 63, 77–9, 81, 90, 111, 155, 166, 169, 174
  Grundrisse 21, 47–8, 51–2, 85, 111–12, 119, 167, 168
  The Holy Family 175
  '"Notes" on Adolph Wagner' 83–4, 113
  The Poverty of Philosophy 111, 112
  'Theses on Feuerbach' 2, 169
materialism 24–5, 28, 137–8, 143, 176, 182
  aleatory 19, 22, 26–7, 161, 162
  defined 171–2
  and Marx 2, 26, 71–2, 102, 120–1, 124, 130, 174, 179

  and post-structuralism 2–3, 54, 71–2, 115, 120–1, 150–3, 160–1, 163, 172–3
messianicity 4, 67, 71, 85–9, 91, 93, 95, 104, 113, 114, 184
micropolitics 127, 144, 145, 157, 189
mode of production 26, 58, 79, 109, 119, 140, 190
Montag, Warren 26, 28, 160, 179, 183
Mullarkey, John 149–50

Negri, Antonio 6, 26–7, 102, 121, 122, 123, 147, 187
New Right 142
Nietzsche, Friedrich 9, 24, 43, 98, 101, 107, 125, 151–2, 163, 180
  and Hegel 131–3
  influence on post-structuralism 14–16, 29, 33–4, 36, 53, 162, 179
  and Marx 103, 104, 107–11, 132–5, 136, 146, 153, 169
Norris, Christopher 32, 33, 35, 181
nouveaux philosophes 10, 16, 45, 59, 66, 100, 122, 156, 158, 178, 186, 189

ontology 2–3, 162, 163, 173, 174, 175
  Deleuze on 126, 130–1, 143, 147, 150, 154, 164–5, 188
  Derrida on 4, 66, 67, 72, 75–85 *passim*, 86, 93, 130
  Foucault on 4, 98, 114, 119, 122, 124, 130, 186
  idealism and 2–3, 25, 36
  Lyotard on 44, 48, 50–5 *passim*, 63, 64, 66, 86, 122, 130
overdetermination 25, 26, 27, 72, 160, 161, 179
Owen, David 123

PCF *see* French Communist Party
philosophy 83, 84, 90–3, 110, 124, 129–32, 139, 149–50, 152–4, 165–7, 170, 172, 174
  as class struggle in theory 20, 179
  of history 58–61, 63, 67, 85, 89, 114, 124, 133, 167

idealist philosophy *see* idealism
materialist philosophy *see* materialism
  and onanism 90–1
  postwar French philosophy chapter
    one *passim*, 101
post-Marxism 5–6, 177, 190
post-modernism 29–35, 40, 60, 171,
  180, 183
post-structuralism *passim*
  definitions of 13–17, 156–60
  distinctions within 162–5
Poulantzas, Nicos 115, 185, 187
power 3, 16, 34, 78, 88, 92
  Deleuze's concept of 143–5, 147–8,
    151, 164–5
  Foucault's concept of 4, 100, 102,
    107, 114–22, 144, 147–8, 164,
    170, 171, 187
  Marx's concept of 100, 117–18,
    119–20
  see also bio-power
Protevi, John 69, 185

repression 100, 114–15, 118, 136,
  143–7
reterritorialization 137, 139, 140, 142,
  145, 146, 149, 152, 153
revolution 77, 87, 91, 106, 112, 143,
  146–7, 148–9, 151, 154, 157
  Lyotard's renunciation of 38, 41, 42,
    45, 66
Rorty, Richard 9, 30, 91, 171, 180, 181
Ryan, Michael 76, 183

Sartre, Jean-Paul 9, 10, 11, 12, 16–17,
  41, 72, 95, 100, 178, 186
Saussure, Ferdinand de 12, 14, 16, 178
Schrift, Alan 178–9
Sim, Stuart 177
Smart, Barry 177, 185, 187

Smith, Adam 96, 137–8, 189
Smith, Daniel W. 163, 189
Socialisme ou barbarie 40–2, 45, 48, 49, 56, 60
Stalinism 10, 18, 20, 22, 32, 41, 59, 158
Stirner, Max 77–80, 81, 132, 169
structuralism 8, 9, 11–19, 21–2, 25, 28,
  32, 46, 158, 160, 169, 178, 179
subjectivity 3, 4, 114, 118–20, 124, 135,
  136, 169–70, 172, 176, 179

teleology 15, 16, 23, 26–7, 36, 164–5,
  173, 175, 176
  Deleuze on 126, 135
  Derrida on 4, 67, 85–90, 93, 98, 113,
    135, 161
  Foucault on 4, 96, 104–7, 122–3,
    135, 167, 172
  and idealism 3–4, 25, 26, 171
  Lyotard on 4, 48, 49, 55, 64, 113,
    135, 167, 172
  Marx and 26, 109–13, 135, 162, 165
Thoburn, Nicholas 187
Thompson, E. P. 35
transcendence 72, 86, 88, 92, 97–8, 99,
  131, 133, 140, 141, 143, 147, 150,
  163–5
Troubetskoy, Nikolai 12

use-value *see* value

value (exchange- and use-) 48, 49, 68, 76,
  80–5, 113, 142, 143, 171, 182
Veyne, Paul 173–4
Visker, Rudi 123
vitalism 4, 44, 121–2, 126, 146–9, 164–5,
  173

Williams, James 55, 61

Žižek, Slavoj 127

Made in the USA
Middletown, DE
20 October 2023

41124492R00119